The Specter of Salem

The Specter of Salem

Remembering the Witch Trials in Nineteenth-Century America

GRETCHEN A. ADAMS

THE UNIVERSITY OF CHICAGO PRESS   CHICAGO AND LONDON

The University of Chicago Press, Chicago 60637
The University of Chicago Press, Ltd., London
© 2008 by Gretchen A. Adams
All rights reserved. Published 2008
Paperback edition 2010
Printed in the United States of America

19 18 17 16 15 14 13 12 11 10   2 3 4 5 6

ISBN-13: 978-0-226-00541-6 (cloth)
ISBN-13: 978-0-226-00543-0 (paper)
ISBN-10: 0-226-00541-0 (cloth)
ISBN-10: 0-226-00543-7 (paper)

Library of Congress Cataloging-in-Publication Data

Adams, Gretchen A.
    The specter of Salem: remembering the witch trials in nineteenth-century America /
Gretchen A. Adams.
        p.   cm.
    Includes bibliographic references and index.
    ISBN-13: 978-0-226-00541-6 (cloth : alk. paper)
    ISBN-10: 0-226-00541-0 (cloth : alk. paper)   1. Witchcraft—Massachusetts—Salem—
History—19th Century.   2. Trials (Witchcraft)—Massachusetts—Salem—History—19th
Century.   3. Salem (Mass.)—Social conditions.   I. Title.
    BF1576.A33   2008
    133.4′3097445—dc22

                                                                    2008028178

⊗ The paper used in this publication meets the minimum requirements of the American
National Standard for Information Sciences—Permanence of Paper for Printed Library
Materials, ANSI Z39.48-1992.

FOR MY HUSBAND, MARK CARTER BOND

Contents

Acknowledgments   ix

Introduction   1

CHAPTER 1. Mysteries, Memories, and Metaphors: From Event to Memory   10

CHAPTER 2. Memory and Nation: The Early Republic   37

CHAPTER 3. Not to Hell but to Salem: Antebellum Religious Crises   64

CHAPTER 4. Witch-Burners: The Politics of Sectionalism   94

CHAPTER 5. Witch-Hunters: The Era of Civil War and Reconstruction   119

Epilogue: The Crucible of Memory   149

Notes   159

Index   217

Acknowledgments

I am an unusually fortunate person because I have so many people to thank, and it is my privilege to do so here. Each of them has my sincere gratitude for all favors large and small, academic and personal that contributed to this project from its first appearance as a conference paper through its many incarnations until it became a book. I suspect that anyone who knew it in its earlier stages will not recognize most of it in its current form, and some of the generous people listed may not even remember a casual reference passed along at a library or comment made at a seminar; but I thank them nonetheless. In most cases they took the time and interest to treat an unknown graduate student seriously and taught me more than a bit about what we should all do as scholars outside the archives and the classroom. Since this project concerns to a fair degree "memory," I hope mine (and my notes) is as good as it should be.

It is customary, but in this case also a real pleasure, first to thank Ellen F. Fitzpatrick. Ellen has all the qualities anyone could want in a mentor, but perhaps best of all, she has imagination. When I came to her with an idea but precious little evidence, she saw the potential as well as the pitfalls. Many others would have steered me on to a safer topic, but Ellen issued the warnings and stood back. She always encouraged me to follow my own curiosity to its own ends. I realize now that one of those safer topics would have been easier for her as well. Ellen Fitzpatrick is a generous as well as a rigorous scholar and everything since has been built on that foundation. Consistently helpful and deserving of thanks once again are J. William Harris, Robert M. Mennel, Cynthia Van Zandt, and John R. Ernest.

For assistance that ranged from reading or listening to portions of this in various stages, general encouragement, suggestions, copies of items found during their own research, criticism, translations, and conversations about the project at venues that ranged from conferences to seminars, research libraries, e-mail and even kitchen tables, many thanks to a long list of people that includes Evan Haefeli, Jill Lepore, Jim Cullen, Holly Snyder, Robert Allison, Richard Wightman Fox, Cathy Corman, Alan Taylor, Vince DiGirolamo, Janet Coryell, Roger W. Bowen, Jennifer Fronc, Douglas Seefeldt, W. Jeffrey Bolster, Benjamin Ray, Laurel Ulrich, Marla Miller, Stephen Nissenbaum, Joanne Thomas, Melissa Homestead, Matthew Warshauer, Eric Altice, Elizabeth Reis, Harry Richards, Michael S. Foley, Jane Kamensky, Carol Karlsen, Udo Hebel, James Mohr, Matthew Dennis, Catherine Allgor, David Snead, Donald Walker, Mark Stoll, Laura Prieto, and Woody Holton. And though I doubt he would recall a book assigned in a graduate course at the University of Oregon almost ten years ago, Jack Maddex was the one who originally sent me down this fascinating road.

Generous financial support from a number of institutions made the initial research possible, but each grant also came with the enthusiastic assistance of knowledgeable people that made it even more valuable. This project was started before "keyword searchable" digital collections were in more than a "beta" phase and was revised and refined when I was in a location with no access to those subscription databases. For that reason libraries and librarians have played a critical role as I spent months skimming entire runs of newspapers and periodicals looking for appearances of Salem witchcraft. It would have been faster and (much) easier to do this sort of project now but not nearly as interesting.

The Boston Athenaeum and Stephen Nonack, its librarian without peer, were the first to assist financially and have remained boosters of this project all the way through. I sincerely thank them. The Friends of Longfellow House and the wonderful Robert Mitchell; the American Historical Association; Smith College; the University of New Hampshire Graduate School; and the University of Glasgow all provided research funds at critical moments. The John Nicholas Brown Center for the Study of American Civilization at Brown University provided the best possible working environment and privileges at Brown's incredible libraries. This project would have been very difficult to complete without the resources and assistance of the unique collection of people on the staff and in residence at the JNBC in 2000. The then director Joyce Bothelo and her staff, Denise Bastien and Alex Dunwoodie, cannot be thanked enough. Also, the great staff at the John Hay and John Carter Brown Libraries were immensely helpful. Particularly helpful at the latter was Richard Ring. The staff of the Monroe C. Gutman Library at Harvard University has my sincere appreciation for the extraordinary efforts they made when I arrived during commencement week with a long list of schoolbooks I needed to consult and a very short time to do it. Despite their own difficult schedule of public events that week, they set me up, made sure the microfilm came to me quickly, and in short gave me every assistance and courtesy.

The American Antiquarian Society awarded me a month-long fellowship and then probably wondered if I would ever leave. Much of the research and most of the writing was done during extended stays in Goddard-Daniels House and in Antiquarian Hall. My only regret these days is that I am two thousand miles away. There is no finer place to research such a project and no finer group of people to work with. It is difficult with this group to determine where the intellectual and professional thanks end and the personal thanks begin. Most of the fellows that were in residence with me during both my official and unofficial stays are thanked elsewhere, but I will express my genuine gratitude for the many kindnesses and incomparable knowledge of the permanent staff, including Caroline Sloat, John B. Hench, Joanne Chaison, Marie Lamoreaux, Dennis Laurie, Laura Wasowicz, Jim Moran, Bill Young, Caroline Stoffel, and Alice Gardiner.

The list of people I can thank as this project went into a much longer stage of refinement and revision in the past few years is considerably shorter, but my gratitude is equally sincere. I owe several colleagues, anonymous readers, and students a great debt for helping me think my way through the book by raising questions, lending their expertise in specific fields to a review of various sections, and expressing their enthusiasm about the manuscript. The first was the only person besides my editor, the readers for the press, or my tenure committee who actually read this entire book in manuscript—not once but twice. M. Catherine Miller has been a terrific friend and mentor even after her recent retirement. She read the entire manuscript very carefully and thoughtfully, helped me navigate my way through the two very different perspectives of my readers' reports for the final revision, and then read it again before I sent it off for the last time. Best of all, she does not substitute praise for honesty. Everyone needs a reader like this, and I am grateful I found one. Another former colleague, Patricia M. E. Lorcin, who has since moved to the University of Minnesota, generously read an early version of the first two chapters, has assisted me in several other professional matters, and is another example of collegiality at its best.

Bernard Rosenthal and Margo Burns likely know more than anyone about the documents related to the 1692 trials themselves. Working with them on the *Records of the Salem Witch Hunt* for the past five years has been an enriching experience both personally and professionally. Bernie and Margo's generosity extended to granting my last-minute request to read and comment on my section related to the trials themselves, and I greatly appreciate it. Two former students who have gone on to their own teaching or graduate careers deserve some sincere thanks as well. Cecilia Gowdy-Wygant spent part of one summer as a graduate research assistant sorting and abstracting old photocopies of articles for me. And though I suspect it is the most boring work she will ever do with or without pay, she was always cheerful and always wonderfully thorough. Jonathan Crider kindly read one chapter I was trying to revise and raised some questions that helped me think my way through an impasse.

Two people who deserve every superlative available cannot even be thanked by name—the anonymous readers for the University of Chicago Press. They both paid my manuscript the compliment of close, intelligent readings that took the project on its own terms rather than on the proverbial "book they wished I had written." No one could hope for more from an evaluator. The suggestions were substantive, detailed, clear, and smart. That my manuscript was entrusted to such fine readers should not have really surprised me. It is emblematic of the care with which the project was handled from the moment Robert Devens contacted me to say that the University of Chicago Press was interested in the book. This book is 100 percent better for his influence and his editorial guidance. I am better for his endless patience and wicked sense of humor. As if the editor and readers were not enough, Emilie Sandoz, Alice Bennett, and Mara Naselli made the production stage of the process infinitely more transparent and easy as the manuscript moved into production. My agent Lisa Adams at the Garamond Agency deserves thanks for many things, but one is for leading me to Chicago.

Most personally satisfying to thank are those who fall into the category of both of colleague and friend. I have been fortunate to have some of the very best from graduate school onward. David Chapin, Kate Clifford Larson, and Kurt Graham are historians whose work I admire, whose judgment I trust, and whose friendship just makes life better in every way that matters.

The group always thanked last should, in a perfect world, be thanked first. These are the family and friends who often have an interest in the author and not the subject, but for whom the author's obsession is enough. I am particularly fortunate in having a marvelous extended family and equally marvelous friends. Michelle and "the little Grahams," Jon Miller, and Spencer Larson were generous with their time, their ideas, and with letting me drag away their respective spouses for extended conversations about history and still always welcomed me back into their homes. My cousins Joe and Sheila Fournier provided a wonderful break from writing when I was in Providence. Louise Wheeler and Bruce Parker did the same when I was in the Washington, DC, area. My very dear in-laws, Beverly and Lloyd Bond in Oregon, saw much less of me when researching, but they always were sure I would finish and finish well. I am only sorry that Lloyd did not live to see the book in print after all. My sister, Linda (Adams) Arnold, has always been a rock. Her confidence and practical assistance have meant the world to me, and its a pleasure to thank her publicly for years of support. And no, Linda, I made no last-minute discovery of "witches" in the family—it's all Plymouth and Maine in those years, I'm afraid.

There are three more people who deserve all the thanks in the world. Two, my husband, Mark Bond, and my son, Drew Galvan, sacrificed all of those things that people sacrifice when they live with a historian whose research is far from home, and still they encouraged me to keep at it. The third, my grandfather, Howard Palmer Oldfield, did not live to see this project even begun. But whatever I have done, it has always been because of them and their faith in me.

Introduction

Metaphor ... is also a priest of interpretation; but what it interprets is memory.
—Cynthia Ozick

The specter of Salem witchcraft haunts the American imagination. Few historical events have provided such a wide range of scholars, dramatists, fiction writers, poets, and amateur sleuths with a subject that so stubbornly resists a final resolution. Although barely nine months passed from the first accusations of witchcraft to the last, those nine months of accusations, confessions, denials, trials, and executions have spawned a vast literature that for three hundred years has sought to fix blame or find reason for the ordeal of the Massachusetts Bay Colony witchcraft trials of 1692. But Salem witchcraft has presented two historical mysteries. The first has centered directly on the events of 1692: What happened in Salem? Or more accurately, "why" did things happen as they did in 1692? The second (and arguably more intriguing) question is, Why have Americans preserved the memory of Salem and excavated it so persistently?

This book does not consider the "why" of the terrible events that took place in Salem in 1692. Readers looking for extended analysis of the outbreak of witchcraft in seventeenth-century Salem should refer to the huge historical literature devoted to that fascinating and elusive episode in early American history.[1] But most people are familiar, at least in part, with the basic outlines of the Salem witchcraft trials. In 1692 two young girls were struck with a strange and disturbing set of symptoms that ranged from fevers to hallucinations and what were described as "fits." Medical and religious consultation arrived at a diagnosis of witchcraft. Three local women who fit the traditional profile of accused witches (older women who were personally difficult or otherwise marginalized) were quickly accused and arrested. The normal course of events in such cases would be the arrest, trial, and either acquittal or conviction and execution of the three. But this investigation accelerated to determine if a wider conspiracy of witches was attacking the colony. Before the court was suspended in October 1692, the destruction to the community was staggering, with a toll that included two hundred accused (most of them arrested and imprisoned), nineteen hanged (including a minister), and one man pressed to death with stones during interrogation. At least four died in prison awaiting trial, and several prominent members of the community fled the colony to avoid either arrest or trial.

The bare bones of the story alone constitute a sensational set of facts with a ready-made potential for drama. But other known elements in this 1692 episode are tantalizing: the seemingly copious body of contemporary materials, from trial transcripts to published commentary, that record the events but do not satisfactorily explain them; the disturbing knowledge that those who pled innocent were executed while those who confessed their guilt lived; and especially significant, both in contemporary commentary and in later assessments of the episode, that while traditional procedures were followed in the initial examination of the two little girls, traditional judicial procedures regarding a category of evidence known as "spectral" in such cases were not followed. All of these elements became essential points of departure for historical inquiry and literary invention over the next three centuries.

The "story," then, of witch-hunting in 1692 Salem is one whose outlines are familiar despite the accumulation of narrative inventions and analytical conclusions in print over the intervening centuries. The tragedy has at different times been judged by both amateur and professional historians to be the result of religious fanaticism; power-mad ministers; hysterical girls; local disputes; mass hysteria; misogyny; anxiety caused by political turmoil, frontier life, and Indian wars; hallucinations caused by rotting grain; psychological distress; or even a result of the persecution of "real" witches. Although literary scholars have found much about Salem's life to investigate as a plot device for a variety of imaginary literatures either set in the contemporary context of the trials or translated into allegorical tales within more modern settings, historians have for the most part concentrated on investigating the events of 1692 in their most immediate context. Far less familiar, despite its pervasive presence in ordinary social and political discourse in the United States, is the history of Salem witchcraft as a cultural metaphor.[2]

Virtually every modern American is familiar with Salem as a popular metaphor for persecution. Ask any American when that association began and he will undoubtedly point to the 1950s era anti-Communism crusade. While McCarthyism reigned in Washington, congressional witnesses routinely decried the frenetic "witch-hunt atmosphere," and commentary on the investigations used such titles as "Salem, 1950." Ultimately works like the 1953 drama *The Crucible* cemented the association in the contemporary mind as innovations in mass media such as wire and syndication services and television provided both new levels of repetition and new venues for dramatic (and even comedic) variations on a theme. In fact Salem's witch hunt quickly became such a byword for the ongoing investigations into political subversion in the United States that FBI director J. Edgar Hoover was reduced to publicly denying that his agency operated under the influence of "hysteria, witch hunts, or vigilantes." But the very familiarity of Salem as an analogy for the 1950s red hunt obscures not only its use in a similar "red scare" in the 1920s but its longer, richer, and more varied metaphorical life.[3]

In 1692 in Salem, Massachusetts Bay Colony, charges of witchcraft separated the godly from the ungodly in the mind of the community. In the centuries afterward, in other moments of cultural crisis (most notably those involving religion or politics), the metaphor of Salem witchcraft has served much the same function. Beginning when the trials were still in living memory, Americans referred to the excesses of Salem's witchcraft trials in public debates over such things as smallpox inoculation, religion, and revolution. Their descendants brought it to their own public arguments about sectional dominance, new religious and reform movements, capital punishment, sexual harassment, gay rights, terrorism, and a myriad of other contemporary issues. In each case, in every era, Americans evoked Salem witchcraft to vividly illustrate the folly of a course of action by either fellow citizens or their government that they believed to be extreme, irrational, and capable of destroying the nation itself.

The Specter of Salem traces the metaphorical life of Salem witchcraft. The seeming ubiquity of Salem as a metaphor for persecution, intolerance, and bigotry is a legacy of the shaping of the memory and the metaphor in an earlier national moment. This book focuses most directly on how, in the political and social crises of the nineteenth century, the unlikely example of the seventeenth-century witchcraft trials in Salem, Massachusetts, became a common symbolic point of reference for Americans.

At the heart of this story is the creation of the United States in the late eighteenth century. As the founders of the first modern nation, post-Revolutionary Americans sought ways to generate the affective bonds of nationalism. The creation of a universe of symbols that encompassed those drawn from the recent Revolutionary War as well as the colonial past was aided by the growth of print culture and the promotion of what Benedict Anderson has defined as an "imagined community" among a widely dispersed and generally literate people.[4] The critical intersection of the project of political socialization with print was through education. The lack of organized public school systems militated against a uniform curriculum geared toward nationalist ends. The gap was bridged by a synergistic relation between a government that required the creation of a political citizen and an increasingly entrepreneurial marketplace. Among the printed speeches, sermons, and other literature meant to inculcate a unifying set of national values was the common schoolbook.

Widely embraced by adults as a way to educate the "rising generation" in the obligations of citizenship in a republic, American schoolbooks represent a neglected source within a wider print culture for tracing the construction of a collective national memory in the early United States. Schoolbooks reinforced norms, warning against deviance by showing the path to righteousness, and they played a crucial role in establishing the memory and meaning of symbols meant to serve as positive, moralized examples for the development of nationalism. Within the wider nation-building project, Salem witchcraft became an unlikely but active symbolic story and a permanent part of the collective social memory of the colonized past.

In the formal study of the collective memory of any society, too often the focus is narrow and oriented toward how the use of a particular narrative of the past serves the needs of the specific contemporary moment in which it is recalled. Alon Confino has rightly argued that when an artifact of cultural memory is studied in a contextual vacuum, the spotlight is on the "construction, appropriation [and] contestation" of the memory within that specific appearance.[5] But in expanding the view to consider the full context within which a specific social memory is recalled and used, it is also important to recognize that such memories have their own history of use. Different elements of a narrative record can be emphasized or suppressed to suit new needs, but ultimately, to be effective or enduring, new incarnations of a specific cultural memory like Salem witchcraft must fit the logic of previous uses, because collective memories themselves have a history of use and meaning.[6]

Collective memory in the United States, like the studies of it, tends to coalesce around symbols designed for emulation.[7] Those that have received the most skilled and innovative attention are (with a few notable exceptions) those that have risen to iconic status as *affirmative* symbols in American culture.[8] Richard Slotkin's consideration of the American frontiersman Daniel Boone makes this point well. Slotkin's articulation of the way collective memory was used in the early United States as a moral map to guide a community to appropriate solutions in times of stress is a useful comparison with the concurrent rise of the use of Salem witchcraft. The power of the myth of Boone, Slotkin argues, lay in its ability, when invoked during crises, not only to remind all concerned of "local values or cultural assumptions" but to act as "the vicarious resolver of the dilemmas that preoccupied that culture."[9] Boone's example, then, suggested a course of action that readers might emulate to strengthen or affirm the bonds of community in moments of crisis. The metaphor of Salem, by contrast, resolved cultural dilemmas not by suggesting a course of action but by warning against one. Unlike the Boone narrative, the Salem narrative offered examples of action that led to disgrace and disaster: frantic townspeople acting as a hysterical mob, and fanatical ministers trying innocent people on superstitious grounds with evidence of a crime only the most credulous could believe. It was not a course of action that recommended itself to anyone. In its role as a *negative* symbol, Salem witchcraft was as useful as any heroic model, by articulating the inevitable consequences of an ill-advised action.

The processes by which collective memory is formed are as impossible to completely trace and account for as are those that form an individual's memory and sense of her own past. What we can do is to examine the traces left in cultural sources to determine what was considered important enough to remember as a culture, how meaning was shaped, and to what end those memories were employed. Salem witchcraft presents a unique problem. There is no record of memorial activity (the most common route to remembrance) following the trials and only a very brief contemporary skirmish over which version of the story would become dominant in print. Yet despite almost a century between the end of the trials and the project of political and cultural nation building, and with only some scattered accounts in print, historical narratives that included the Salem trials appeared with increasing frequency in the 1790s as both adult and schoolroom histories became a fundamental part of the project of nation building. It is clear from the beginning that the example of Salem, as a model of the social costs of undesirable behavior, served well those who sought to promote habits of mind in tune with Enlightenment values of reason and order. As the memory of Salem witchcraft itself moved from the periphery to the center of cultural memory with the creation of distinctly "American" history and symbols, it became a useful cultural boundary marker between the rational present and the superstitious, disorderly, and even brutal past.

Historicizing the origin and evolution of Salem witchcraft as a cultural metaphor when it was most vital as an "agent of moralized fear in political speech" shows how dynamic collective memory can be, since it not only expresses anxieties but shapes the reality within which it operates.[10] Metaphor as an artifact of collective memory "transforms the strange into the familiar" and, as such, functions as a literal call to action.[11] As George Lakoff and Mark Johnson have argued, metaphors are "the words we live by" because they are grounded in the "most fundamental values in a culture."[12] They shape reality and response. Perhaps the most vivid example of how this worked in the nineteenth-century political sphere is in the use of Salem in the 1850s and 1860s. As Salem became an important rhetorical device during the Sectional Crisis and the Civil War, the association of specific social, political, and even physical threats ("They began by burning witches, and they will end by burning us!") by metaphorically identifying the abolitionist with the "Puritan" and presenting "witch burning" as a the inevitable historical consequence of Northern (or "Puritan") ascendancy shaped social and political reality for pro-slavery audiences. People barraged with a decade or more of such associations realistically came to believe that they were at personal risk from such an eventuality and were encouraged to act on the threat. The process was shaped by decades of similar associations of Salem with a darker side of American experience and built on earlier, familiar representations of this element of the colonial past.

The story of the movement of the 1692 Salem witchcraft trials from the periphery of memory in colonial histories to a metaphor that by the mid-nineteenth century was central to nationalistic political discourse can be traced in print. Published sources include pamphlets, schoolbooks, newspapers, magazines, orations, and imaginative literature. From the floor of Congress to the pulpit, the after-dinner speech, the commemorative address, the schoolroom, the editorial page, the personal diary entry, and the stage, writers, speakers, and politicians in the nineteenth century employed the Salem metaphor to address a variety of concerns within a seemingly endless series of controversies.[13] To paraphrase Merrill D. Peterson, this is not a book about the history of Salem witchcraft, but a book about what American political culture has made of Salem witchcraft.[14]

*   *   *

Chapter 1 considers the role of cultural memory and the ways it is formed. At the heart of the discussion is the 1692 episode as a narrative created in print while events were still a matter of public dispute. Following the threads of the most prominent competing narratives (Cotton Mather's *Wonders of the Invisible World* and Robert Calef's challenge to that version, *More Wonders of the Invisible World*) as well as the traces of public opinion left in the petitions to the government by individuals and families damaged by the episode, we can see how those versions shaped the memory of Salem by the time of the American Revolution nearly one hundred years later.

Chapter 2 considers how Salem was embedded in the creation of a distinctly American national mythology in the wake of the Revolution and explores the role of both print and region within that creation. Circumstances of temperament, infrastructure, and political ambitions favored New England authors and publishers and the narratives they had self-consciously collected since settlement. For this reason the Puritan of Massachusetts Bay Colony was presented as the central American founding figure and was assiduously promoted in the plentiful histories that poured from the region's presses. Schoolbooks played a central part among the commemorative, historical, and literary projects that transmitted and established the standard narrative of Puritan founding from 1790 to 1860. The availability of schoolbooks produced for the elementary level, and the context within which they were produced, distributed, and used, gave their morally driven narratives significant cultural weight. Rather than being a problem within this newly fashioned national narrative, Puritan Salem's 1692 episode of witch-hunting provided an opportunity to demonstrate the moral progress inherent in the transformation from colonies to nation. Thus, as the past provided the character of the hearty pious settler for emulation, it also provided an equally vivid cautionary tale.[15]

Chapter 3 traces how in the 1830s the metaphor of Salem witchcraft moved out of histories and literature and into public discourse. Salem's witchcraft trials warned of the political consequences if a nation became overwhelmed by "fanatical" followers of new religious movements such as Spiritualism and Mormonism. The rhetoric of opposition drew on themes familiar from the rampant anti-Catholic sentiment in the United States but found its most telling illustration of the dangers of religious "delusions" and "fanaticism" in movements arising from Protestant roots in the 1692 witchcraft trials in Salem. Salem's example provided reporters, editors, and even average citizens with a symbol that had the authority of historical precedent. As the specter of Salem was raised in these debates, a strong reminder was issued that there were indeed limits to acceptable modes of American religious expression.

The most persistent idea about Salem witchcraft in the American imagination is the claim that witches were burned in 1692. This addition to the story of Salem did not come from any historical or fictional account but was born in the highly charged political rhetoric that preceded the Civil War. Chapter 4 details the use of Salem witchcraft by Southern editors and politicians as a regional slur to answer abolitionist charges about the cruel nature of slavery. As a rebuttal to antislavery claims about the innate brutality of the slave states, pro-slavery writers and politicians used Salem to define first abolitionists and finally all Northerners as Puritans. The specific use of the charge that witches were burned in 1692 Salem also provides an interesting view of the cultural costs when historical events are lost to collective memory. The Negro Plot of 1740 in the colony of New York, as some contemporaries noted, had striking parallels to events in Salem fifty years before. Slaves convicted in the alleged plot were indeed publicly burned at the stake. By the 1850s, however, this potential counterillustration to arguments that described lynching and other brutality in the Southern slave system was largely unknown, leaving a potentially effective and persuasive historical example unused in favor of the more distant and less germane example of Salem.

Chapter 5 delineates the ways the meaning of Salem's metaphor shifted during the Civil War and Reconstruction years as Northern commentators adopted it to marginalize their own radical factions. In these years the metaphor's meaning increasingly emphasized the Puritans' "bigotry" and "intolerance." The consequences of this rhetorical strategy and its wartime use by both sides had two enduring consequences for the meaning of the metaphor of Salem in political culture and for the figure of the Puritan in American memory.

First, the old schoolbook Puritan was severely damaged as a symbol within national iconography and gave way to the infinitely less complex Pilgrim of Plymouth Colony. While the old conflation of the two symbolic settlers often continued in popular use, increasingly, Salem and its Puritan forefathers were being relegated to a secondary role in the narrative of national founding and a more permanent role in collective memory as a cultural cautionary tale. In this new formulation, Salem's 1692 witch hunt became emblematic not of the extremism of those in the community with potentially dangerous or disruptive beliefs and behaviors but of the excesses of the "witch-hunters" who did not prosecute in their official roles but, instead, *persecuted*.

The epilogue briefly considers the post-nineteenth-century life of Salem as a metaphor that is most familiar to modern Americans. Within the various crises from Prohibition to anti-Communism, terrorism, and presidential impeachment, within hours of an event one can find–thanks to on-line and televised news commentary–some appeal to Salem's example to restrain government powers or to quell popular opinion when it threatens to drive political decisions. Looking at the critical events of the past few decades through newspaper database keyword searches alone, we can do a roll call of sorts of disaster and disgrace with an appropriate reference to Salem. Cultural crises and political scandals have existed for the entire life of the nation and assuredly will continue to emerge. While Salem has endured as a metaphor because of its flexibility in expressing cultural anxieties and warning against extreme behaviors or beliefs by citizens or even the government, it is only in the moral-political realm that it, by the beginning of the twenty-first century, expresses anything more than a fear of government powers. In this way the final chapter of *The Specter of Salem* reveals how the cultural memory of an event, like the episode of witch-hunting in 1692 Massachusetts, often has a longer-lasting effect than the event itself.

CHAPTER ONE

Mysteries, Memories, and Metaphors

From Event to Memory

In January 1692 Samuel Parris, the Puritan minister of Salem village in Massachusetts Bay Colony, faced a crisis with the two children in his household. His nine-year-old daughter Betty and eleven-year-old niece Abigail Williams were acting in alarming ways and complaining of a variety of conspicuously painful physical symptoms. John Hale, a minister from a neighboring town, later described the apparent agony of the two children, whom he said were "bitten and pinched by invisible agents." Hale was clearly affected by seeing the two little girls suffer through attacks in which "their throats choaked, [and] their limbs wracked and tormented so as might move an heart of stone."[1] The Parrises did what any concerned parents would do: they cared for the sick girls while they prayed and fasted, hoping for a recovery. The illness lingered for weeks. When the symptoms did not abate, Reverend Parris consulted a local physician. After the examination, the physician concluded that the little girls were the victims not of physical or mental illness but of witchcraft.

A charge of bewitchment in such disturbing cases was not unheard of in the Puritan colonies of New England. Belief that Satan was close at hand and able to act within the physical world was real. When Cotton Mather later wrote of the outbreak, he related that during the Salem examinations there was sworn testimony that "at prodigious witch-meetings the wretches have proceeded so far as to Concert and Consult the Methods of Rooting out the Christian Religion from this Country." This statement was not simply a justification for the trials but an appeal to his readers—an appeal that was familiar and logical to those who had long heard their own ministers preach about the dangers of this new land. It certainly would have reflected readers' own anxieties about what might lie in wait in the dark woods beyond the dooryard.[2]

Although the outline of the events that made up the witch hunt in Salem are familiar in some form to most modern Americans, it is worthwhile to briefly discuss what happened in 1692–93. Just as there was a social context for the use of Salem witchcraft as a metaphor in the nineteenth century, there was a social context for the charges, the trials, and the various ways the episode was remembered in the years immediately after the trials ended. The individual motivations of the accusers, the witnesses, and the clergy, as well as the broader social and political contexts of the episode, inspire continuing debate and, despite the huge number of studies in print, are likely to persist as a subject of scholarly and popular interest. Before later generations saw interpretive significance in the larger social and political context of the episode, seventeenth-century Puritans saw in those same events their own signs that Satan might well be launching an invasion of their colony.[3]

The Massachusetts Bay Colony's Puritan inhabitants were always alert to the "signs" that served as markers for God's pleasure or displeasure with them, and in 1692 those signs were plentiful. Political turmoil since the 1680s, in both England and New England, left the colony without a charter and briefly without a governor. In addition, Essex County was on the northern side of the settled area. The ongoing war with Indians on the northern frontier and the ever-present threat from the bordering French colonies were other sources of anxiety. Local and individual tensions over landownership, the appointment of Samuel Parris as minister, and other church-related issues, as well as personal feuds and the sense among many that the religious mission and faith of colonists were in decline made them more alert to any signs of God's displeasure or the devil's predations. Each of these contemporary difficulties not only posed an immediate threat to life and property but created a psychological framework wherein the appearance of witchcraft was not only possible but likely.

Still, while witchcraft was a capital crime and something to be feared, it was believed to be rare and limited; most commonly an outbreak was confined to charges leveled against an individual or a very small circle of witches. In the entire period of settlement before 1692, fewer than one hundred people were prosecuted, and only sixteen are known to have been executed. The one-year ordeal of the Salem witchcraft cases, by contrast, resulted in the imprisonment of two hundred, the execution by hanging of nineteen, and the death of one man, Giles Corey, for refusing to speak.

By 1692, learned jurists and theologians in the metropolitan center of the kingdom were split over many of the finer points of recognizing and prosecuting witchcraft. The debates were academic and as yet had little effect on either the law or the everyday beliefs and experiences of most people. In more rural areas of England, and certainly in the remote, closed society of religious dissenters living on the outer edge of the empire in New England, the threat of "Satan's malignity" was real and always potentially close at hand.[4] Descriptions that included words like "malignity" were more than simple rhetoric. Witchcraft, or *maleficium*, was a cancer with the potential to devastate a community by destroying lives and property. When presented with a charge of *maleficium* by someone claiming to have been afflicted, ministers proceeded carefully to rule out mental, physical, or emotional causes for the accusation. The traditional methods for testing the veracity of the alleged victim's claims included the same steps of fasting and prayer taken in the first weeks in Salem by Samuel Parris and his colleagues. But when all considered and learned opinion concluded that witchcraft was at the root of the children's suffering over several long weeks, there was nothing to do in 1692 but to discover the agent of their torment before more destruction was brought upon the community.

Following the diagnosis in February 1692, Reverend Parris and his colleagues pressed Betty and Abigail to name their tormenters. Under the intense pressure from the adults in their household and community, they did. The girls named Tituba, a slave Parris had brought to the colony from Barbados.[5] Two other women, Sarah Osburn (who would die in jail) and Sarah Good (who would be tried and executed) were also named as witches. Justices of the Peace John Hathorne and Jonathan Corwin issued warrants for the arrest of the women named.

Tituba's March 1, 1692, confession included the critical fact that she had signed a "book" (indicating a formal covenant with the devil), and more important for the course of the trials, indicated that there were still more witches abroad. Tituba testified that there were nine "marks" in the devil's book, including those of the already accused Good and Osburn. Throughout her recorded testimony she repeated Satan's threats about the consequences of failing to do his will. Most dramatically, Satan told her on the very morning of the examination that if she testified, "he would Cutt my head off."[6] From the perspective of her interrogators, the significant element of her testimony was not the dramatic threat Tituba repeated but the startling news that there were as many as nine conspirators. Although others would later make claims of hundreds, this self-confessed witch had provided information that by itself expanded the hunt.[7] Still, while the word of a slave and the claims of children too young to testify under oath were chilling, they were but not enough by themselves to cause real panic.

The key element in turning accusations and arrests into prosecutable cases is found within the warrant for the arrest of Sarah Good on February 29, 1692, the day before Tituba's examination. Listed in the warrant is the first complaint that can be considered to be made by an adult: seventeen-year-old Elizabeth Hubbard claimed she too was "molested by Satan."[8] Although more children and adolescents would bring charges against other community members through the spring and summer months, the most critical to the legal processes were the large number of men and women in the community who accused and testified and those who controlled the courts. Authority at every stage of the episode in Massachusetts Bay Colony was ultimately in the hands of adults, not children.

But the little girls from the initial incident (Betty Parris and Abigail Williams) and the other "afflicted girls" (like Ann Putnam Jr.) who are the focus of so much speculation in later histories of the trials do deserve some consideration. Were the young girls of Salem involved in some sort of occult or folk magic practices? Or did they learn of the symptoms of bewitchment from published accounts and use them to gain attention? The first issue is easily discounted; this version, popularized most widely in the 1860s by minister-historian Charles Wentworth Upham in *Salem Witchcraft*, originated in earlier elementary school histories. Whether Upham picked this up from those earlier histories in print or whether it might have been local lore (he was a Salem native) by the mid-nineteenth century is not clear. What is apparent is that most historians and writers who later followed Upham seem to have been influenced by his extensive use of trial records. But no evidence exists in the seventeenth-century records to implicate Tituba or any other adult in introducing or encouraging any "occult" practices within any adolescent circles in Salem contemporaneously with the 1692 charges.[9] In regard to claims that reports of early witchcraft cases in circulation in the colony prompted the girls' initial symptoms and accusations, the problem becomes, Which witchcraft cases? Cotton Mather's own account of the 1688 case of the four Good-win children in *Memorable Providences* was indeed circulating in print and likely was an object of discussion in the region—particularly in the household of a minister like Parris. But it would hardly be necessary for children to hear of a past case when there were other active accusations of witchcraft being pursued in the neighborhood of Salem in the winter of 1691–92.[10]

Just as witchcraft was a reasonable, if rare, diagnosis for the affliction of the children in the Parris household, those first accused fell into so-cial categories that made them the "usual suspects" in any occurrence of witchcraft in a community. Sarah Good and Sarah Osburn were females who either were paupers or were old and, in general, as marginal to their communities as the slave Tituba. Sarah Good, in fact, had once before been a suspect, which left her at particular risk for further accusations. If any people had reason to be resentful about their lot in life and open to overtures by Satan, both popular and clerical wisdom in Puritan New England assumed it was women like these.

As with all witchcraft charges, those in Salem were strongly related to gender and social class. Women were far more likely to be accused than men. Most historians agree that about 80 percent of accusations were di-rected at women; the majority of men accused were kin to those women. John Proctor's case is a good example of how men became the objects of witchcraft accusations. The conviction and death sentence given to Proctor's wife alone could eventually bring suspicion on him within the dynamics of seventeenth-century witchcraft allegations. Despite popular assumptions in later times, that Proctor drew attention to himself by his public distain for the charges and by his signing of a petition in support of Rebecca Nurse, these were contributory factors at best. It is clear from a comparison of the signatories of the petition in support of Nurse that neighbor did not fear to publicly stand for neighbor even in a crisis of this magnitude. Rebecca Nurse, a pious, respected member of the commu-nity fell so far outside the socially understood definitions of a likely witch that thirty-nine of her neighbors protested the charge using their longtime knowledge of her character as a defense.[11] But whatever combination of circumstances brought accusers to name John Proctor, none of the other petitioners were accused. We can also see in the case of the known es-capees from Salem and the ultimate disposition of some of the charges that the wealthy (Philip and Mary English) and the famous and influen-tial (Captain John Alden) at least appeared to be treated with more care, if not actively assisted in their flight.[12]

It was May when the newly appointed royal governor Sir William Phips arrived in Massachusetts Bay Colony, and the Salem court had already been at work for two months. Phips arrived to find a colony already in crisis. He met the threat head-on by ordering that those imprisoned be secured by chains and moved to the strongest jails in the colony. Those experienced in witchcraft outbreaks understood from the testimony of victims that witches had enhanced strength and so were a special threat to the community. Governor Phips also appointed six of his council to sit in a special Court of Oyer and Terminer (literally, "to hear and to determine") to investigate what clearly had provincewide implications. William Stoughton, lieutenant governor of the colony, was made chief justice, and Phips requested that Boston ministers guide the court on the best methods for discovering who truly were witches.

The establishment of a special court to hear the cases points to another issue frequently ignored or distorted in the matter of the 1692 cases: the extensive and formal legal procedures that were followed. The records remaining three hundred years later are incomplete, but they do show clearly that the cases were investigated and tried by jury. There was no "rush to judgment" in the modern-day meaning of the phrase. Examinations of witnesses, grand jury indictments, jury trials, and long stays in prison were the fate of many of the two hundred or more arrested.[13] Arrest warrants, indictments, recognizes, depositions, and other legal documents familiar not only to the legal authorities of seventeenth-century England but to the modern American as well are all available for the cases tried in 1692. Those in later times who attempted to unravel the chain of events and understand the Salem episode were hampered not by lack of legal evidence but, instead, by an inability to understand how a court of law could read a "guilty" verdict on a witchcraft charge. Unless, of course, those involved were deceived by witnesses, operated under some sort of "delusion" themselves, or corruptly perverted justice to serve the interests of the colony or the church in the episode. John Hale's statement five years later might be either the cry of a man trying to justify his own role in a matter that had become controversial or a reasonable reminder to the lay community of the duty he faced as a minister in 1692 when a charge of witchcraft had been made. The investigation and the trials, Hale wrote, were "a conscientious endeavor to do the thing that was right."[14] And by mid-June of 1692, it is also reasonable to argue, the authorities were indeed attempting to use the best information and practices available. The legal proceedings had been taken from the local to the provincial level, and the advice of the leading theologians in the colony was formally sought in order to follow the most correct procedures in this civil-religious crime.

On June 15, 1692, the Boston ministers completed the "Return of Several Ministers" for Governor Phips. They detailed the best contemporary wisdom on how the court should proceed in response to the crime of witchcraft. The ministers urged the court to use "very critical and exquisite caution" in the use of "spectral" evidence, that is, evidence most often observable only by those afflicted. Such evidence was considered by all experts to be an indication that an accused might be practicing witchcraft but in itself was not reliable *proof* of witchcraft. The devil "sometimes represented the shapes of persons not only innocent, but also very virtuous," the ministers reminded the court.[15] The English standard was for spectral evidence to be supported by empirical evidence that all could see and weigh. In the seventeenth century this could include physical signs ("the devil's mark" or "witches' teats"), being witnessed calling on Satan or unspecified "spirits" for assistance, or a confession.

Despite the ministers' warning to the court, spectral evidence was clearly a significant or even critical part of the cases against those convicted in Salem. Witness testimony about midnight attacks by accused witches was important but was not the only way spectral evidence entered into the trials as evidence. Perhaps the most insidious appearances were the apparent manifestations of witch attacks during the court sessions themselves. The effects of the alleged torments of the afflicted that could be seen by adult witnesses in the courtroom were included within the complaint in the indictments. In effect, witnessing an individual's claiming spectral torment while in court became empirical evidence at Salem, contrary to established legal and clerical opinion in such cases.[16]

Cotton Mather, in modern times the Puritan clergyman most closely associated with the 1692 trials, and most often the target of blame, began his association with Salem witchcraft as the primary author of the June 15, 1692, "Return of Several Ministers." Although his official account of the trials for the colonial government (*Wonders of the Invisible World*) provided the source material for the creation in much later times of his postmortem reputation as their architect, his first duties were warning the court of the potential for error. In that role, ironically, Mather was arguably the author of the only method of escaping certain execution once an accused went to trial. He recommended to the court that defendants whose witchcraft-related crimes were "lesser" not be executed upon conviction; more significantly, if the accused confessed and made a "solemn, open, Public and Explicit renunciation of the Devil," her life should be spared.[17] This letter was not publicly distributed, but those facing trial would soon see the pattern, starting with the very first examinations and trials. The slave Tituba, who spent a year in a colonial jail, was examined, confessed, and was not executed (it is not clear from records if she was ever indicted by a grand jury). Rebecca Nurse simply maintained her innocence. She had no prior reputation that might implicate her in such charges, and no regular evidence was offered. She was executed. Bridget Bishop also declared her innocence to the end. Bishop, however, faced evidence that supported any spectral evidence offered. That she had been accused years earlier provided critical circumstantial evidence, and sworn testimony to her possession of puppets by witnesses in the Salem trials provided enough empirical evidence for any witchcraft charge. Spectral evidence also was offered at Bishop's trial, but she was doomed before that was entered. Bridget Bishop was convicted of witchcraft and hanged in June 1692.[18] Five more of the accused were convicted and hanged in July, five died in August, and the final eight executions were done later in August. By the middle of October the trials were temporarily suspended, and the witchcraft outbreak in Massachusetts Bay Colony began to collapse.

It is clear from the record of the official actions of Governor Phips in mid-October that there were serious concerns about the scope and conduct of the trials. All of those concerns centered on the controversial issue of spectral evidence. The governor canceled the scheduled October sitting of the court, and he wrote to the Privy Council in London on October 12, 1692, informing the government that he had done so because of the dubious value of spectral evidence. Phips said, "I found that the devil had tak[en] upon him the name and shape of severall persons who were doubtlesse inocent." Phips distanced himself from the situation that by any measure was causing as much uproar in the colony as any invasion of witches. Phips was also careful to detail the steps he had taken to reduce his own culpability for the trials in London's eyes. Although he was en route to the colony when the first arrests began, he also made sure to give the impression that he had little to do with them once he arrived. He used the ongoing war on the northern frontier as a reason for his absence during the summer (according to the records, he was actually in Boston that summer). In case any of the debate about the use of spectral evidence in the trials reached London, Phips dismissed its importance to the cases already adjudicated by saying that convictions had been predicated on "the accusations of the afflicted and then went upon other humane evidence to strengthen that."[19] In short, Phips presented himself as a man in control of the situation–at least once he was back in Boston from his claimed service at the battlefront—who prudently suspended the proceedings to await instructions from the home government once trials appeared to have become controversial in the colony.

But the judicial machinery still rolled forward on the cases already in the system, and new accusations were made. Many of the accused were still imprisoned in October, and in December the colony created yet another court (the Superior Court of Judicature) that had among its responsibilities the disposition of the remaining cases. More than fifty defendants were tried between January and May 1693, but only three accused witches were convicted in trials that strictly adhered to the traditional rules of evidence. All the defendants in these cases had confessed to witchcraft.

Those still languishing in the colony's jails and those who had earlier faced arrest but temporarily fled the colony required legal closure to resume their lives, even if the trials appeared to be all but over at the end of 1692. Those who had the means to escape to New York earlier in the summer, like Captain John Alden and the Englishes, apparently felt it was safe to return. Alden returned to face the court in December, was released on bond, and by April 1693 no further legal action was pending against him. Although the Englishes were accused, there is no record extant of a "true bill" being voted by the grand jury. Philip English also petitioned the courts well into the eighteenth century for damages related to his ordeal, without any reference to trials or verdicts. All the imprisoned, including those who were found innocent or never brought to trial, remained in prison until their families or some sympathetic member of the community paid the jailer for their keep. Victims and their families petitioned the colonial government well into the eighteenth century for restitution and for reversals of attainder on estates. Some would even petition the state of Massachusetts into the twenty-first century for the clearance of convictions. Though the jails were beginning to empty a little more than a year after the first arrests, the political and social consequences were far from over.

The scope of the 1692 witch hunt had been unprecedented in colonial British America, and some of the same elements that led to the acceleration of the hunt in the early spring contributed to Phips's suspending the court by early fall. Chief among these were the credibility of the accusers and the targets of the accusations. While, as Mary Beth Norton has shown, the predominance of women and children believed to be victims in the earliest wave of attacks provided very sympathetic victims, they were also the easiest to discredit as the movement to question spectral evidence gained force. Certainly, as Norton notes, "few as yet charged them with dissembling," because most of those who commented in print believed that they were confused victims of Satan's deceit or even potentially in league with Satan themselves.[20] Confusion or being themselves under the control of Satan through their inherent weaknesses of age and sex could also explain the other serious concern about how the accused were too often outside of any understanding of who was a likely witch.

Those accused in the earliest wave of accusations (like the slave Tituba or the sharp-tongued pauper Sarah Good) were the "usual suspects" in any witchcraft outbreak simply because of their condition in life and the resentments it might spawn in them toward the more fortunate members of their community. Such women, it was thought, might be bitter enough or weakened enough to allow Satan to hold sway over them and to follow his bidding to attack neighbors and kin. Minister George Burroughs, pious Rebecca Nurse, Reverend John Hale's wife or any number of the good church members of Massachusetts Bay Colony and their families who were accused at some point during the outbreak in 1692 were not thus motivated. And accusations of a crime that was understood by all to have its roots in personal animosity against a stranger like Captain John Alden brought additional confusion to the proceedings as they spread through neighboring towns. In short, the established and understood signs by which to identify those who would do *maleficium* were eliminated for one short season, and everyone was potentially at risk. If everyone could be guilty, some had to wonder, then was it possible that no one was guilty? Certainly twenty-six men in the neighboring town of Andover asked this question when protesting the cases against their neighbors in mid-October 1692. When capital cases were built on "the Accusations of children and others [who are] under a Diabolicall influence," they wrote in their petition to the General Court, the result was a situation where "we know not who can think himself safe."[21]

Coming to terms with the trauma of the witchcraft episode was necessary for the entire community because of its scope and the risk it had posed to all. In a society that believed the devil could be physically present, the discovery and execution of a limited number of witches might be expected. While the discovery of such a crime was a personal tragedy, it also averted a community disaster. The long duration of the siege (by

Satan or by the government in the name of rooting out Satan) and the seemingly uncontrolled sweep that left all at risk (from the disaffected marginal inhabitants of the colony to the prosperous and pious) had everyone groping for a way to incorporate the recent experience into their lives. Defining the experience of the trials in their aftermath was critical— not simply cathartic, but essential for the reintegration of lives directly affected and for the general reconciliation of faith with experience. Colonial officials needed both socially and politically to assert the propriety of their actions and judgments in order to maintain their present and future authority. Those they governed, traumatized by a season of vulnerability and community losses, needed the acknowledgment that errors had been made before they could reestablish the familiar patterns that constituted their identity as a community and sustained their trust in authority. How that process would be accomplished by those who shaped the narrative of the trial experience while it was still in "living memory" largely set the terms of that reconciliation and determined how the episode would be remembered long afterward.

Despite the turmoil of the actual trials and the highly literate community within which they occurred, the temper of the general population of Massachusetts Bay Colony in relation to the events of 1692 can only be pieced together. In fact, reconstructing the social context of the aftermath of the trials can be more difficult than reconstructing the trials themselves. One historian of seventeenth-century witchcraft, Richard Godbeer, likened his experience of working with contemporary trial transcripts to watching "narrow-beamed spotlights that play upon an otherwise darkened landscape" as the accused and their accusers "made brief and dramatic appearances in the records at the time of their trial and then returned to obscurity."[22] Nevertheless, there are ways to recover how the experience was being interpreted and remembered as it ended. Such evidence exists within four categories: the petitions for restitution, pardon, and reversal of attainder; the narratives of the trials published by ministers as the trials ended; the public acts of contrition by the community and individuals involved in the legal processes; and finally, the emergence of counternarrative in print form by 1700. In these sources there is sufficient evidence to determine popular opinion about the ordeal of the community, general assumptions about how the law against witchcraft should be applied, and what the protectors of the court and government believed it was necessary to defend about the witchcraft trials. By evaluating the existing sources in these categories, we can gain some sense of how public sentiment changed and how a particular narrative of Salem's colonial witchcraft trials entered national memory a century later.[23]

Petitions provide the most direct sense of public opinion regarding the trials. There are petitions to Salem court supporting those imprisoned; but more important, as the trials ended there are individual petitions to the General Court seeking redress. Trial transcripts, however, are highly mediated. Testimony in any trial is limited not only by the nature of the questions to which the witnesses and defendants are asked to directly respond but by the mediated record of their responses. This is particularly true in the seventeenth-century witchcraft trials. The recorder for the court was often either a member of the panel of judges (most notably John Hathorne and Jonathan Corwin) or had kin among those who were witnesses, accusers, or accused (Samuel Parris and Thomas Putnam fall into this category). This naturally raises questions about their biases and makes considering recorded testimony more complicated than simply recognizing that such untrained recorders were only approximating any verbatim transcripts of testimony. Petitions, however, are self-generated documents. Though some might have been completed for individuals by other members of the community, they can reasonably be considered to have been done at the direction of the petitioner and to contain his or her sentiments. As a common English practice, petitioning was encouraged, provided it addressed the government "Christianly and respectively." The practical value for the government in allowing such petitioning was to turn potentially "dangerous dissent into lawful and manageable channels."[24]

There are still in existence seventy-three petitions from the suspension of the trials in October 1692 to the last filed by immediate family members of the accused in 1750.[25] The language used in the petitions for pardon, restitution, and other requests to void judgments is an intriguing source of evolving public opinion—in particular, the words the petitioner chooses to identify the legal matter on which the appeal was being made, and the grounds on which the petitioner believes relief should be granted. Key to determining public temper is the rapid change in descriptive language about the trials and their participants. During the witchcraft trials, and even as they were being temporarily suspended by Governor Phips in October 1692, petitions conformed to a technique based on defending the subject against the basic charge of witchcraft on the grounds of known good character. The petition of the twenty-six men of Andover on behalf of their neighbors follows such a form. The petitioners first carefully affirmed their own piety and their respect for the law, since they "would not appear as Advocates for any who shall be found guilty of so horrid a crime." Appeals in this vein were based on common understanding of who was likely to be a witch. "Our friends and neighbours have been misrepresented," one petition began, and detailed lifelong good behavior, church membership, and "blameless conversation." And for those they named who had confessed to the crime of witchcraft? "We have reason to think that the extream urgency that was used with some of them" by family and interrogators provoked confession as a desperate measure. In other words, they were urged to confess by friends and family in order to live, or they were subjected to extreme methods of interrogation. Most important, the Andover petitioners got to the heart of their own confusion and anxiety about the episode when they complained, "We know not who can think himself safe, if the Accusations of children and others [who are] under a Diabolicall influence shall be received against persons of good fame."[26]

Although the appeal to character appeared within petitions well into the eighteenth century, it quickly disappeared as the sole point of defense. Even when petitions were pointed in their criticism of the trials and referred specifically to public knowledge that the trials were defective, they often still included a defense of the community reputation of their loved one. In 1711, the family of the executed minister George Burroughs argued that "the influence and energy of the evil spirits [was] so great...as to cause a prosecution to be had of persons of known and good reputations." Although petitioners were quick to see the advantage in using public discontent and government defensiveness about the conduct of the trials in their appeals, the continued inclusion of an appeal to character even as a secondary defense served both personal and procedural arguments. It was often the last chance to publicly assert the good reputation of a lost loved one (or to rehabilitate one's own), even while it reminded the government that the abuse of spectral evidence in the Salem cases violated the legal requirement for empirical evidence in such cases. Witchcraft was a crime rooted in character and conduct observable to all.[27]

By December 1692, only two months after the suspension of the trials, criticism of the process itself crept into petitions, and known good character was minimized or eliminated as the primary grounds for relief. This language became the standard basis for requesting relief in petitions related to the trials through the eighteenth century. It reflected a profoundly changed social and political context. The late fall of 1692 brought publications by ministers who openly addressed questions in the community about the value and use of spectral evidence. Whatever the general mood, the appearance in print of replies to "concerns" brought that issue into the open and made it available to petitioners. The December 1692 petition of Abigail Faulkner reflects such an application. She claimed that some who named her had formally recanted their testimony, but she also boldly challenged the nature of the trial evidence, saying she had been "condemned to die having had no other Evidences against me but ye Spectre Evidences."[28] Certainly Faulkner could not have hoped for an approval of her request if she raised a challenge that was radical. Such a challenge would be considered neither "Christianly" in tone nor appropriately respectful toward the government, as a petition must be by its very definition. What did allow Abigail Faulkner and others to use such language was that these issues already had been raised publicly in print—often, in fact, by ministers.

By December 1692 at least three publications by prominent clergymen had attempted to define the proper role of spectral evidence. After 1700, when Robert Calef's blunt full-length history of the trials challenged them on just these grounds, other petitions moving toward the General Assembly invariably included claims of deceit by witnesses based on either their own false natures or Satan's influence. Faulkner's own 1700 and 1703 petitions are even more direct in their assertions of falsehoods than in the winter of 1692: "My selfe was accused by ye afflicted who pretended to see me by theire spectrall sight." Faulker declared in her later petitions not only that the court was incorrect in the weight it gave to spectral evidence, but that witnesses had lied in providing it.[29] In 1710 Abraham Foster's petition for restitution of his mother's cost of imprisonment during the trials, referring to the unreliability of spectral evidence, used a phrase that was by then a standard distillation of the argument. Foster complained that his mother's 1692 conviction was the result of "such evidence as is now Generally thought Insufficient."[30]

The petitions languished in the General Court during the 1690s and on into the first decade of the next century. Massachusetts Bay Colony, however, did compile an unusual record of public attempts to reconcile the trauma of the witchcraft trials with community dissatisfaction in their aftermath. Witch hunts were not new to Old or New England, and the suspicions were more likely to linger than to disappear with an individual's acquittal. Or they might be redirected toward the surviving family of an executed witch. In this witch hunt, however, everything was reversed. Rather than targeting the accused and their survivors for more signs of *maleficium*, the community offered them a form of support in rebuilding their lives. Even though the Salem episode was only one item in a list prepared five years later for reflection on a general day of fasting called by the governor for January 14, 1697, it nonetheless was on the list. On the appointed day Samuel Sewall, one of the original trial judges, stood with his minister before the congregation of his Boston church and asked forgiveness for his role in the trials. Twelve of the trial jurors also marked the day by publicly signing a statement admitting that they now believed there had been "insufficient basis" for the 1692 witchcraft convictions and repented of their own part in the episode. The very existence of government action and individual repentance in print or public confession provides additional hints about the level of grief and anger that lingered in local memory. And as the century closed, petitions continued to make their way to the General Court in ever increasing numbers.[31]

In 1703 the petitioners gained support for their requests from ministers in the region (including Joseph Green, Samuel Parris's replacement in Salem village). In their own petition the ministers affirmed that "neighbours of good conversation" had been imprisoned in 1692 owing to "the complaint of some young persons under Diabolicall molestations." By 1703 even ministers could argue that it "hath been Acknowledged, that there were Errors and mistakes" in the trials despite the care taken by the court.[32] The General Assembly of the colony at long last responded in that year as it cleared the convictions of some petitioners. It also made a limited acknowledgment of error by saying in the bill that "it is Conceived by many worthy and pious Persons that the Evidence given . . . was weak and insufficient as to Taking away the lives of Sundry so condemned"— although it had not yet granted any of the petitions for financial relief.[33] However, by the first years of the new century it was settled opinion at all levels of society that "errors and mistakes" had been made in regard to the Salem trials. As ministers joined petitioners from their communities to request that some restitution be made to families impoverished by seizures, by 1709 even Cotton Mather, the 1692 government's chief defender, was calling on the government to act. Finally, in 1710 the legislature named a committee to review the petitions. One year later, in October 1711, just a few months shy of a full decade after the witch hunt began, a committee began holding sessions in Salem to determine financial compensation. Except for Philip English, only those whose petitions were in regard to condemned or executed witches were awarded any compensation. In the act passed to appropriate funds, the General Court acknowledged that something had gone amiss in 1692, but it still neatly deflected blame. Those who petitioned got some practical relief, but if they were looking for an apology, the government was still not offering one. "The Influence and Energy of the Evil Spirits so great at that time acting in and upon those who were the principal Accusers and Witnesses proceeding so far as to cause a Prosecution to be had of persons of known and good Reputation; which caused a great Dissatisfaction and a Stop to be put thereunto until their Majesty's pleasure should be known therein."[34] Satan and those in his thrall were responsible, not the officials of the colony or its courts. The act also formally recognized that there was public turmoil over the trials. But according to this bill the government's only role was successfully bringing the unfortunate matter to an end.[35]

Thus the petitioners' ability to openly question the conduct of the trials themselves changed the terms of appeals from the character of the accused to the character of the trials. While the suspension of the trials may have emboldened some who were angry to challenge the government in the very petitions that sought favors, it is more feasible to conclude that the immediate publication of ministerial accounts that tried to justify the trials in late 1692 opened the door for individuals to question them and finally gain some public redress. Within those ministerial publications about the trials were elements that directly addressed ongoing public dissent about some aspects of the 1692 trials.

During the most active period of court proceedings, any attempts at public debate over the validity of government action in the matter of witchcraft had been suppressed publicly and dramatically. In June 1692 William Milborne, a Baptist minister in Boston, was briefly arrested for claiming that the trials were conducted in a way "whereas several persons of good fame and unspotted reputation stand committed to several gaols in this Province upon suspistion of sundry acts of witchcraft only upon bare specter testimonie." Governor Phips issued an order for his arrest, citing writings "conteining very high Reflections upon the Administrations of Publick Justice." Milborne paid his bond of £200 for the "said Seditious and Scandalous Papers or writings."[36] At some point between May and October, Phips had issued a general ban on publications, as he reported in his October letter to the Privy Council. "I have alsoe put a

stop to the Printi[ng] of any discourse one way or the other that may increase the needlesse disputes of people upon this occaision because I saw
a likelihood of Kindling an inextinguishable flame if I should admit any
publique and open Contests."[37]

Phips's order notwithstanding, by fall of 1692 there were a number
of manuscripts in circulation among the influential and educated in the
colony, and nearly all were designed to establish an official narrative of
the motives and actions of the clergy and government.[38] Several ministers,
including Increase and Cotton Mather, were preparing books in defense
of the colonial government and its church. All were, in fact, authorized (at
least secretly) by the governor and were indeed published in the weeks
around Phips's letter to England. In each case, publication locations or
dates were falsified to avoid the appearance of violating the publication
ban even while the government was actively suppressing the publication
of dissenting arguments.[39]

Despite their explicit purpose of justifying the traumatic events of
the past nine months in the service of protecting the community, each of
the ministers specifically addressed the issue of spectral evidence. Increase
Mather presented his arguments about witchcraft and spectral evidence
before some ministers of the colony and gained the concordance of many,
who were subsequently listed in the printed version as endorsing his argument. He justified the process of witch-hunting through a discussion of the
theological literature about the nature of the devil and the traditional legal methods for discovering and defining witchcraft. As Increase Mather's
manuscript circulated before publication, it gained more endorsements
and was read from many pulpits in the colony.[40] His often-quoted line,
"Better that ten supposed witches should escape, than that one innocent
person should be condemned," was the sort of statement his son Cotton
(noticeably missing from those who endorsed the book in print) feared
would give support to those who wished to "cavil and nibble" at the justification for finding and trying witches and the methods of doing so.[41]

The closest thing to an "official" narrative of the trials was Cotton
Mather's own *Wonders of the Invisible World*. Written at the express
request of Samuel Sewall and Lieutenant Governor William Stoughton
(respectively, a member of the Court of Oyer and Terminer and its chief
justice). They hoped to quell the public uproar by reasserting the dangers of witchcraft and the propriety of the methods used in the current
witchcraft cases.[42] Despite Mather's own warnings in June about the place
of spectral evidence in witchcraft trials and the court's obvious failure to

adhere to the guidance offered, his book was a classic defense of the institutional structures of colony and church.[43] Cotton Mather's goal was not to split hairs over spectral evidence but to offer his readers a broader perspective. His preoccupation was "the whole PLOT of the Devil, against *New-England,*" and he insisted that Satan's possibly using the innocent to confess (or to be under the suspicion of their neighbors) was a tactic as dangerous to the survival of the colony as any other sort of diabolical attack he could launch. Mather was persistent in his demands that readers understand the nature of the threat at Salem. Confessions made there confirmed the worst possible situation for the survival of the colony. It was not merely that a few weak individuals had been persuaded to covenant with the devil but that "at prodigious Witch-Meetings the Wretches have proceeded so far as to Concert and Consult the Methods of Rooting out the Christian Religion from this Country." It was testimony that the conspiracy was vast and that Satan meant to do no less than destroy the entire North American Christian community. Perhaps, he wrote, some methods of the court could be called "disputed," but they were nonetheless methods used before in witchcraft trials.[44] Mather's argument is pure orthodoxy: to find and punish those covenanting with Satan in order to save the afflicted and protect the community was the duty of the court, and that duty was done with diligence. It was an argument that would likely have been sufficient and widely approved in 1691, but one that had proved dangerous to the pious in 1692.

Mather's history of the Salem trials dodged any discussion of the more controversial arrests and convictions that plainly troubled many who petitioned for their neighbors. Instead, he took as his case studies individuals like Bridget Bishop or Martha Carrier (or even the controversial minister George Burroughs, who had his own well-known controversies with his family and his community)—those whom anyone in seventeenth-century Puritan Massachusetts could see as potential witches. By failing to make any case at all for the accused who drew community support during their ordeal, like the widely supported pious Rebecca Nurse, he could not help but fail to convince men like those from Andover who asked in their own petition: "Who can think himself safe?" Ultimately, Mather's failing was that he did not do what his brethren did in 1692—defend the Salem trials as possibly flawed but ultimately fair and necessary—but Mather chose to dismiss the public's most pressing fears. Under Mather's argument, the message to readers was that they might find themselves the subject of witchcraft accusations in a similar episode where a good reputation could not provide a shield against malicious or even "diabolicall" accusations. Mather's own correspondence plainly shows the public reaction to his book and his own complete inability to understand that reaction. He wrote to his uncle John Cotton that he met nothing in Boston but "sinful and raging asperity."[45]

Samuel Willard, another Puritan minister in the colony, occupies an intermediate position within this list of contemporary authors. His publication about the trials, *Some Miscellany Observations on Our Present Debates Respecting Witchcrafts, in a Dialogue between S. & B.*, carried no authorial designation, and the title page gave its origin as Philadelphia. Willard endorsed Increase Mather's *Cases of Conscience* and even provided an introduction for it in the same month his own book was published. But Samuel Willard himself was a seasoned minister with serious concerns about the use of spectral evidence in the 1692 trials. He had experience evaluating similar allegations of witchcraft in the 1670s in a previous pastorate in Groton, Connecticut. In that case Willard defused the situation by using the traditional methods of skepticism and patience with the accuser. In his work on the 1692 trials, he affirmed the dangers and reality of witchcraft in the world as he provided an imaginary debate between "Salem" and "Boston" on the theological and legal issues surrounding witchcraft. Within his book, however, his speakers raised points of argument that could only inflame the debate within the colony. He stated that some persons in Massachusetts Bay Colony said of the Salem accusers that they were "scandalous persons, liars and loose in their Conversation, and therefore not to be believed."[46] Willard suggested that perhaps the devil had not covenanted with the accused but, in his natural inclination to deceive and confuse, had actually recruited the accusers and compelled them to implicate the innocent. Willard raised the issue at the heart of the problem of spectral evidence. Such people have "by their own account given themselves up to the Devil, the Father of Lies; and what Credit is to be given to the Testimony of such against the Lives of others?"[47] If Samuel Willard stands as an intermediate presence in the posttrial narratives, it is between the orthodoxy of Cotton Mather and challenges that arose from nonministerial sources.

Some influential criticism emerged in print only indirectly in the years following the trials. Thomas Brattle, for instance, circulated a copy of a letter among a select group of men in Boston in October 1692. The surviving copy of the letter, reputedly sent to an unnamed English correspondent, became a significant source for later historians and stands as one of the few contemporary examples of the opinion of a Massachusetts Bay Colony resident not writing in defense of his own role during the episode. Thomas Brattle was an educated member of the Massachusetts Bay Colony elite. A merchant with a Harvard degree, he eventually became a fellow of the Royal Society for his work in mathematics and astronomy. But before we label him a "man of science" and find in his criticizing witchcraft trials the actions of a rational man in an irrational and superstitious age, we need to understand that his criticism is quite specific and is located in the problems related to the conduct of the trials, not the idea of witchcraft itself. Thomas Brattle, in fact, was a pillar of his local Puritan congregation and, by his own statement in the letter, did not aim to "cast dirt on authority" by voicing his concerns about the course of the trials. Uninvolved personally, Brattle supplied his own narrative from a different perspective than those caught in its judicial apparatus as he point by point dismissed claims made by trial witnesses as fanciful–such as the idea that mere glances by the accused could send anyone into "fitts." He wrote what everyone who was familiar with the requirements of the law already knew: the court's over reliance on unsupported "spectral evidence" seen and heard only by the witnesses was legally incorrect. To Thomas Brattle the court procedures themselves were so contrary to established practice and so dire in their consequences that they did not merit the name of law but instead "deserv[ed] the name of Salem superstition and sorcery." Brattle worried that such irregularities would cause "the reasonable part of the world" to "laugh" and think that the problem in Massachusetts Bay Colony was not that the accused were possibly witches, but that the men supervising the trials were "possessed, at least, with ignorance and folly." What Brattle did in his letter, as Bernard Rosenthal has argued, was to make "the seventeenth-century case against the proceedings," but in 1692 he was making it to a limited circle. Thomas Brattle's criticism and language gained a wider audience only in 1700, when Robert Calef of Boston used it as a source for his radical challenge to the publications by Mather and others tied to the government.[48]

Historian Samuel Eliot Morison famously said of Robert Calef that he "tied a tin can to Cotton Mather which has rattled and banged through the pages of superficial and popular histories."[49] Robert Calef was, like Mather, a respectable and educated man of the community, but by profession a merchant rather than a minister. Although Calef finished his own

manuscript in 1697, it was not published until 1700, by an English printer
who took on the task no printer in Massachusetts Bay Colony dared do.
Calef, the first nonministerial author of a narrative of the 1692 witchcraft
trials, was unsparing in his assessment of the trials and their participants.
The very title of his book, *More Wonders of the Invisible World*, mocked
Mather. The five years between the trials and his writing of the manuscript
obviously provided more than enough time for communal reflection and
reconsideration.[50]

Robert Calef used accounts he gathered from court records and from
victims and their families. Though Calef's position was peripheral to circles of power in the colony, his use of these accounts made him the public
voice of the accused and their families. Robert Calef's blunt posttrial assessment of the participants and their motives drew from Brattle, from
trial records, and from living victims and witnesses to the events. He
plainly blamed the witchcraft accusations on "a parcel of possessed, dis-
tracted, or lying Wenches." It was their deceit that "let loose the Devils of
Envy, Hatred, Pride, Cruelty, and Malice . . . disguised under the Mask of
Zeal for God." Thus Calef's account of the trials created a seventeenth-
century lexicon of Salem witchcraft that launched provocative words like
"zeal," "infatuation," "delusion," "superstition," "folly," and "ignorance"
into the published accounts of the trials as early as 1700. Reaction by those
most implicated in the operation or public defense of the trials was swift
and angry. Cotton Mather bitterly complained about Calef in his diary (as
he would rail against other Salem-based criticisms until his death in 1728)
and, with a few allies, provided a public rebuttal in *Some Few Remarks
upon a Scandalous Book*. The authors noted with obvious satisfaction
that "we heard that our Booksellers were so well acquainted with the Integrity of our Pastors, as that not one of them could admit of any of those
Libels to be vended in their shops." Increase Mather (president of Harvard College and father of Cotton) had a copy of the Calef book burned
publicly at the college.

Neither merchant Calef nor mathematician Brattle denied the possibility that men and women might covenant with the Devil and practice various
forms of *maleficium* on their neighbors, but they did doubt the veracity of
the accusers and the weight given to spectral evidence within the trials.
Their position on the witchcraft trials was logical among believing men
of their time and place. But whatever their own intentions, they provided
language that would be selectively used with different implications by other
men in later times. If anything, Calef and Brattle were the harbingers of a

new order where ministers would become more subordinate to such worldly men in the daily operation of society and government.[51]

Controlling the narrative about an event, as Governor Phips and the ministers instinctively understood in 1692, gives hope of controlling any collective social memory of it. The initial narrative of events in particular stakes out a moral territory that defines prevailing mores and affirms existing standards. Memory distills experience by "selectively emphasizing, suppressing and elaborating different aspects" of the historical record. Referring back to the historical record is a critical source of legitimation for the lessons the community is meant to derive from the original event. Later authors who chose Calef's history of the trials as their own source material explained that choice by framing him as a contemporary truth-teller who lived through events without personal involvement and who used official records and eyewitness accounts to challenge the narratives published by the colony's ministers. Robert Calef's own intentions ultimately became unimportant. Calef matters to later users of his narrative only in terms of how his account and even elements of his biography could be shaped to suit contemporary desires for a historical authority to support their own arguments.[52]

As the eighteenth century progressed and the trials began their retreat from living memory, Salem's witch hunt was enshrined in general histories of the British North American colonies, and historians had no compunctions about freely assigning blame and naming villains. Daniel Neal, an English clergyman who wrote a history of the Puritans in 1720 while the trials were still fully remembered, took Cotton Mather as his authority for the general history of the colony (in particular, *Magnalia Christi Americana*). Neal departed from Mather abruptly and solely on the issue of Salem's witch hunt, on which he resorted to the more agreeable (to the tastes of an eighteenth-century Londoner) Robert Calef. All the confessions and accusations, Neal wrote, "seem to me...the effects of a distemper'd brain." Another London resident, Thomas Salmon, wrote in his own history that he believed Salem minister Samuel Parris was "the prime author of the delusion." George Chalmers, a Baltimore Loyalist who returned to England on the eve of the Revolution and shared neither denominational nor regional ties with the Massachusetts Bay colonists, called the witch hunt "a kind of madness" perpetrated by a "credulous court" with the "greatest zeal and dispatch." Isaac Backus's 1784 history of Baptists in the colonies made a point of saying what later generations of American elementary school textbook authors would: that England had far more witchcraft executions. And then he made sure his readers knew there was no evidence that the Baptists had any role in what he called "those confused and bloody proceedings."[53]

In the case of physician William Douglass we can find both Salem's appearance in local histories and one of its first uses as a rhetorical weapon within a public controversy. Douglass begged the readers' pardon for his decision to exclude an extensive treatment of Salem witchcraft in his 1749 history of British North America and thus for leaving to others the details of what he called Cotton Mather's "amusements...[like] witches." Yet Douglass could not resist commenting on the trials, which he judged in medical terms to be "horrid inhuman murder, by colour of law...perpetrated upon many ignorant maniacs, and other persons affected in their nerves and called witches." Douglass, however, was hardly a disinterested historian when it came to Mather or his public actions. During the 1721--22 smallpox epidemic, Douglass had argued publicly, angrily, and at length with inoculation enthusiast Cotton Mather. James Franklin's Boston newspaper the *New England Courant* had taken up Douglass's cause against the untried and potentially dangerous smallpox vaccination scheme. The preface to the antivaccination pamphlet Douglass published in 1722 specifically used Salem against Mather in a manner that foreshadowed its use in later public controversies when both the events of 1692 and the epidemic of 1721-22 were long out of living memory. Douglass's pamphlet condemned three "infatuations" that New England could claim as her own: the persecution of Quakers, "the hanging of those suspected of Witchcraft about the Year 1692," and now the reckless inoculation proposal.[54]

William Douglass was not the only one to apply Salem witchcraft in a printed challenge to Mather during the epidemic. As part of the ongoing dispute, the newspaper's regular contributor Nathaniel Gardner wrote a parody of the pro-inoculation dialogues that had been recently published by Cotton Mather and other ministers. Gardner's version asks, "I pray, Sir, who have been instruments of Mischief and Trouble both in Church and State, from Witchcraft to Inoculation?"[55] For James Franklin, along with his younger brother Benjamin and their friends, his interest in this fight was more about challenging local authority than advancing scientific principles. As Perry Miller commented in regard to the local memory of the witchcraft trials and Cotton Mather's role in them, the youthful staff of the *Courant* "knew what the people thought, saw [their] chance, and thrust it home" specifically to discredit Mather in this latest public crisis.[56]

In one of several ironies, Mather here was (at least in retrospect, with inoculation now a standard medical practice) in the role of the champion of science while Benjamin Franklin, who would be considered a man of science later in life, was in the camp of the seemingly reactionary and even superstitious portion of the population. It required a bold group of young men like the Franklin brothers, with both means and motive, to taunt Mather with Salem witchcraft in the 1720s when many survivors and participants were still alive—or at least to do so publicly in print. If the temptation to make a similar parallel between contemporary controversies and Salem did occur to others in these decades when the event itself was still well within the living memory of the community, it seems that simple prudence rendered them more reticent than the Franklins and their friends with the *New England Courant*.

Given the emergence of Salem witchcraft as a useful metaphor in the 1830s in public debates over new religious movements, the "Great Awakening" of the 1730s to 1760s seems like an obvious place to find earlier parallels drawn between the perceived threats that might arise from the excitement of the revival experience and the witch hunt. But it is dangerously reductive to consider the differences between "Old" and "New Light" factions as being simply a function of "enthusiastick" behavior during services. Both sides actively appealed to the past for authority— they particularly noted Cotton Mather's own lament about the decline of pietistic fervor in New England—for their own approaches to religious renewal. The difficulty inherent in using Salem's witch hunt as a negative illustration while simultaneously appealing to the same Puritan past as a model for the return to faith can itself explain its absence from debates in the eighteenth century. A more logical explanation, however, is the dramatic change one hundred years brought in terms of audience and forum for controversies about revivalism.

One hundred years later, during the cycle of revivals labeled the Second Great Awakening, the terms and location of debates over religious practices and their implications for society had changed. In the eighteenth century fewer printed arguments appear to be directed outside ministerial or well-educated circles. In the nineteenth century, critics directed their concerns about the potential political and social consequences of revival fervor to a broader public audience—an audience that, in what was also a vastly expanded world of print, also was familiar as well with a historical example like Salem witchcraft that offered contemporary lessons. For whatever reason, Salem's episode of witch-hunting appeared so seldom in the eighteenth century as an example of where excessive religious "enthusiasm" might lead society that it is difficult to find any at all.[57]

As the contentious 1760s and 1770s brought political matters in the British colonies to outright rebellion, Salem was scattered among the examples chosen to illustrate how dire the situation had become. The impetus for this obviously was not only the political radicalism that centered on Massachusetts but the publication of an influential history of the colony that refreshed public memory about the trials. In 1767 Thomas Hutchinson, former royal governor of Massachusetts Bay Colony, published the second volume of his massive *History of the Province of Massachusetts.* Included in the latest volume was the history of the Salem trials. Hutchinson had used original trial records (many of which were destroyed or lost when a mob invaded his home in a "Stamp Act" protest in 1765), commented on earlier narrative versions of the trials, and clearly found Robert Calef to be the most authoritative seventeenth-century guide to the history of the trials.

Hutchinson provided a lively judgment-filled narrative that freely took issue with previous historical accounts of Salem witchcraft. Although many, like William Douglass in his 1749 history of the British colonies, savaged colonial officials over witchcraft trials (like his adversary Cotton Mather from the 1720 smallpox controversy), Hutchinson nevertheless condemned Douglass's own reasons for condemning the trials. Douglass, trained as a physician, concluded that Salem itself was a town that regularly produced "hysterias" and "hypochondrias." But Hutchinson (not a physician) dismissed this and made his own medical diagnoses of the maladies affecting the accusers. His conclusion was that the entire community suffered only temporarily from "bodily distempers" as a direct result of the stress of potential accusations. Further, anyone connected with the accusations or the trials was, to Hutchinson's mind, variously "credulous," guilty of rank "imposture," or simply operating under a "delusion."[58] Thomas Hutchinson's version of the Salem narrative remained the favored source for other histories well into the nineteenth century, but it also coincided with the increased use of Salem as a metaphor within political jabs aimed at Massachusetts radicals during the Revolutionary era.

The circulation of a popular history of Massachusetts Bay Colony in the late 1760s that clearly condemned a previous episode of "zeal" by its colonists clearly appealed to some in far less radical Philadelphia. One man, taking the opportunity to frame a call for an American-based bishop for the Anglican community in the colonies within his censure of present-day New England radicalism in politics, suggested that one benefit might be controlling the religious zeal that often erupted out of the same colony. After all, he argued, "who knows whether the New Englanders will remain content... and will not again hang Quakers [and] witches?"[59] John Leacock, a Philadelphian active in the Sons of Liberty, wrote doggerel and satirical pamphlets commenting on the political events of the day. His target was "extremes in all forms," and in a dig at radical Boston he chose "Matherius Cottonius, the former high priest... [of] the righteous, God's chosen people." Leacock concluded by asking if there is not still in "the land of New England" a "witch" to tell the future. Living outside the region was not a prerequisite to using Salem to express anxiety about extremism. In 1776, with the Revolution fully under way, Alexander King, a Connecticut physician and patriot, found his tyranny and historical illustration much closer to home. The local committee of safety drew his ire in a diary entry for its excessive zeal in routing out those who might harbor Loyalist sentiments. King claimed that the climate in the Suffield area was such that any "inadvertent expression" might bring calamity to a household. Such a climate of public opinion, he said, reminded him of "the time of imaginary witchcraft at Salem." Then too, men had neither "sense enough to perceive the impostures [nor] resolution enough to stem the torrent."[60]

Among the few metaphorical uses of Salem that appeared in over nearly a century, one exchange stands out—as much for its participants as for its use. In a manner that would become familiar within public controversies in a little more than fifty years, John Adams and Daniel Leonard staked out opposing positions, each recognizing in contemporary circumstances echoes of earlier events in Massachusetts. In the dispute about taxation on the eve of the American Revolution in 1774, Loyalist Daniel Leonard (writing as "Massachusettensis") defended the British government's imposing a duty on tea. He warned readers that future generations would be "amazed" at the "unaccountable frenzy" raised over a mere "three-penny duty on tea." Such a state of "distraction" among the people over such a minor thing, he warned, would be seen as "more disgraceful to the annals of America than that of the witchcraft."

In his responses as "Novanglus," John Adams also evoked Salem, this time to warn about the "passivity" of Massachusetts Bay Colony in accepting a new charter in the 1690s in spite of its "abridging English liberties." Such passivity, he claimed, had "less to be said in excuse for it than the witchcraft" that was also a product of that time. Salem appeared in

Adams's diary that same year in an entry marking the third anniversary of the Boston Massacre. As he reflected on his role as defense attorney for the British soldiers, he wrote that in retrospect he believed it to be "one of the most gallant, generous, manly, and disinterested actions of my whole life." The conviction and execution of the soldiers, he continued, would "have been as foul a stain upon this country as the executions of the witches anciently."[61]

In these late eighteenth-century appearances of Salem's witch hunt in print, whether in political commentary or in histories as a lesson to be remembered and heeded, there are some common threads. The use of Salem revolves around the period's concern with political unrest, focuses on the public excitement that drove accusations, and reveals how the memory of the 1692 events was being transmitted. Each of the references is made by a man who is either known to be well educated or, in the case of the anonymous *Pennsylvania Gazette* letter writer, can reasonably be assumed to be. Each man also presumes, in his public use, that there is at least a limited audience that will understand the allusion with just a brief phrase or two of description. By 1776 the trials were more than eighty years in the past. Although one or another of these men might have learned their history from local tradition, several lived at a distance from Massachusetts, so their knowledge likely derived from one of the histories in print. With the availability of general histories that overwhelmingly favored the Calef interpretation, those who drew on Salem witchcraft as a warning could also presume that readers would at least be aware of his perspective. Such events, all the published histories since Calef's book in 1700 already concluded, were products of the failure to maintain control of a situation, of a loss of reason, or of excessive religious "zeal." Just as participants in the 1692 trials were described in these narratives as suffering from "delusions," "fanaticism," "superstition," "ignorance," or even lying, so too would those involved in the nineteenth-century controversies and public excitements be described by opponents who drew direct comparisons with Salem's witch hunt. Political and social developments after the Revolution created an environment where history would be seen as a source of authoritative examples of both virtue and vice. In that search for the foundations of national character, many would find the memory of Salem's witch hunt a useful symbol to mark the cultural boundary between the virtuous national present and the superstitious, disorderly, and even brutal colonial past.[62]

CHAPTER TWO

Memory and Nation

The Revolution and the Early Republic

In one of the most dramatic and memorable scenes in American literature, guests arrive at Colonel Pyncheon's new home only to find their
host dead from mysterious causes. Despite, or perhaps because of, the
large crowd of excited witnesses, rumors and myths about the cause of
Colonel Pyncheon's death instantly arise, and they persist for generations.
The stories link his death to his role in the local witchcraft trials; people
believe that the curse Matthew Maule laid on Pyncheon at the hour of his
execution has finally been fulfilled. Condemned to death on Pyncheon's
accusation of witchcraft, Maule cried out to Pyncheon as he faced the gallows, "God will give you blood to drink!" Excited tales from witnesses
to the evidence of Pyncheon's fatal hemorrhage immediately conjured up
details of violence done by a spectral hand. The most fantastic was the "fa-
ble of the skeleton hand, that the Lieutenant Governor was said to have
seen at the Colonel's throat, but which vanished away, as he advanced
farther into the room." Such a story, readers were informed, might be
the sort of "tradition which sometimes brings down truth that history has
let slip"; but then again it might be, as such things more commonly are,
merely part of "the wild babble of the time."[1]

The vignette is from Nathaniel Hawthorne's *House of the Seven Gables*,
and though neither Salem nor the year 1692 is ever explicitly mentioned,
the curse itself might be familiar to readers well versed in Salem witchcraft
history as the one the condemned Sarah Good actually laid on minister

Nicholas Noyes in 1692. Certainly the average reader who came upon the scene in the opening pages of the novel in 1851 would not have needed many details to instantly recognize the author's historical allusion. For despite Nathaniel Hawthorne's nearly complete identification with Salem witchcraft as a plot device after *The House of the Seven Gables*, he was a latecomer to the subject of Salem in the nineteenth century. In fact, to illustrate his tale of the destructive burden of the past on the present for readers of his own day, he could have chosen no better or more familiar theme.

An American who happened to see Cornelius Mathews's drama *Witchcraft* in the 1820s or to read Harry Halyard's *The Haunted Bride* in the 1840s or even *The House of the Seven Gables* in the 1850s would be well prepared to follow the plot and to see the moral implications embedded in the stories. The American audience in particular would be well acquainted with Puritan Salem from their schoolroom histories alone. That literature and history were more companionate than competing genres through most of the century created a symbiosis. This mingling of history and literature was also evident in the professional relationship between two of the most famous authors of nineteenth-century Salem-related texts, Nathaniel Hawthorne and Samuel Goodrich.

In 1836, when Hawthorne was fifteen years away from publishing *The House of the Seven Gables*, his chronic financial problems led him to take on the editorship of *The American Magazine of Useful and Entertaining Knowledge* for the salary of $500 a year. His tenure at the magazine was not happy. He repeatedly complained to his older sister Elizabeth that his employer, publisher and schoolbook author Samuel Goodrich, was a sharp bargainer who had taken advantage of Hawthorne's desperate state. "Concoct, concoct, concoct, I make nothing of writing a history or biography before dinner," he said bitterly. Meanwhile, Goodrich became a wealthy man, employing not only Hawthorne but also other celebrated nineteenth-century writers such as Catherine Maria Sedgwick. After ghostwriting one of Goodrich's popular "Peter Parley" series of histories in 1837, Hawthorne expressed his annoyance in even stronger terms. Goodrich, lived only, Hawthorne groused, to "feed and fatten himself on better brains than his own."[2]

This literary contretemps is an interesting moment of intersection for several reasons. Although no one is more immediately associated in the modern popular mind with the memory of the Salem witchcraft trials than Nathaniel Hawthorne, few nineteenth-century Americans were more responsible for nurturing that memory than Hawthorne's erstwhile employer, Samuel Goodrich. Their individual projects provided a narrative of the nation's past that advanced a compelling tale of Salem witchcraft to a receptive audience and invested that narrative with morality. On close examination, the lessons about Salem witchcraft that Hawthorne, Goodrich, and scores of other nineteenth-century authors advanced were identical, whether promulgated in fiction or in schoolroom histories. All of them carried explicit denunciations of the trials framed in dramatic moral terms. And all were directed toward a single goal: the contrast between the dark colonial past and the bright promise of the national future.

The unlikely example of Salem witchcraft as one dividing line between the colonized past and the national present emerged from a deliberate effort to create a national mythology in the decades after the Revolution. Old traditions and ceremonies needed to be transformed with new American content and symbolism. Existing loyalties to colony and Crown had to change as Americans were politically socialized from subjects into citizens. New traditions based in common experience, disseminated through print and framed by the common points of reference, could supply what Jeremy Belknap (both a historian and a founding member of the Massachusetts Historical Society) optimistically called the "new republican adhesives" to replace the old bonds of community based in ethnicity or religion. As affirmative symbols were drawn from the memory of both the Revolutionary and colonial experiences, so too were negative symbols. Within this framework of creating a usable past for a durable American nationalism, the Puritan past eventually came to underpin a broader national identity.[3]

Deliberately transforming Revolutionary ideology into national ideology was meant to support the political structures of government with a complementary cultural foundation. The search for examples of "virtue" to serve as models for citizens also produced historical examples from a more distant past meant as contrasting lessons in the social costs of undesirable behavior. How Salem witchcraft provided Americans with a useful cultural boundary marker between the rational, independent present and the superstition-filled colonial past is best understood by examining how the foundations of nationalism were constructed and disseminated in the first decades of nationhood.

In the complicated social context for the creation of the cultural nation, various factions competed for their own visions to prevail. Some sought to "strenuously repudiate the 'burden of the past,'" while others looked to the authority of the past for validation. This situation created a complex relationship with the past in a population whose hallmark would soon be its collective capacity not simply to look toward the future but at times seemingly to live in the future, yet who had an enormous appetite for historical books, societies, and commemorations. The rhetoric that poured from the presses in broadsides, pamphlets, and newspapers during the Revolutionary era provided a vocabulary of concepts that had yet to be fully defined or internalized. Lacking history, memory, or tradition, the new citizens of the new United States would have to invent all three to transform Revolutionary ideology into national values.[4]

Solving the tensions between abstract ideas and practical experience during the war years involved using local culture as the primary location for nationalizing celebrations and commemorative activities intended to internalize appropriate ideas and behaviors. As a post-Revolutionary popular political culture was nurtured, a "shared political language" emerged that had profound consequences for the political socialization of Americans. The didactic aspects of performative nationalism affected not only the local participants in civic rites and their immediate audience but also a larger national audience through print, with newspapers doing much of the work to create not only a collective consciousness but a republican one. From about forty newspapers in 1776, the number grew to more than one hundred in 1790 and over two hundred by 1800. As newspapers became the principal source of information for most people in the United States by the beginning of the nineteenth century, they took on an instructional role by printing entire programs, orders of ceremony, and patriotic oratory. They became the way most Americans learned the correct conduct at public political celebrations as well as the appropriate ideas to adopt.[5]

The keystone memory that the entire new American symbolic structure relied on was the common experience of the American Revolution. Creating unity from a war that in some areas was as much a civil war as it was a war for independence from Great Britain's imperial control was difficult. While many outright Loyalists had fled or had been deported, many whose support of independence had been ambiguous remained. Jealous local and regional interests also needed to be consolidated into a national identity with a common present and a common future. The tenuous nature of national unity is suggested by the careful construction of symbols for the nation itself. The repetition of the motif of "thirteen" for the original rebelling colonies, the appeals to ancient republics for lineage, and the motto *e pluribus unum* (which expressed a hope rather than what any thinking person truly believed in the 1790s) were all created toward that end. In such a context, civic festivals and commemorations provided the opportunity for Americans to begin not only imagining themselves as a community but, in also acting as one, to perhaps develop the habit of unity. The values embedded within the idea of republican virtue were added to those newly defined ones in activities commemorating the war and the men who fought it.[6]

Memory was "created by countless small-scale local commemorations, [and] oddball newspaper articles" as well as by the publication of veterans' memoirs. Attending plays and reading memoirs or novels that included Revolutionary War subjects reinforced ideas about the values inherent in war service and sacrifice and so had a different performative aspect. The role of consumer also let people participate through routes other than civic festival culture as they bought and read the proliferating biographies, memoirs, and histories. All these means created powerful symbols and helped create, in the highly literate United States, "a national and nationalistic political culture whose primary medium was print."[7]

The repetition of specific terms provided an instructive repetition in newspapers as well. It was in the public press that the dual narrative of "sacrifice" and "virtue" first found its expression. By converting wartime self-sacrifice into the "habitual virtue" of sacrificing personal "interest" for the "commonweal," it was widely believed, they might ensure a stable, enduring republic. The critical problem was not that anyone disparaged the *idea* of virtue. However, even before the war had ended many were beginning to believe it was a value frequently praised but seldom practiced. Samuel Adams worried about men who were "commercial and interested" and who were likely to form "a joint Combination of Political and Commercial Men" from New York and the south to dominate the government. By the mid-1780s, he admitted defeat to the forces of "luxury" even in formerly radical Boston itself. In this culture of nationalistic commemoration, the ultimate example of the failure of virtue and thus the inevitable consequences to society of the triumph of self-interest was, of course, Benedict Arnold.[8]

The case of Benedict Arnold raises questions about the role of the negative symbol or cautionary tale like Salem witchcraft within the creation of American nationalism. The hero of Ticonderoga and Saratoga, and one of the most trusted of George Washington's generals, Arnold abused his position as military governor of Philadelphia, became mired in debt, and after sixteen months of secret negotiation for the surrender of West Point (of which he had recently been given command), he sold the information to the British. Those valorizing the heroic events and individuals connected with the Revolution could either deliberately ignore General Arnold's treason as an embarrassment or use it as a cautionary tale. They took the latter course. The man his fellow general Nathanael Greene called "once his country's Idol, now her horror," provided postwar service as a symbol of exclusion from the project of national unity.[9] His crime provided such an unequivocal definition of betrayal that his very name became synonymous with treason.

Arnold thus stood as a national boundary marker between individual virtue and vice, demonstrating how symbols designed to marginalize deviance within national collective memory are as effective as creating symbols meant to consolidate unity. In memory, Benedict Arnold's crime was against the symbolic foundations of the war and the core value underpinning both Revolutionary sacrifice and the republic it created: "virtue." As the American Revolution was used to define the nation's values, Arnold's failure to restrain his self-interest made him personify the threat to the moral basis of its founding. Thus Benedict Arnold served as an object lesson for citizens of the ostracism that would result from transgressing social boundaries. His personal weakness served collective national memory by its stark contrast with the true patriot's virtue. The strong negative symbol, therefore, circumscribes social boundaries as effectively as the affirmative symbol.[10]

Edward Ingebretsen identifies those cultural symbols that separate the socially "sacred" from the "taboo" as serving the function of expressing "moral outrage" within a culture. Framed in language meant to "demonize and alienate," the subjects of such language are rhetorically marked as outside defined social boundaries while marking all others as safely inside.[11] As such, it can be argued, designated cultural "villains" (both living and in collective memory) are often most effective symbolically within political rhetoric when constructed as one-dimensional. Removing ambiguity draws a brighter line between the prescribed normative and condemned deviant behavior and values, allowing more effective parallels between the historical example and the contemporary target. Toward this end, narratives about the Revolutionary experience often erased mention of Arnold's earlier service or heroism, placing not only his conduct but his character in permanent opposition to desirable national values. Arnold became a highly effective national symbol because he could be cast as an uncomplicated and irredeemable symbol of treachery.[12]

Although the memory of the Revolutionary experience provided a useful narrative for defining a set of desirable national values, there were limits to its utility as a source of national myths in the decades right after independence. Events and individuals connected to the Revolution not only were still alive or in living memory but were often engaged in ongoing political or personal disputes. To complicate matters, those who promoted casting the recent Revolution as "the fruit of a long past spent in toil, sacrifice, and devotion" created a narrative of national founding that required showing its course from origins to fulfillment. Many involved in the nationalizing project became preoccupied with the British colonial past despite the contradictions of seeking validation within a historical record that was simultaneously used to justify the Revolution itself.[13]

Those selectively using the colonial past both to explain the need for Revolution and as the source of the virtues that secured independence sought to separate the settler colonists from their government in national memory. For those authors and orators, the result was a narrative tradition that, in the political rhetoric of the day, looked to "the people" themselves for evidence of nascent "American" characteristics in the colonial period. By 1828, men like Supreme Court Justice Joseph Story would regularly applaud what he defined as the realistic foundations of the origins of the United States. The story that could be told of America's founding was not, like Europe's, located in "traditionary darkness" or in "imaginary personages" but in real people who could serve as inspiration.[14] But by the end of the 1820s, statements like Story's were a measure of the success of creating a usable colonial past in the decades since the Revolution.

Immediately after the Revolution the question might well have been (even in a nation formed entirely of former British settler colonies), Whose colonial history? Some of the former colonies had relatively stable, homogeneous populations, with common religious beliefs and a long residency on the continent. Others had significant diversity and frequent influxes of new arrivals from England and northern Europe. Variations in economic and social development and traditions as well as large populations of Indians or enslaved Africans (neither group given any real consideration) all provided challenges to anyone looking for a truly shared past. But by 1800 it was clear that one region, New England, was using its material advantages and its political ambitions to fill that cultural void. It was within this New England–based attempt to turn real British colonists into symbolic American settlers that the memory of the 1692 Salem witchcraft trials emerged as a negative symbol.

As a region, New England had national ambitions and boundless self-confidence, with a highly developed economic and institutional structure to back them up. New Englanders were indeed well situated to find the promise of national greatness within the memory of their colonial past. In terms of British North American settlement, the region had a mature society. Its long history as the primary location of colonial scholarship and printing provided the materials, and its own religious and cultural traditions created a useful orientation in an era of self-conscious national defining.

The unofficial campaign to create "New England as nation" did construct a practical cultural authority that would linger into the twentieth century. But at the same time, the effort to write the nation's past as the New England past was not simply an alternative to a national influence that increasingly eluded New England states at the ballot box. For many of those contributing to the project, it reflected a sincere belief in keeping with their Federalist thinking: that the route to permanent stability for the nation passed directly through the village green of a Massachusetts or Connecticut town thriving under the "conservative values of hierarchy, deference, and civic virtue."[15] Providing idealized visions of the order and prosperity of the conservative colonial theocracies of Massachusetts to serve as models for the nation was also an attempt to address contemporary concerns. It was a historical example that counteracted what many Federalists saw as the chaos of the Revolutionary years and the equally chaotic new society it created. The moral implications embodied in what would later be called the "errand in the wilderness" of the Massachusetts settler generation, created as a common point of reference, served a variety of interests and would become one of the cornerstones of the idea of American "exceptionalism."[16]

Those who worked to shape the nation's colonial past into New England's image within their narratives of founding concentrated on creating a collective representative figure. For those in the Revolutionary generation hoping to promote republican virtue, the seventeenth-century Massachusetts settler was an attractive symbol. The Puritans, as well chronicled by themselves and their descendants, articulated clear moral principles and a sense of providential destiny. They were portrayed as dedicated to order, stability, morality, congregational governance, and education–the same values being promoted as desirable in citizens after the Revolution. Republicanism itself, in fact, has been called a "more relaxed, secularized version" of Puritanism.[17] That these colonial communities could be aligned to new nationalist aims to provide a sense of native timelessness to values that could serve the nation was critical to their utility as symbols. The qualities found desirable in the symbolic Puritan, particularly "self-restraint and attention to duty," were central to ideas about republican virtue and thus resonated across a broad spectrum of the population no matter who was endorsing them. The promotion of New England (or more precisely "Massachusetts") as the true birthplace of the nation assigned the Puritan the role of American "Adam."[18]

From the end of the Revolution to the end of the Civil War it was the Puritan, not the Pilgrim, who emerged as the dominant symbolic Massachusetts settler. In print and oratory, the sturdy "virtue" promoted as central to a republican consciousness was attributed primarily to a "Puritan" colonial past. The 1620 immigrant to Plymouth Colony was certainly always given full credit for his earlier arrival on American shores and his admirable piety in the plentiful national histories that detailed American colonial founding. But in the early national imagination, the Plymouth Pilgrim and his less prominent and dramatic presence in the publicly available historical record was increasingly merged into a generic "Massachusetts" historical mythology as completely as the former colony of Plymouth was folded into Massachusetts Bay Colony by the English government in 1692. Although many have traced commemorative activities by the Pilgrim Society or used the New England Society's annual celebration of the Plymouth landing to argue for the centrality of the Pilgrim in national memory, they also note the persistent conflation of the Puritan and the Pilgrim even by these knowledgeable descendants. In the common schoolbook and in countless other uses, the Pilgrim became a sort of "advance man" for the Puritan who arrived on American shores nearly a decade after. In the first half-century or so of nationhood, it was the Puritan who dominated in tales of colonial founding meant to warn or inspire. It was the dominance of the Puritan in histories, literature, and the press over the first half-century of nationhood that lent such power to the later use of the Puritan image, and Salem in particular, as a weapon in pro-slavery rhetoric directed at New England abolitionists in the 1850s and 1860s.

The reality is that in the antebellum period even those who had the most reason to recall that Massachusetts Bay Colony and Plymouth Colony were different entities casually "aspirated the Pilgrims and the Puritans in one breath."[19] It was a conflation of convenience, not calculation. A good example of this common practice comes from a juvenile book, *History of*

the Pilgrims, or A Grandfather's Story of the First Settlers of New England.
Despite the unequivocal subject given by the title, the author asks the
readers, "Tell me what you think of these Puritans yourselves?"[20] This
Puritan focus was reinforced as they became the subjects of drama, verse,
and fiction, in more than one hundred books on New England themes
that were published between 1815 and 1860. Very few took Plymouth as
their theme, preferring the dramatic possibilities in the historical record
of Massachusetts Bay Colony and its Puritans. But the problem with using historical figures as mythic characters is that "history" (the record of
actual events) often intrudes at inopportune times. Just as the creation of
the symbolic Puritan was a product of specific historical circumstances, so
too was his demise. What benefited the Puritan settler as a candidate for
founder in the imagination of authors of both schoolbooks and fiction to
the 1860s is the same thing that later killed him off in favor of his milder
brother in Plymouth—an extensive recorded history.[21]

Among all the commemorative, historical, and literary projects that
transmitted the narrative of national founding as originating in Massachusetts, however, schoolbooks are of special interest in the period 1790
to 1860 for their particular place in the early national American imagination. It is through the common schoolbook that we also find Salem at the
convergence of the project to define national character and the New Englanders' aggressive promotion of their own past as the nation's past. The
shift in the collective memory of Salem witchcraft from a relatively minor historical episode of colonial witch-hunting to a permanent metaphor
in cultural memory was not inevitable—even with the rise of the Massachusetts settler as the central founding figure. Salem's witch hunt, already associated with undesirable behaviors and beliefs in existing histories of the colonies, became more widely known and more deeply associated with emerging national values because the Puritan past served as a
common point of moral reference in the basic schoolbook.

The availability of elementary schoolbooks, and the context within
which they were produced and used, gave the narratives a cultural weight
that only newspapers could hope to match. As popular periodicals, national
histories meant for the adult market, and American drama and literature matured and multiplied from the 1820s onward, the history of Salem
witchcraft would appear within their pages. But it always reinforced the
conclusions repeated within the schoolbook for almost a generation. In
the 1830s the familiar schoolbook example of Salem began to creep into
public discourse as a metaphor within debates about various social and

political controversies. But that cultural presence and the terms within which it was expressed were built on what nineteenth-century Americans already collectively remembered about Salem. And that memory was learned from their schoolbooks.

One schoolbook author speaking to the 1845 meeting of the New Jersey Teachers and Friends of Education asserted their value in national life from the perspective of two generations of independence, by stressing that it was from "those unassuming companions of the schoolroom, and not from those more elaborate writings which grace the libraries of the men of wealth and the professional scholar, that the great mass of our citizens must ever derive their knowledge of the character, toils, and privations of our fathers, and the origin and nature of our free institutions."[22]

As a category that Noah Webster included in his compendium of "useful knowledge," history was indeed considered culturally important. It was used to present examples of unambiguous virtue to help cultivate the same in the generation born to liberty. Such literary efforts could be considered, in the first decades after the Revolution, an intellectual form of taking possession of the nation. Historians have often commented on the conservative nature of these books promoted as "guardians of liberty," arguing that they could be "more accurately be described as guardians of tradition," although it is difficult to see a firm American "tradition" to guard in the dynamic period from 1790 to 1860.[23] Rather, the books are more accurately described as a part of the process of creating a tradition that could serve as a national collective cultural memory of the past.

Prominent thinkers in the post-Revolutionary era believed that education was important in nationalizing the population. Philadelphia physician Benjamin Rush famously advocated education as a mechanism for turning children into "republican machines." He envisioned "republican seminaries" that would educate by proper principles that ultimately would "render the mass of the people more homogeneous, and thereby fit them more easily for uniform and peaceable government."[24] This common linking of virtue with education also merged with the substance of American education, which was predicated on a seventeenth-century belief that the "mythic significance of becoming a literate, catechized, and Bible-reading people was freedom from 'popish tyranny.'" The belief in "the centrality of moral progress over time" made not only schoolbooks but adult histories concentrate on moral lessons. Noah Webster's statement that "the virtues of men are of more consequence to society than their abilities" reflected a mind-set that dominated not only late eighteenth-century political ideology but the resultant nineteenth-century American theory of education.[25] In shaping the past as a frame of moral reference, however, they could not help but shape memory.[26]

In the first decades of independence a wide variety of American texts were produced for the adult and juvenile markets in the United States. Their goals were overtly nationalistic, and authors announced their intentions in prefaces. Noah Webster's speller and general reader, *A Grammatical Institute of the English Language,* published in 1783, was the beginning of the Massachusetts schoolteacher's long project to produce a dictionary of the American language. Webster believed it was important to define an American English as the only appropriate vehicle to express distinctly American ideas free from what he termed the "corruption and tyranny" of Europe and its "debased" culture. His ardent belief in the idea of a republican education for a republican citizenry required books with an appropriate ideology and a sense of America's singular destiny. Noah Webster reminded Americans that "it is the business of *Americans* to select the wisdom of all nations...to add superior dignity to this infant Empire and to human nature." A few European selections might be appropriate within readers, but in the opinion of Webster and men like him, books imported from Europe or reprinted in America without alteration clearly could not provide the lessons needed to create affective or intellectual bonds of nationalism.[27]

Geographies were the first domestically produced books that aimed to present practical knowledge within a national context. Jedidiah Morse, a Congregational minister from Massachusetts, published his enormously popular *American Geography* in 1789. It performed a critical service immediately after the Revolution by encouraging readers to visualize one unified nation. Certainly maps of the former colonies separately or together were in print, and nothing had changed in settled regions to account for the popularity of the original edition or Morse's various later versions for the juvenile and the adult markets. But politically, just about everything had changed. Through the *American Geography* individuals could visualize themselves in relation to citizens in other states fixed in space within this new entity, the United States of America. Histories first followed as sections within geographies and quickly appeared as separate volumes, fixing the nation and its people both in time and in the imagination.[28]

The importance of schoolbooks in the nineteenth-century American cultural landscape lay not only in their content but in their reach. Elementary primers and other schoolbooks were, "along with the Bible, the 'stock book' in the bookshops and general stores of the village," which accounts for their also being the most widely read books of any genre in the United States before the twentieth century. They were used both for private instruction and in schoolrooms. The importance of formal education for nationalizing the population and buttressing that nationalistic sentiment with desirable moral values was more often stated than made material. In 1827 Massachusetts was the first state to establish an education commission and a free public school system, with educator Horace Mann as secretary. It was also the first to require history as a subject in schools, precisely because it was considered useful for the future citizen. In addition, by 1839 Massachusetts had created a state normal school to train teachers. Other states were slower to set up formal structures for state oversight. Pennsylvania established such a system in 1834, Vermont in 1850, and Iowa in 1858, for example. The southern states had no long-standing tradition of public education at the town level, and settlements there were farther apart. Many white southerners were privately educated or attended academies, which by 1850 enrolled some 70,000 white students. Even public school systems left schoolbook adoption to the individual, and the teacher worked with whatever books students brought to school.[29]

Since schools through most of the nineteenth century taught by rote memorization, inculcating the "lesson" of Salem was not only effective but permanent, if we can believe Daniel Fenning's statement to parents and teachers in his 1799 speller. Fenning promised, in terms that echoed philosopher John Locke's, that early instruction was important because "the mind of the child is like the soft wax to receive an impression, but like the rigid marble to retain it." But whether this statement was something he believed or simply a marketing ploy, the pedagogical approach of rote memorization ensured that children would indeed, as a part of their education, memorize the "facts" about heroism or treason in the American Revolution or of the terrors of Salem witchcraft. More significantly, children would also memorize the moral lesson presented in vivid language within each history lesson.[30]

This catechistic approach was necessary because teachers often were imperfectly educated. In the example of Salem's witch hunt, children were expected to answer such questions as, What were the effects of this delusion? What strange delusion seized upon the minds of the people? What is now thought by people of America on the subject of witchcraft? How many were executed? What of the delusion elsewhere? In Europe? Was

belief in witchcraft general in that age? The "correct" answer was to re-
cite the appropriate passage in the text, where the themes of "delusion,"
"infatuation," and foreign origins for the witchcraft episode are conspicuously repeated and, as in the examples here, use the words from the
main text as "prompts" in the review questions. The specific language
used about Salem's witch hunt was coupled with an insistence that, in retrospect, a "season of error" obviously defined the seventeenth-century
episode in an otherwise admirable community. Within this system of instruction, schoolbooks did not just universally teach American children
about the events at Salem in 1692; they provided explicit lessons to be
drawn from those past events and pointed out what those lessons meant
in the present.[31]

Although the common schoolbook was meant to be a nationalizing
influence, the dominance of New England–based authors and publishers
within the trade provided a distinct narrative driven by regional memory.
Some authors were college-educated ministers and some pursued teaching as a vocation, but printers and other literary entrepreneurs with little
more education than their potential students increasingly entered what
was rapidly becoming a lucrative profession. The period after the War of
1812, in particular, marked the rise of a class of self-made men and women
who offered as their credentials not degrees but prefaces that stressed
the nationalizing goals of their offerings and their own virtuous dedication to disinterested public service. Both New Englanders from elite, educated backgrounds and those without them were ready in large numbers
to take advantage of the emerging opportunity and would produce most
of the 113 schoolbooks published in the United States up to 1860. In fact,
the six best-selling authors of histories for the classroom between 1821
and 1861 (Salma Hale, Charles A. Goodrich, Samuel G. Goodrich, Jesse
Olney, Emma Willard, and Marcius Willson) were all native New Englanders.[32]

The methods used in writing textbooks not only allowed men and
women of limited education to become authors but also contributed to a
stability in the narrative line about Salem or any number of other historical events. Many authors (like Benson Lossing or Samuel Goodrich) explicitly referred to themselves not as "authors" but as "compilers." Compiling consisted essentially of wholesale adoption of other books in print,
with little or no modification. As Lossing plainly stated in his preface,
"We freely appropriated to our use the fruits of the labors of others."[33]
The boy of 1820 could easily find the same version he read in grade school

in a later printing—for instance, in his grandson's new edition of the same schoolbook in 1860. Of course, given that schoolbooks were individually purchased and owned, it may well have been the very same family copy that grandfather had used.

Although the post–Civil War era saw a new crop of books whose view of what constituted "useful knowledge" or desirable narrative elements changed to emphasize a more civics-based narrative, the persistence of older editions in schoolrooms kept the antebellum versions alive and influential right up through the end of the century. The 12 million or more volumes of Samuel G. Goodrich's Peter Parley series of schoolbooks sold in the United States included full accounts of Salem witchcraft in the various histories and in the nonfiction Tales series, whose sheer numbers testify to its influence. When one considers that family members and neighbors used the same copies for generations, the potential influence of the most popular schoolbook versions increases all the more.[34] This uniformity over time more firmly embedded the language of a particular view of the events of 1692 in the American mind just as the method of instruction reinforced the details of the moral lesson. For the average literate American, these books "delineated...an idealized image of both himself and of the history that had produced the admired American type."[35]

The schoolbook genealogy of that "admired American type" led directly back to the colonial settlement of the seventeenth-century colonies that would become Massachusetts. The settlers of Massachusetts Bay Colony and Plymouth Colony were offered as the ideal for a collective representative American figure with a decided focus on the Puritan. That Virginia was settled in 1607, thirteen years before Plymouth Colony and twenty-one years before the first of the Massachusetts Bay Colony settlements, might appear to present a problem. No textbook, no matter what its author's biases or origin, disputed Virginia's "pride of place" as the first permanent English colony on mainland North America; they just doubted it was worthy to claim it was the cradle of national leadership when the virtues of the settler generations were compared.[36]

Virginia's founding and settlement in the histories produced for children before the Civil War could be summed up by a page heading in Emma Willard's 1846 *Abridged History of the United States*: "Bad Settlers." Virginia's men came to the New World not out of virtuous motives but out of "self-interest" and "extravagant hopes of sudden and brilliant wealth." And although in her section on Anne Hutchinson's trial for heresy Puritans received the heading "Religious Feeling. May Become Perverted," the text leaves no doubt as to her meaning. Puritans made errors, but only by taking a good quality (piety) to its extreme. Jamestown's "bad settlers," however, when left alone by Captain John Smith, fell into "disorder and misrule." When faced with the consequences of their actions, "the spirits of the people were broken." Samuel Goodrich, as he so often would do on other historical subjects in his many juvenile histories, colorfully regaled readers with the perfidy of Virginia's first colony, which in his version ultimately and "miserably perished." Goodrich built his narrative on an account of the colony that described Virginia settlers as "poor gentlemen, tradesmen, servingmen, libertines, and such like," so he was no more surprised than Willard that the Virginia colonists fell into a general mood of "despair." Such men had no resilience in the face of hardship because of their selfish motives for immigration.[37]

The judgments of Willard and Goodrich are not necessarily a product of their personal hostility toward Virginia; nor are these narratives peculiar to books published in the 1840s. The same sort of narrative can be found in Salma Hale's gold-medal-winning 1826 history. Again, only Smith's "persuasions and threats" could get work out of settlers who were prone to "disorder and confusion" generated by their "raging passion for gold." In his 1807 account of the founding of Virginia, Noah Webster provided a terse narrative conducive to memorizing and reciting facts, but among those facts is his judgment about the character of Virginia's first colonists as "disobedient and refractory." Benson Lossing continued this narrative emphasis in the 1850s by offering a description of Virginia as populated with "dissolute scions of wealthy families" who often "came to avoid punishment for crimes at home," men who in their moral degeneracy "regarded Virginia as a paradise for libertines." Lossing carried on the tradition of praise for John Smith by noting that the moment Smith left the colony, settlers dissolved into "every irregularity of life," and their reckless consumption of supplies created "the starving time." Virginia's sole saving graces in all the schoolbooks are that it is English and Protestant and that it eventually established the rudiments of representative government with the House of Burgesses in 1619. Although representative government in Virginia was in place one year before Plymouth Colony was settled, the disapproval of the initial Jamestown settlers' passive acceptance of a royal council and failure to set up a local government were seen in these nationalistic nineteenth-century texts as dangerously submissive to "the tyrant's will." The one unequivocal point of approval is for Captain John Smith, who had the gumption to take the lazy colonists in hand and make them work at gunpoint. Clearly, beyond John Smith's energetic imposition of order, the average school history found little for the child to emulate in this group of settlers.[38]

The construction of the Massachusetts past follows a similar track by embedding a moral tale within the account of the settlers' response to their hardships. But unlike the stories of Virginia, this one was celebratory. The seventeenth-century Massachusetts settler received much more praise in school histories and was covered at greater length, while Massachusetts itself was presented in a detailed account that stressed its importance relative to the other British colonies. Although the combination of topics included in any of the histories makes any real comparison difficult, any analysis of space devoted to the two regions consistently yields a bonus of as much as two to one for the colonies that would become the state of Massachusetts. And that critical detail helps make the United States of the antebellum schoolbook into a paradise of Massachusetts values. Plymouth Colony would rise to more prominence in school histories after the Civil War. In the earlier schoolbooks, the Pilgrim most often functioned as a sort of advance party for the Puritan migration. The child was assured that the Plymouth colonist was a "type of Puritan," and almost invariably the narrative moved directly into the main migration of Winthrop's party in 1630. Thus it was the seventeenth-century Puritan alone or as a composite settler of Plymouth and Massachusetts Bay Colonies, not the profligate Virginian, who was held up as the proto-republican model of virtue. Or, or more tellingly, it was not the independent man of Roger Williams's colony of Rhode Island or even a New England regional composite.[39]

The symbolic Massachusetts settler, then, who would do so much double duty as the collective representative of virtuous citizenship and as an object lesson in the consequences of vice in and out of schoolbooks, had his own founding narrative that readers were invited to identify with in every appearance. When the Massachusetts settlers met "incredible sufferings from cold, snow and rain," unlike the unfit Virginians, "they were not discouraged." When "disease and hardship thinned their ranks," their reaction was not the "despair" of the Virginia schoolbook settlers; readers were assured that they "bore all with equal firmness." Thus the sections on the Massachusetts colonies focused on the underlying moral condition that provided their strength of body and character. Rather than "starving times," the faithful Massachusetts settlers were rewarded for

their virtuous motives by continuing to "advance in the attainment of stability and prosperity." In contrast to the indolent Virginians, the schoolbook *Mayflower* passengers were busy during their voyage to the New
World creating "a voluntary government before landing, upon purely
democratic principles," which was the event within which any detailed
discussion of Plymouth was almost invariably located. These hearty Massachusetts settlers, who were themselves victims driven across the vast
Atlantic far "from all the civil parts of the world" by vicious persecution, were lauded because they "resisted oppression in England, suffered
hardship and braved death to enjoy their religion unmolested." Through
the narrative of being tested and found virtuous, schoolbook authors presented New England as worthy of being the proverbial "nursery of men."
These common narratives displayed the regionally driven effort to construct a national past with Massachusetts's founders at the center, but
in their similarity they also display not so much a conspiracy as a similar set of sources, home-region biases, and the realities of the publishing trade. The steady post-Revolutionary rhetorical drumbeat of "virtue"
was maintained when considering colonists' motives for New World migration: the Virginians were unfit for even symbolic national leadership
because they were founded by "self-interested" men, while New England was shown to be fit through its history of virtuous self-sacrifice for
principle.[40] What other sort of people could provide the examples of
virtue sought by Joseph Emerson, whose textbook companion to a popular juvenile history asked students, "Why is our history next in importance
to sacred history?" The answer was simple and was reflected not only in
heroic tales of the Revolution but in the Massachusetts settlement narratives: "Because God has not dealt so with any other nation."[41]

In presenting the Massachusetts settler as the fount of all American
virtues, all the histories had to struggle to account for the episode of witch-
hunting at Salem. In the end, though, Salem witchcraft proved to be a
boon to the schoolbook authors who competed for a share of the growing market. While most authors, like Emma Willard, offered to "sow the
seeds of virtue, by showing the good in such amiable lights, that the youthful heart shall kindle into desires of imitation," others, like Charles A.
Goodrich, suggested that "pictures of the vicious, ultimately overtaken by
misery and shame" could provide an equally strong lesson.[42] Embedded
in celebratory narratives of Puritan founding, Salem stimulated the moral
imagination by pointing to the results of failing to maintain the advocated
critical national values as clearly as Benedict Arnold did in the narratives

of the Revolution. Along with the language meant to create affirmative symbols, then, was the equally important cautionary tale from history designed to serve as a negative symbol. Through such clearly drawn moral condemnations, schoolbooks helped inscribe the boundaries of acceptable or desirable behavior and the signs by which to recognize upright citizens.

The schoolbooks of the first half of the nineteenth century would selectively invest Salem witchcraft with meanings that reflected contemporary anxieties. It illustrated the dangers inherent in failing to control the passions, in bowing to the tyranny of leaders, in rejecting reason and order, and in accepting foreign influences, and it was always presented as a contrast to the progressive national present.

Virtually all the authors of antebellum school histories included Salem. Frederick Butler, in his 1821 history, gave the Puritans unstinting credit for laying "the foundation of the United States of America," then said he found the witchcraft episode so "disgraceful" that he wished it "buried forever in oblivion." But even Butler lacked the temerity to eliminate at least a reference to a historical episode that had "become a subject of public notoriety" (not to mention the sort of colorful incident that helped sales). Butler's method was to wash his hands of it while directing readers who felt compelled to know more to Thomas Hutchinson's *History of Massachusetts*. Charles Prentiss wished "in silence and sorrow, to pass all notice" of Salem but admitted that "truth and impartiality compel us, most reluctantly, to give a very brief account." Among the antebellum textbook authors, Prentiss and Butler were decidedly in the minority. Colorful stories of the past were a key element of most texts. The overwhelming choice of the schoolroom historians who wrote before 1860 was to praise the Puritans for founding the nation while using Salem witchcraft as an opportunity for a related lesson about American moral progress.[43]

The primary purpose of education was to cultivate virtue, and so the books situated children in their society with clear lessons about their place in it. Children were reminded that they should be seen but not heard. Expectations of duty, honesty, and respect for authority were taught with examples that made it clear that virtue was rewarded (like the "frugal and honest" Massachusetts Bay Colony settlers whose fidelity brought "prosperity") and that evil deeds brought swift punishment. Schoolbook authors regularly warned children that vice would lead to ruin or death. Such remarks supported the standard New England–based, Calvinist-inspired schoolbook morality of a world where "the misfortunes of men [are] mostly chargeable on themselves." Thus bad behavior was depicted as willful and a result of either bad character or parental indulgence. Salem's seventeenth-century children provided a perfect illustration within that context. The children of Salem, wrote Salma Hale in 1825, were "hardened by impunity and success" as they expanded their circle of accused witches. William Grimshaw, whose history Abraham Lincoln praised as central to his own childhood reading, did not disguise his disgust that "children, not twelve years old, were allowed to give their testimony." The whole thing, Jedidiah Morse claimed, was a result of "fraud and imposture, began by young girls, who at first thought of nothing more than exciting pity and indulgence." From the heights of the nineteenth century, the lesson taught by many books was that in 1692 "the most effectual way to avoid an accusation was to become an accuser"—fostering the notion that craven self-interest, not religious belief, drove the Salem witch hunt.[44]

Dishonest testimony had tragic results, but another form of self-interest and a warning about the excesses of nonrepublican governments was that durable republican trope, the tyrannical ruler. Textbooks that did not single out culprits in the upper levels of Massachusetts Bay Colony society often alluded to simply "superstitious ministers and magistrates." Those that did specify who was to blame often claimed that local minister Samuel Parris was personally motivated by a "terrible vengeance." According to several authors, Parris, the "chief agent in the beginning of this frenzy," was widely known to contemporaries as being so bitter about conflicts in his congregation that "it had even attracted the attention of the General Court." Cotton Mather would attract more of the blame by the second half of the century, but he did draw some condemnation in the antebellum period for what one book labeled his "compound of ignorance and learning, of bigotry, spiritual pride and inquisitorial malice" in conjunction with the trials and their aftermath. Samuel Goodrich blamed Mather specifically not only for keeping the trials and executions moving forward but for his role in "deceiving the public" about his own involvement through his "artful appeals and publications."[45]

The "inquisitorial malice" in one of Samuel Goodrich's schoolbook descriptions of Mather's actions is particularly telling as an intersection of several negative themes in circulation in the early nineteenth century. To illustrate the extremes of brutality possible at the hands of authority, it was hard to come up with a more freighted example in colonial or antebellum America than the Roman Catholic Church. As we shall see in the public controversies of the 1830s–50s, to show the dangers some beliefs posed to the independence of the individual, Salem witchcraft was often framed in the language of the rampant anti-Catholic strain in American society. Certainly such references would resonate with antebellum readers, for whom the Inquisition was synonymous with brutality.

The reference to the Inquisition also brings up the role that "foreign" influences play in the interpretation of Salem's witch hunt, particularly in contrast to the "American" identity of the colonial Puritans. The selective use of the colonial past in nationalist narratives in any genre allowed authors to situate virtue or vice geographically. Seeing how schoolbooks implicitly shifted the geographic or political identity of Salem witchcraft is critical to understanding the role of their colonial sections as nationalist primers. In accounts of colonial heroism or fortitude, the subject was implicitly identified as "American" whether the protagonist was a resident of "Delaware" or "New England." The Puritan congregational structures were presented not only as proto-republican, but as the result of the sort of innate character traits that motivated immigration to the New World. But laws that prosecuted people for ridiculous things like witchcraft were exactly the sorts of Old World dangers supposedly left behind with independence. In Jedidiah Morse's popular *American Geography,* first published in 1789, he reminded readers that Salem witchcraft was "the practice of the courts...regulated by English law and custom." Hannah Adams did the same in her 1807 abridgement of *History of New England.* Samuel Goodrich regularly stressed to his readers that New England witch-hunting "was not an invention of their own. They received their notions from England." Even when Massachusetts colonists were not reported to be directly under the influence of English customs or law, children were instructed that witchcraft persecutions had been "common in Europe for centuries" and that, as regrettable as the twenty deaths at Salem were, "thousands were executed in England and other countries" for the same offense. And so, in the case of New England, John Howard Hinton sniffed, "neither England nor any other nation is entitled to cast the first stone at them."[46]

The questions provided for student review within textbooks or in companion volumes reinforced this essentially foreign nature of Salem's witch hunt: "What most excellent English judge repeatedly tried and condemned persons for witchcraft?" Another asked, "Why did our forefathers believe in [witchcraft]?" and provided in the key (as for all the questions) an answer that children were meant to repeat directly from the text: "They received their notions from England." Marcius Willson, one of the most popular authors, reminded children that "belief in witchcraft was then almost universal in Christian countries." Noah Webster concluded that, on balance, "the colonies were no worse than the mother country." William Grimshaw made a distinction between the barbarity of European trials and Salem by describing the fate of witches in England, where the court "consigned its victims to the flames." By making Salem a distinct location and by universally including the justification that belief in witchcraft was part of the "superstition of the age," the lesson of Salem could be used as a measure of American moral progress because, in these narratives, Salem witchcraft happened *in* America but it was not *of* America.[47]

The nationalistic bent of nineteenth-century schoolbooks emphasized both material and moral progress, and the story of Salem provided a baseline for measuring how far Americans had come from what they labeled the "superstitions" and the overall brutality of the past that still trapped those under the tyrannical rule of kings and popes. Most books emphasized that children lived in a better age than their counterparts in 1692 Salem. The authors of the elementary texts were especially enthusiastic about including Salem witchcraft because it provided such good opportunities to draw parallels between the past and present. Francis Lister Hawks, writing as "Uncle Philip," told the readers of his schoolroom history that "your Uncle Philip has too much sense to believe in magic, charms and witchcraft." John Hinton mourned the Puritan lack of knowledge about "the structure of the human mind," which provoked such outbursts of passion as witch-hunting. Jesse Olney cautioned children that "we must remember, that this was an age of superstition." Samuel Goodrich in his *First Book of History for Children and Youth* promised his young readers "the most amusing and instructive portions" of history, then told them how children in Salem "pretended" to see evil manifestations and caused people to hang "for a crime that was only imaginary." Most authors ultimately reassured their young audience with the statement that "we ... know there is no such thing as witchcraft."[48]

Schoolbooks all followed this model of providing accounts that reserved a full understanding of Salem and its tragedy not for its seventeenth-century colonists involved in the trials but for more enlightened and progressive nineteenth-century readers. Samuel Goodrich gave one variation on a common theme when he reminded children that "it was a common error of that age" to believe in witchcraft. And still, he went on, "we cannot but wonder that our ancestors should have believed in it, and that many persons should have been hung, for a crime that was only imaginary." His brother and fellow schoolbook author Charles A. Goodrich informed his readers that this belief in witchcraft was universal and simply "taken for granted." Jesse Olney made the same point when he explained that although it "is astonishing to us that our forefathers with all their learning should have been thus deluded...we should remember that this was an age of superstition." Therefore, though the ancestors of nineteenth-century Americans may have been trapped by the intellectual limits of their world, it was neither their fault nor of their creation.[49]

Schoolbook authors were also in agreement that Salem witchcraft was a result of "manias," "delusions," "infatuations," "excitements," and other terms that implied a loss of reason. Abiel Holmes wrote that Salem "furnishes an affecting proof of the imbecility of the human mind, and of the powerful influence of the passions." William Grimshaw described the witch hunt as "an agitation, a terror in the public mind...driving the people to the most desperate conduct." In Charles Goodrich's view, one of the responsibilities of the present generation was to look upon this episode "with gratitude to their freedom from those delusions." In schoolbooks it was the "spirit of the age," an "intolerant spirit," an "age of superstition," or "the prevailing credulity of the age," all working on "minds not sufficiently enlightened by reason and philosophy" to produce the "popular delusion" that was Salem witchcraft. Most troubling was the relationship between the Puritan founder as a symbol and the implications of Salem. Charles Goodrich clearly expressed his expectation of finding "madness and infatuation" in the remote past, at least from those he called "weak, illiterate, and unprincipled." To look at Salem in 1692 through a historian's eyes, though, meant that he found it among those he defined as men "of sense, education, and fervent piety," and he conveyed a warning that others would use in relation to popular "excitements" in his own time. When passionate behavior overruled reason among those considered modern sensible men, it threatened all of society just as it did in 1692–but with less justification.[50]

New Englanders' influence in the schoolbook market as well as their orientation toward American history was consolidated by source materials that were very often written by New Englanders as well. The volume of Thomas Hutchinson's *History of the Province of Massachusetts* that included the period of the Salem trials was written and originally published in the late 1760s but came to the notice of nineteenth-century authors of both adult and juvenile histories when it was included in an early issue of the *Proceedings of the Massachusetts Historical Society*. By that time the former royal governor of Massachusetts Bay Colony had died in exile in England, but neither his death nor his Revolutionary-era Loyalist politics were a bar to his being used for nationalistic purposes. In fact, his status as a colonial governor appears to lend a certain authority to his judgments. Authors ranging from Abiel Holmes to George Bancroft quote him extensively and approvingly—mentioning his official title—within their own similar narratives of Salem witchcraft. Though Hutchinson wrote his history during the mid-eighteenth century, their publication on the eve of the Revolution, when his contemporary reputation in Boston was at its lowest point, brought his public influence on the narrative of the 1692 trials clearly within the nineteenth century. Hutchinson was popular with these later historians because he shared their disdain for the witchcraft trials and carried the authority of an educated colonial voice. If no member of the seventeenth-century government of Massachusetts Bay Colony ever explicitly condemned or apologized for the episode, a later colonial governor, it seems, would do just as well.

Thomas Hutchinson appealed to nineteenth-century historians and compilers in other ways too. In evaluating the trials' catalysts and the motivations of their participants, he shared the disgust for witnesses that Robert Calef expressed in his 1700 book—and that any number of authors and readers shared by the early nineteenth century. His narrative conveyed a sense of outrage about the trials, forcefully expressed in his summation of the character and fate of those involved: "None of the pretended afflicted were ever brought upon trial for their fraud, some of them proved profligate persons, abandoned to all vice, others passed their days in obscurity or contempt." The familiar judgments about "credulous" authorities and witnesses who were either guilty of "imposture" or in the thrall of a "delusion" riddled Thomas Hutchinson's narrative as well. Although the claim about the accusers' fate is dubious history, it was in its own right (and as "compiled" within any number of nineteenth-century histories) a highly effective and reassuring moral narrative.[51]

George Bancroft, the most influential historian of the nineteenth century, made good use of Hutchinson's original narrative and of the other versions in print. Bancroft's own success as a historian of the United States (and particularly in his treatment of historical episodes such as Salem witchcraft) owed much to his ability to "enunciate with conviction, elegance, and learning what nearly everyone already believed." Bancroft, the first American trained to be an "objective" or "scientific" historian, was nevertheless an ardent nationalist who was shaped by his Massachusetts origins as clearly as any other regional author. In his chapter "Witchcraft at Salem," Bancroft deftly synthesized earlier accounts that ranged from the seventeenth-century trial records to Thomas Hutchinson's history, applying familiar language as he judged the trial and its participants harshly in every line.

Witnesses in Bancroft's version "told stories yet more foolish than false," while Samuel Parris, the town's minister, operated not from belief in witchcraft but out of "special hatred" and "blind zeal." Confessions were sought by the "malice" of ministers on behalf of "angry" neighbors. According to George Bancroft, those in Salem who were especially at risk for witchcraft accusations were people who were "uninfected by superstition." He created an anachronistic segment of the population of Puritan Salem who "rebuked the delusion" out of disbelief in witchcraft itself and who ultimately faced the gallows themselves to preserve the authority of ministers who controlled by encouraging such "delusions." Samuel Parris, the target of most of Bancroft's ire, pushed for the execution of one woman whose guilt the jury had doubted because, according to the historian, "She must perish, or the delusion was unveiled." In Bancroft's history, Salem, and indeed Massachusetts, was saved not by "the English law, word for word as it stood in the English statute book," but rather when "the common mind was disenthralled, and asserted itself," when the people "refused henceforward to separate belief and reason." Bancroft combined the themes familiar from more than a generation of histories for the classroom and the adult library while bringing the nationalist views of progress in religion, politics, and society together in appealingly vivid and unequivocal terms that suited the worldview of antebellum Americans.[52]

As national histories rose in importance through the first half of the century, so too did a national literature. As those in the early decades of independence had hoped, American writers in all genres found in the colonial past rich topics for fully imagining the "American type." By midcentury many notable nineteenth-century literary figures, including New England natives John Neal, John William De Forest, John Greenleaf Whittier, and of course Nathaniel Hawthorne produced major novels using the witchcraft trials as significant plot elements.[53] They and many lesser writers found in the 1692 trials that "rare deposit in historical memory which is simultaneously dark and heavy, though not nearly explained completely by established facts." Each author that approached Salem in the antebellum years was preoccupied, in Lawrence Buell's words, with the inherent "gap between the enlightened present and the Puritan past."[54]

The first literary treatment of Salem witchcraft was a forgettable (and indeed largely forgotten) 1817 epic poem by Jonathan Scott, *The Sorceress, or Salem Delivered.* Scott's poem was published early in a period when American writers were seeking native subjects to self-consciously create a specifically American literature. Although Congressman Rufus Choate, in calling for a national literature in 1833, suggested that more use be made of early New England history, he warned against unworthy topics like Salem's witch hunt. Recounting such topics in Massachusetts's colonial history "chills, shames, and disgusts us." The more heroic material of founding could, he said, would "impress the facts, the lessons of history more deeply ... into the general mind and heart."[55] Nevertheless, what discomforts the descendant often makes the best dramatic tension in literature. Those in every genre of imaginary literature took to Salem's witchcraft episode with the same orientation and the same enthusiasm as the schoolbook authors. Within the New England literary world in particular, the common connections and influences abounded, and the orthodoxy with which the Puritan past was presented as a paradoxical model was consistent in histories and in literature.

Between 1817 and the publication of *The House of the Seven Gables* in 1851, Salem witchcraft served as a subject for at least two stage plays, a half-dozen or so novels, a variety of short stories, and several poems.[56] Puritans in fact would provided fertile ground for tales that provided both explicit and implicit contrasts to the moral progress made with independence. The Puritan past was still close in time, and its presence as a plot device and subject of moral instruction in national histories gave it an immediacy to nineteenth-century Americans.[57] Perhaps Hawthorne himself best summed up the fraught relationship between the nineteenth-century American and the historical Puritan in a frequently quoted line: "Let us thank God for having given us such ancestors; and let each successive generation thank him, not less fervently, for being one step further from them in the march of ages."[58]

But ultimately what Nathaniel Hawthorne did so successfully in *The House of the Seven Gables,* as well as in a number of short stories, was to use this particular historical episode to explore the nineteenth-century impulse to present the Puritan past as one to be both emulated and repudiated. In doing so, he highlighted that inherent tension between the national present and the colonial past.[59] But by the time *The House of the Seven Gables* was published in 1851, that foundation had been laid by more than fifty years of schoolbook histories and reinforced by similar perspectives in other adult and juvenile literature. Those earlier works had conditioned readers in a way that made the story familiar and exciting and helped to make it Hawthorne's best-selling novel. When Hawthorne gave readers a vicarious thrill by bringing the threat of Salem forward into the lives of fictional contemporary descendants of the original trial participants, he also connected with another way the threat of Salem resonated with the reading public. Between 1830 and 1850, the contemporary specter of Salem witchcraft had already come out of the books and into public discourse to express Americans' fears about various domestic threats to their faith in reason and progress. When anxiety about the course of a new cultural movement or political controversy arose, the average American did not have far to go to find a handy historical parallel to express quickly and completely the nature of his fears. If the concern threatened his sense of himself as part of a new nation that was moving forward, the metaphor of Salem witchcraft functioned well as a universally familiar shorthand for the social and political costs of sliding backward into a colonial world of irrationality, tyranny, and superstition. It did so with the language and ideas of the schoolbook, which provided such "useful knowledge" and a bridge to a distinctive American memory.[60]

CHAPTER THREE

Not to Hell but to Salem

Antebellum Religious Crises

In November 1834 the *New England Magazine* included in its "Comments on the Times" an account of a sensational trial then under way in New York City. The charges were embezzlement, fraud, and murder. The defendant was a man who styled himself "the Prophet Matthias" and who had despotically ruled a small but devoted household of believers for two years. Matthias, before becoming the self-described "Spirit of the Truth," was carpenter Robert Matthews from the Hudson River Valley region of New York. His story unfolded in new competitive daily newspapers such as the New York *City Sun* during the fall of 1834, and as the more scandalous details of life in Matthias's "kingdom" emerged, Americans were riveted by his story. The tale was propelled into national prominence by the combination of an alleged murder, rumors of sexual misconduct, and the bizarre doctrines and person of Matthias himself. Scandalous characters and public sensations like Matthias, who committed "uncleanness, seduction, and adultery...in the name of the Lord," sold newspapers for the new "penny press." And as all the dailies would do in other public controversies and scandals from that point forward, the New York *Daily Tribune* promised to "cheerfully publish all new facts."[1]

The anonymous author of the *New England Magazine* article, like most of the public, undoubtedly learned most of what he knew about Matthias's trial from these new daily newspapers. In covering the trial of Matthias, reporters and editors scrambled to find new ways to describe his cult in order to keep the "news" fresh and papers selling. The details of the case and the language are similar in the two sources, and "compiling" was as prominent a feature of newspaper and periodical composition as it was for schoolbooks. More strikingly, in virtually all the print sources of the period, the language used to judge Matthias, his religion, and his followers bears a close resemblance to that found for more than a generation in the imaginary and pedagogical literature about Salem witchcraft. And during the course of the coverage, Salem itself would appear. The press's fascination with the Matthias case serves as an early map of the themes and language that would become familiar as Salem witchcraft became an increasingly useful cultural metaphor over the nineteenth century.[2]

The 1834 *New England Magazine* article labeled Matthias an "imposter" and scorned his middle-class followers as men whose "credulity and confidence knew no bounds." But as another publication noted, Matthias's believers were, after all, only partially culpable, since "nothing but insanity accounts for the hideous delusion."[3] In the popular schoolbooks and general histories in circulation by the time of the Matthias case, the damage done in Salem in 1692 was also said to be due to the actions of certain "impostors" in the community who acted upon similarly "disordered imaginations."[4] Only insanity or "religious delusion" could account for solid middle-class members of the New York commercial community like Benjamin Folger and Elijah Pierson surrendering their money, their independence, and in Folger's case his wife to a man calling himself the "Prophet." Pierson's death under mysterious circumstances and the collapse of Matthias's odd little kingdom at Mount Zion, on the banks of the Hudson River, had themes that the new dailies rightly expected would sell papers. The rumored sexual arrangements, the possible murder of Pierson, and—most important of all in an age of religious revivals—the ability of an uneducated rural eccentric to persuade two "men of education, good sense, and knowledge of the world" to follow him played on readers' anxieties. Beyond the immediate scandal, this component of the episode had broader implications for society in a time when various unorthodox religious practices and social change were causing concern.[5]

Some more unambiguously connected Salem to the current scandal. In 1835 William L. Stone, who wrote extensively on the case, charged Matthias with heading a religion whose very essence was a "series of delusions originating in fanaticism" as he also explicitly introduced the theme of Salem witch-hunting. Referring to strong religious beliefs that drove men to particular and disturbing actions, Stone reminded his readers of the model of the Puritans and their penchant for "persecutions for witchcraft in the early days of New England." The Prophet Matthias's followers, like those early New England men, may "have been impelled by a strong but mistaken view of duty." Stone not only wrote a book about the scandal (*Matthias and His Imposture's* [*sic*]) but also reported on the trial for a New York daily, the *Commercial Advertiser*. Three years later, in 1838, Stone published the novel *Mercy Desborough* using Puritan witchcraft trials as a subject. Stone clearly had in mind Matthias's follower Anne Disbrow Folger when he chose his sympathetic main character's name from an obscure colonial Connecticut case that occurred at the same time as the trials to the north in Salem. The choice of setting should not, however, be taken as the attempt to insert a competing narrative into the public imagination. The Connecticut cases were in Puritan courts and Puritan towns, and the narrative elements Stone offered were "Salem" right out of the familiar accounts in print in the 1830s. Stone, a childhood friend of Anne's husband Benjamin Folger, was sympathetic to the Folgers in all of his published writing.

William Stone was at the forefront of a fashion of using the witchcraft trials of 1692 to frame moral lessons about contemporary scandals and events, in a way that echoed schoolbook language. The rise of the daily newspapers provided a more immediate and more widespread forum for discussing such issues, and the papers relied on an evolving narrative to sell the latest edition. Stone and others suggested that the Matthias cult was one of the disturbing new religious movements that exemplified a lurking potential for a lapse into a foreign, superstitious past that Americans believed they had grown beyond with independence. Salem's episode of witch-hunting provided a vehicle for articulating concerns about cultural developments.[6]

As a new symbol emerging within the American cultural idiom, Salem witchcraft certainly did not appear everywhere or even in every public controversy. New religious and reform movements in the 1830s and onward raised anxieties about disruption of the established social order. Some people expressed their fears using the familiar example of the seventeenth-century Salem witchcraft trials already present in schoolbooks and in the developing national imaginary literature. For that reason, tracing the appearances of a specific collective memory like Salem witchcraft in public discourse can itself be useful by "articulating the connections between the cultural, the social, and the political" as old themes are linked to new fears. That both adult and juvenile literature framed the

Salem trials in terms that reflected contemporary social and political anxieties likely moved some to reach for that episode as a cautionary tale, as it likewise prompted authors of schoolbooks to repeat the example in each new edition. The increasing public turmoil in the 1830s gave many Americans new reason to fear slipping backward into a world of monarchy, irrationality, backwardness, or foreign influence. The cultural memory of the witchcraft trials of 1692 provided a warning about the limits of tolerance when practices and behaviors fell too far outside the norm, even in a society that prided itself on personal liberty.[7]

Salem's 1692 witch hunt proved to have more cultural staying power than the more contemporary scandal of Prophet Matthias. In what has aptly been called an "antebellum spiritual hothouse," the variety of religious and quasi-religious movements in the decades between the Revolution and the Civil War seemed endless. In that context, when many Americans appeared to their neighbors to be forsaking established Protestant denominations for unusual doctrines and practices, it is not surprising that Salem witchcraft came to mind. Spiritualism, Mormonism, Millerism, and a host of other religious and quasi-religious movements from the 1830s onward all drew the comparison with Salem witchcraft from their critics for their allegedly erroneous (and even dangerous) beliefs and practices.[8]

As ministers, politicians, and an assortment of citizens—ranging from those writing "Letters to the Editor" in local newspapers to the author of the three-hundred-page polemic—would repeatedly ask about religious movements in the nineteenth century, Where was the celebrated "progress" of man? It was one thing for the "excitable portion of the community"—whose ignorance prevented them from distinguishing true beliefs from "miserable delusion"—to follow a Prophet Matthias, a William Miller, or a Joseph Smith; it was quite another when the Folgers of the nation fell under their spell. Perhaps human nature remained impervious to improvement, as the *New England Magazine* suggested, when men of the caliber of Folger and Pierson were vulnerable to delusions hardly less absurd than in the time of witchcraft. Although the anonymous writer did not specify Salem or a New England—based witchcraft episode, the language used in the passage hints at it. And with Salem witchcraft serving time and again as a familiar symbol of Old World "delusions" in their schoolbooks, certainly antebellum Americans could make the connection for themselves.[9]

The Prophet Matthias would quickly recede into obscurity both as a public figure and as a news item, appearing only in the occasional list of dark "pedigrees" for other religious controversies. For example, a minister in the 1850s complained about the "spirit messages" that might come from Spiritualists advocating "Free-Loveism" along the lines of "the Prophet Matthias and his adherents." Charles Leland, in his ongoing battle against the teachings of the Latter-day Saints in the 1860s, managed to resurrect the dimly remembered Matthias along with the by then common example of Puritan extremism in the Salem trials. Leland traced a lineage for the Mormons that ran from "ultra Puritans in England" through colonial New England to the late "Matthias with his 'Impostures.'"[10]

Critics of new religions focused on swaying public opinion by defining spiritual innovations as not "religions" at all. In this context, as David Brion Davis has argued, Americans were a tolerant people because they accepted those who exercised their freedom of religion in appropriate ways. But the religious, social, and even political movements that were considered "delusions" or products of "fanaticism" by the nineteenth-century American Protestant population were many. In print genres ranging from periodicals and sermons to monographs, speeches, and editorials, critics challenged religious innovators who undermined "American" values. They persistently complained that the faithful had lost their reason because of their involvement in religious sects and worried about the "foreign" doctrines and practices introduced by a religion that might threaten republican principles. From the 1830s through the end of the century, the delusions and excesses of Salem witchcraft provided an effective point of reference for those who publicly struggled with such questions.[11]

Positive religious models for Americans were, of course, constantly and deliberately offered in oratory, iconography, and commemorations, and particularly in schoolbooks. By the late 1830s, school geographies, histories, and readers had already established narratives highlighting a cluster of American virtues centered on the idea of an independent, rational, and progressive people. The rote memorization that prevailed through most of the century reinforced appropriate beliefs on subjects like religion. Antebellum school histories most specifically emphasized that the United States was a moderate and tolerant Protestant nation with a divinely appointed destiny. The moral dimension of nineteenth-century primary education in particular was explicitly based on that central tenet. The issue of "toleration," a perennial schoolbook virtue, at least in the abstract, proved especially important to the debate about emerging religious and quasi-religious movements. Mitchell's *Geography* modeled the overarching idea of the limits of toleration: while "every man may worship

God according to the dictates of his own conscience," only "Christianity" provided the proper "basis of the government and institutions." The profusion of Christian-based movements spread across American society would test even that principle by raising the question of how to define Christianity itself.[12]

The "vivid outburst of popular spiritual syncretism" of the post-Revolutionary era challenged toleration for practices that often had emerged directly out of Protestant traditions and denominations. But just as vigorous was the growth of a vocal opposition to these new movements and what was perceived widely as their "radical challenge[s] to ... religious, sexual, and economic values."[13] As William Hutchinson has noted, neighbors could look with "amused (or bemused) tolerance" on positions considered to be "wildly heretical" until there appeared to be a real possibility that action might spring from them.[14] The ensuing debate about the validity of the emerging religious sects led to pointed questions about what constituted legitimate and desirable religious practices in the new United States. The familiar lesson of Salem witchcraft demonstrated the real potential for even Protestant Americans to lose their independence to a central authority that relied on their surrendering individual will and assuming "fanatical" beliefs—beliefs that, as in the colonial witch hunts, might throw the entire society backward into a world of superstition and tyranny. Examining the literature that defined public opposition to two of the largest "innovations" arising out of antebellum American Protestant communities (Spiritualism and the Church of Jesus Christ of Latter-day Saints), we can see what Salem measured for average white Protestant Americans of the time. Salem's episode of witch-hunting marked the boundary of acceptable Protestant beliefs and behaviors not only by going beyond them but by associating Protestant excess with what they had been taught from the cradle was the greatest threat: Roman Catholicism.

The key to debates about religion in and out of schoolbooks lies in Roman Catholicism's place in the nineteenth-century American imagination. While "Hindoos" and "heathens" provided colorful textbook copy about the challenges facing Protestant missionaries or the exoticism of the world outside the United States, the real danger was generally understood to be the designs of the Roman Catholic Church. Part of the strength of the nation, the child was instructed, was that it was neither tyrannized by the pope nor prey to false religions. By the 1850s, when nativism and battles over various new religions were in full bloom, the foundation had been clearly laid by the relentless anti-Catholicism available in print for decades. From schoolbooks to Sunday School tracts and the casual denigration of Roman Catholicism in fiction, average American Protestants understood that Catholicism was a debased belief system. The pervasive intolerance toward it not only informed their reaction to the church and its faithful but increasingly was applied to Protestant-based religious movements with features similar to those most detested in the Roman Church.

What Catholics would do if they took over the nation was not in dispute. The terrible results were well detailed in literature aimed at every level of readers. It was understood that everything about Catholicism was "inimical to industry, propriety, knowledge, and freedom."[15] The consequences of Roman Catholic cultural dominance needed no analogy for nineteenth-century American Protestants, so Salem witchcraft seldom if ever appeared in anti-Catholic polemics. But the calamitous consequences of similar "extremism" in religions with Protestant roots did require the symbolism that Salem's emerging metaphor offered. As a dramatic illustration of the course and consequences of Protestant religious extremism, Salem was ideal. It was a familiar, native, and Protestant-based cautionary tale that drew on the themes already circulating about the dangers of Roman Catholicism.[16]

Thus tolerance, as described in antebellum culture in general, did not mean allowing license to just any popular religious or political notion. Finding the "truth" was not promoted by "listening to error and falsehood."[17] Most Americans believed, as did one Pennsylvania man, that what society needed most was the "criterion by which we may determine with certainty, who are right, and who are wrong."[18] As Ruth Elson has detailed, schoolbooks in particular presented religion as the best reflection of the level of "civilization" attained in a nation, with American Protestantism representing the highest end of the spectrum. With the world clearly divided into religions that were "true" (Protestant) and "false" ("Hindoos," "Mohammedans," and Roman Catholics in particular), the American child was provided with a standard by which to assess people's spiritual condition and by extension their character. Nothing in the schoolbooks or the general literature available on religion, politics, or society better exemplified the threat to the United States from what Noah Webster had called the "debased culture" of Europe than the Roman Catholic Church. To draw a clear line from approved Protestant-based beliefs to those regarded (at best) with suspicion, the path goes directly through the contemporary anti-Catholic rhetoric.[19]

Anti-Catholicism or "antipopery" was not new in the United States; it predated the Revolution. Indeed, it even emerges within the records of the Salem trials themselves. Just a month before his own execution for the crime of witchcraft, John Proctor petitioned the court on behalf of his son William, who, he said, had been interrogated in Salem using techniques that were "very like the Popish cruelties." Robert Calef repeated Proctor's charge in his own 1700 critique of the trials to highlight the brutality of the examinations.[20] In some New England colonies November 5, the English popular holiday Guy Fawkes Day, commemorating the foiled 1605 plot to restore a Catholic monarchy in England, was even celebrated as "Pope Day." The anti-Catholic bias easily survived the Revolution even though Roman Catholics were a small portion of the population. By the time of the first national census in 1790, there were only an estimated 35,000 Roman Catholics in the total population of 3 million. Most American Roman Catholics were in the former Catholic colony of Maryland, but many states including North and South Carolina, New Hampshire, and Connecticut nevertheless had laws that barred Roman Catholics from public office.[21] This "inherited...fear of Papists and foreigners" merged with expansionism and immigration over the first quarter of the nineteenth century to intensify public fears of a Catholic threat. The material circumstances of national growth that increased the general population to over 12 million by 1830 also fueled a significant increase in the American Roman Catholic population. By 1830 there were an estimated 600,000 American Catholics, largely concentrated in eastern urban areas.[22]

The 1830s were notable for the expansion of the anti-Catholic popular print culture, as well as for physical violence against Catholic communities and institutions. In the same twelve-month period when Matthias's trial testimony scandalized much of the American reading public, the presses of the United States produced a significant number of publications that fed the "no-popery" sentiments among Protestants in both the short and the long term.[23] These included virulent anti-Catholic newspapers like the *Protestant*, which represented only one small segment of what Ray Allen Billington described as the "vast flood of propaganda loosed against the Catholic church in the first half of the nineteenth century." The immense success of Lyman Beecher's *Plea for the West* in the 1830s may have "popularized" the idea that Roman Catholic schools were the keystone of the Roman Catholic plan to take over the United States, but from the educated polemic like Beecher's to the crude bigotry and sexual innuendo of cheap pamphlets, it is not unreasonable for Billington to conclude that "the average Protestant American of the 1850s had been trained from birth to hate Catholicism." The claims of papal political designs on the nation and superstitious practices imported from Rome provided a toxic mix that was relentlessly applied to the descriptions of Catholicism in children's books as well.[24]

Publications from Protestant tract societies such as *Dr. Scudder's Tales for Little Readers, about the Heathen* detailed the exotic practices of the "Hindoos" and the Chinese to created a colorful context within which the Protestant missionary struggled against the "midnight of pagan superstition." The constant use of words like "heathen," "pagan," "superstition," and "idolatrous" to describe practices of non-Christian belief systems often cleverly intersected with similar uses in anti-Catholic literature. The association was often more explicit. Roman Catholics were consistently described as no better than those who practiced "the religion of the Hindoos, the Chinese, or the followers of Mohommed."[25] Publications aimed at adults played on the general American belief in the efficacy of education. In reminding readers that the Roman Catholic Church hierarchy craved a docile ignorant worldwide population, they warned of the church's alleged desire to create one through the devious means of "schoolbooks printed and put in circulation in Catholic countries... and books of devotion printed in the United States."[26]

A steady stream of invective against Roman Catholics included alleged exposés of the "dens of vice and iniquity" that were monasteries and convents to highlight both the "foreign" and the "immoral" nature of the church and its threat to social order.[27] Publications that claimed to expose the brutality and immorality of convent life gained favor in the early 1830s as well. These were framed by a variety of scenarios of cloistered life, but all reached the same conclusion—convent life was unnatural.[28] Some secular publications rejected the more "indecent and dishonest polemics that war against the Church of Rome," claiming that all faiths were guilty of excess or error at some time in their histories. In fact, one said, the "Pilgrims of New England might not hear, with complacency, the story of their faith."[29] What did drive the convent exposé genre was sales. The sexual content of these books, "licentious stories under the cover of moral lessons," as one reviewer called them, was certainly central to their popularity in the marketplace.[30] And the narrative of besieged and abused womanhood was also promoted as a measure of a nation's civilization. It was a theme that would recur in a similar exposé genre aimed at polygamous Mormon households.[31]

principles.[42] In fact, when schoolbook author Samuel Goodrich wanted to convey to his young readers the essentially foreign and brutal nature of the Salem witchcraft trials, he assigned to minister Cotton Mather the most damning motive he could find: "inquisitorial malice."[43]

The Roman Catholic response was to make the most of what they framed as the American parallel to the Inquisition. It was the Puritans of seventeenth-century New England who brought persecution to the shores of the later United States, they argued. Beyond the implications about the direct lineage of contemporary Massachusetts convent rioters, Salem provided a case of internal violence as Protestants "persecuting brother Protestants." In the catalog of human brutality, the Puritans left a grim record of "boring with red hot irons the tongues of the inoffensive Quakers, in burning witches." This was no invented claim, the *United States Catholic Magazine* reminded readers—Protestant authors of American histories provided the evidence themselves in their histories. "Read Bancroft, read Goodrich," it urged, pointing to the most popular schoolroom and adult histories. "You will see [it] there inscribed on the historic page." Not only did these very books, the editorial noted, provide the shocking truth about Protestant New England, they were compelled by truth to include "*fact* which reflects immortal honor on our American Catholic ancestry" in Maryland."[44] The Inquisition, by contrast, in the arguments of the Catholic defenders, belonged to a far more distant time and place and was a practice long abandoned. But that claim of temporal distance did no more to stop the invoking of the Inquisition as emblematic of Roman Catholic character and practice than did the insistence by some New England Protestants that "witch hunts" were equally far behind them.

Twenty years after the riot at Charlestown, however, the defenders of Protestant colonial New England were more skilled in publicly debating religious atrocities. An 1854 letter to the editor in the *New York Times* claimed that Protestants had the same capacity for abuse of power when in control as did Catholics. A reader rebutted that statement with the argument that perhaps there were incidents like witch-hunting in New England's history that caused their descendants to "blush," but they were "comparatively few and the prevalence of the delusion short." He offered an ingenious bit of reasoning that displays the ubiquitous anti-Catholicism of the United States in the nineteenth century as well as the pervasive belief in the transforming power of America itself. The defender of New England allowed that English colonists did indeed bring those European-learned practices from the "dark ages," but they quickly realized that they were incompatible with "the genius of the institutions established by our fathers." Should that argument be insufficient, the letter writer further attempted to remove inconveniences like witch-hunting from the American Protestant record by asserting that the Protestant of the seventeenth century was "more near of kin to the Church of Rome" than to the American Protestant of the 1850s.[45]

The evolution of a vocal anti-Catholic sentiment in the United States from the 1830s onward provides a context for the ways many Americans expressed dissatisfaction with developments in Protestant communities during the same period—recurrent themes echoed both in anti-Catholic rhetoric and in print descriptions of events in 1692 Salem. Salem worked as a metaphor for the threat of Protestant extremism because it pointed to specific historical consequences of allowing "fanaticism," "foreign" influences, and "superstition" to prevail. Just as there was no need for an analogous symbol to warn the American Protestant public of the dire consequences should Roman Catholicism succeed in the United States, the church remained a somewhat abstract threat. Although possible Roman Catholic "conquest" of the United States was always openly feared, no Protestants ever seemed to seriously think that somehow they or their neighbors would be caught up in Catholic doctrines and act on them. The "delusions" of Protestant extremism, on the other hand, had a real chance of ensnaring the unwary and inciting dangerous behavior. American Protestants watched each other with a suspicious eye, as popular movements attracting coreligionists brought new ideas and practices to general public attention.

Central to Protestants' discomfort toward other Protestants were the ongoing evangelical revivals between the Revolution and the Civil War that have become known as the Second Great Awakening.[46] At the end of the turbulent 1830s, Joseph Emerson Worcester's *American Almanac and Repository of Useful Knowledge* culled from diverse print sources membership statistics for Protestant denominations in the United States. The various Baptist groups had the most members, with 4.3 million. According to Worcester, the "Mormonites" already could claim 12,000 members in less than a decade of active proselytizing, which was double the number of Shakers and only 3,000 less than the number of Lutherans he identified in the entire country. Of most interest to readers of 1838 (impressive to some and disturbing to others) was the proof Worcester offered for the success of three decades of revivals by evangelizing groups like the Baptists.[47]

The contemporary intersection of backward-looking and forward-looking ideas found a useful expression in Salem's episode of colonial witch-hunting for a variety of reasons. One reason was tension about the place of a variety of supernatural phenomena within Protestant denominations. Belief in various forms of folk magic permeated society as good churchgoers found no inconsistency in using dowsing rods to find water or in consulting the astrological information found in every common almanac to determine the best times for planting, traveling, or even cutting hair.[48] Few people gave much thought to the inherent contradiction between their Christianity and following almanac lore or rituals passed to them in local tradition. But by 1830, when Salem emerged as a rhetorical weapon in public controversies, changes in attitudes toward ideas like witchcraft even in denominations that once openly spoke of the physical threat the devil posed made the witchcraft charge more effective as a slur.

As Christine Heyrman showed in her study of Methodist and Baptist evangelizing campaigns in the southern states from the late eighteenth century into the early nineteenth, both denominations underwent a transformation directed at gaining "respectable" white converts. The desire of preachers to convert the respectable white yeoman, or better yet the wealthy planter, led to a steady downplaying of the "devils" and "wizards" that frequently appeared in early sermons. The "broad repositioning" of both denominations by their more educated clergy by 1820 was a reaction not only to the content of preaching but to the reaction of the desired "respectable" convert pool, who saw the charismatic preaching style and subsequent reaction of the revival audiences as disturbingly "magical and wizardly" in itself. As Methodist and Baptist preachers of the early nineteenth century aimed for respectability in the minds of white neighbors, they increasingly assigned witchcraft and other "superstitions" to African Americans and "simple hearted" whites.[49]

In the same period both the popular press and the histories and geographies produced for the juvenile and adult markets reinforced the idea that witchcraft was a product of mental illness, ignorance, or "pagan" and "uncivilized" societies. In the textbook realm, race was a marker of belief in superstitious things. West Africans were, according to Noah Webster and others, "great believers in witchcraft."[50] In the popular press, Indians and African-descended slaves were assumed inherently to be prey to such "pagan superstition."[51] Certain immigrants also fell into categories where ethnicity (and possibly religion) contributed to the presumed ignorance that led to such beliefs. In a report from New Bedford, Massachusetts, in

1830, a local resident attempted to remove a "hex" from his goat with a cure he said was "used in Ireland." By contrast, a South Carolinian was described in a newspaper as an "eccentric character." Along with his local reputation as a recluse and miser, the article included his status as a slave-holder to built a case for his attraction to superstitious ideas. As a sign of his mental disorganization, he allegedly lived in "a habitation abun-dantly worse than any of those occupied by his negroes," and the shack was filled with "charms" the man believed would keep witches at bay. By 1830, witchcraft beliefs could be held by a white American man only if there was evidence that he was in some way deranged.[52]

The emotional fervor of Protestant revival meetings was unsettling to many observers, who would eventually draw on Salem as an example of where such religious passions might lead. However far Methodists or Bap-tists had moved away from a reliance on supernatural phenomena in this world, their opponents used it against them. Such charges not only had the benefit of casting revival-based evangelicalism as superstition mas-querading as religion, they carried racial and social classifications meant to marginalize believers and repel potential converts. The public disorder that might be spawned by the "frenzy" of the revival was part of a broader concern. Could those who were attracted to the excitement of the camp meeting settle for the approved "steady piety" that helped stabilize the individual and the community? Or would those people look for the next excitement? Even Charles Grandison Finney, one of the leaders of the re-vival movement, came to worry that some "fanaticism" resulted from the "jump and stir" of camp meetings.[53] As some critics worried about the effect on worshipers, still others were apprehensive about the concurrent "swarms of clerical idlers and vagabonds that prowl about the country." A few even feared that the evangelizing movement was nothing but a money-making operation "under the mask of religion." And if any reli-gious goals truly lay behind proselytizing enthusiasm, it was in truth only a design to bring the United States under the "domination of the gloomy bigoted followers of John Calvin." The results of one such seventeenth-century "fanatical" government were well known. When Calvinists and their "savage intolerance" ruled the land, they "flogged, cropped, and hanged the feeble, timid Quakers...and sanctioned the horrible execu-tions for witchcraft in the town of Salem."[54]

The linkage of Salem and the four Quakers executed by Puritan Mas-sachusetts Bay Colony between 1659 and 1661 illustrates the selective na-ture of collective memory. Given the frequent presence of both colonial episodes in the historical narratives for adult and juvenile markets, either could have served as a familiar example of the consequences of Puritan "zeal." But while both episodes offered warnings from the past while allowing the progressive present to draw a self-satisfied compliment, one event became a prominent cultural metaphor and the other, as we shall see, became at best an intensifier of that metaphor. The key to this development is how each episode could be seen to serve (or not serve) the goals of those who brought the Puritan past into public discourse in the early 1830s. The "usefulness" of each event largely depended on how it had been remembered. Salem's "witches" were long gone, but descendants of Massachusetts's Puritan colonists were central figures in the nineteenth-century shaping of the national past. They had created narratives of both seventeenth-century events that affected how each could be used as a historical symbol. In addition, the Quakers were a larger and more influential presence in nineteenth-century America than in seventeenth-century New England. They too had advanced a narrative of their coreligionists' executions to serve their own denominational goals.[55]

The struggle to define the conflicts between Puritans and Quakers, as with the witchcraft trials, began during the original events and continued to develop within collective American memory as it evolved to suit changing social needs. The Quaker campaign to define the arrests, convictions, and executions of four of their coreligionists as martyrdom for "liberty of conscience" appeared to have triumphed, as Americans in the post-Revolutionary era found contemporary social and political value in such an emphasis. To all appearances, the Quakers "won" the struggle for narrative control in the sympathetic portrayal of the four executed members of the sect as early martyrs for the "liberty" that the post-Revolutionary generation valorized. But the victory was less complete than it might appear. The Puritans and their descendants had followed a course of defining the Quaker trials by asserting that "civil disorder" rather than any championing of liberty was at the heart of the convictions and executions. Even histories that found the Quaker executions to be "a disgraceful blot on the annals of New England" had equally harsh words for the conduct of the seventeenth-century Quakers.[56] The Quakers' effort to create a usable past in accord with their own denominational changes centered on downplaying historical realities. The aggressive and often disruptive way Quakers publicly "witnessed" in the seventeenth century was refashioned in Quaker denominational memory by eliminating or minimizing elements of old-style practices—all the better, as Carla Pestana has shown, to create a more sympathetic and "inoffensive martyr" out of Mary Dyer and the three men executed in seventeenth-century Massachusetts Bay Colony.[57] Most important in relation to any potential for neutralizing the Quaker cases as a possible symbol of Puritan brutality was the way the accounts resonated with broader concerns of American society in the 1830s through the 1850s.

Using the British colonial past was popular among a wide variety of Americans as they expressed in print their anxieties about religious extremism, mob violence, and popular reform movements like the abolition of slavery. But it ultimately affected the usefulness of the seventeenth-century Quaker as a symbol. Here the Puritan narrative about the Quakers' disorderly conduct that was carried forward and deepened by the many celebratory narratives in histories (often written by New Englanders) prevailed. The minister Leonard Bacon certainly understood this when he spoke on the subject to an annual gathering of New England descendants in 1838. Bacon agreed that the Puritans were indeed a "persecuting" group by contemporary standards. But he was careful to include the information that was in every schoolbook account of early Massachusetts by this time: putting the onus only on the Puritans for "persecuting" hid the fact that they were a colony governed by laws while the Quakers were disruptive, invading "fanatics" who the Puritans quite reasonably believed were "highly dangerous to society."[58]

The sole category where Quakers served as an independent symbol was appeals by beleaguered denominations who, as did the *Evangelical Magazine and Gospel Advocate*, appealed to the cultural memory of the harsh bigotry "under which Quakers and Baptists were put to death." Since these denominations frequently were described as equally "disorderly," they raised the Quaker cases in a bid for mainstream inclusion, attempting to align themselves with what they saw as historical martyrs for American religious freedom. As the century wore on and Salem became an established cultural metaphor, the Quaker example appeared less frequently.

Even schoolbooks that described the seventeenth-century clash in Massachusetts Bay Colony as a battle between the "fanaticism of the magistrates and the Quakers" were using that construction to put the blame on *some* Puritans and *all* Quakers. Inevitably, despite the repeated condemnation of the seventeenth-century Puritan judicial system, the colonial Quakers of the schoolbook came to sound like the contemporary religious extremists who were the marginalized targets of the Salem metaphor hurled by those in the threatened mainstream.[59] Therefore, while the claim that Puritans persecuted the Quakers could (and often did) embellish their charges of cruelty and fanaticism through the nineteenth century, it was inevitably used as an intensifier.

Aggravating the charge of Quaker violence was the issue of public indecency. In these narratives, female Quakers in particular were viewed as a menace for transgressing appropriate religious and gender boundaries. Jedidiah Morse, in his own popular adult and juvenile books, was particularly outraged by the seventeenth-century female Quaker's "imprudent, indelicate and infatuated conduct." Describing Quakers as suffering from "a species of madness," Morse offered as evidence the case of Deborah Wilson, whose protest went as far as appearing in "the streets of Salem, naked as she was born."[60] The origin of the sect was, as Benson Lossing more colorfully and specifically located it, in "the heaving masses of English society where 'zealous religious women' were common."[61] Even Quaker John Greenleaf Whittier remarked in 1848, with some obvious discomfort, that in such matters as the Puritans and the Quakers, the Puritans (as represented in contemporary narratives) could indeed gain some reputational cover for their own actions in the "fanaticism and folly" that marked the conduct of the early Quakers.[62] As a symbol that could produce outrage and disgust, the Salem "witches" did not carry any narrative culpability for their fate into nineteenth-century national memory. Removing the Quaker cases from active social use still left Salem witchcraft, more than enough evidence to comprehensively condemn the Puritans.

Thus the utility of the Quaker executions as a historical metaphor was limited. To Americans of the turbulent 1830s, the disorderly behavior of the seventeenth-century Quakers complicated their victim status. Their alleged culpability for their fate encroached on the unconditional sympathy that best suits a cultural symbol of oppression. So too, by extension, did the nineteenth-century Quakers' penchant for antislavery activity prevent the American pro-slavery population from seeing them as figures for identification or empathy. Although the midcentury defenders of slavery in print or oratory often included the Quakers in their catalog of sins of the "Puritan North," in this case it is best understood as useful hyperbole. As part of a list of depraved acts committed by the ancestors of Northerners, the Quaker cases intensified the idea that the history of "fanaticism" among such people made them a threat not only to their pro-slavery fellow citizens but even to their ideological antislavery allies.

Describing a seventeenth-century Protestant group as "fanatical" was important, however. It was rooted in the often-repeated idea that Catholics were born and raised within a system that conditioned them to be "serfs" for the pope. Serfs might become violent, of course, as could any mob or army, but only if moved by their tyrant. Protestants, on the other hand, were generally described as individually involved in religious "manias" or "delusions." Almost invariably, the Protestant religious deviant headed toward the margins of acceptable religious beliefs or practices was described as overwrought. To be in the thrall of "fanaticism," as one article by that title defined it, was to be "a man made with wild notions." The regular references to "agitation" and "zeal" expressed a widespread belief that people who were susceptible to the excitement of the revival meeting or new religious ideas were invariably those "whose opinions are so hastily formed, or unreasonably held" as to be unreliable. Such people were likely not only to "break forth into bold assertions" but to take "violent action." Salem worked well to express the various dimensions of these fears. The nineteenth-century commentator assumed that only "delusion" or "fanatical" religious convictions could explain the belief in such things as witches, and once people were under the control of such passions, they might well act like those in Salem.[63]

In rhetoric directed against such groups as the Spiritualists and Latter-day Saints from the 1830s onward, we find useful examples of how Salem witchcraft was used to encompass anxieties about each religion's doctrines and practices and the grave social and political consequences of their widespread adoption. Spiritualism was introduced to the nation a little more than a decade after the Prophet Matthias scandal highlighted the disturbing potential in the Protestant-based religious revivals, new religions, and social movements sweeping America. The foundational belief of the movement was that the spirits of the dead could be contacted by sensitive living persons acting as "mediums." Such "spirit communications" offered messages from departed loved ones as well as guidance on matters that ranged from the spiritual to the scientific. Reports of strange phenomena involving twelve-year-old Kate and fourteen-year-old Margaret Fox of Hydesville, in upstate New York, and their "rapping" communication with the "spirit world" appeared in the *New York Times* in 1849.[64] It took hold of much of the American imagination the next year when the Fox sisters appeared in New York City. They demonstrated their "rapping" and their ability to channel spoken messages from the dead for both selected individuals and sellout crowds.[65] Spiritualism initially appealed to such a broad cross section of seekers that some Americans in the 1850s thought it was foolish to dismiss it immediately with "a shrug and a sneer." Others believed from the beginning that the public

was merely fooled by the "absurdities of modern witchcraft."[66] The be-
reaved were promised another chance to reach departed loved ones.
Those seeking everything from Christian perfectionism to medical treatments and scientific proof of life beyond death gravitated toward Spiritualist demonstrations and séances.[67]

Spiritualism had another benefit that attracted long-term adherents as
well as dilettantes. Like William Miller's movement foretelling the end of
the world in the 1840s, it could be adopted alongside one's primary religious affiliation.[68] In fact Spiritualism, like Millerism, had no institutional
foundation and no set dogma. As more a quasi-religious movement than
a traditional religion, it offered an appealing "extreme individualism" in
practice and belief.[69] Whatever anxieties Spiritualism may have reflected
in its believers, it certainly revealed the anxieties of its Protestant critics.[70]

It is clear that the divisions of opinion over Spiritualism's practices
sometimes brought into public debates the idea of "witchcraft" as a practice rather than "Salem witchcraft" as a metaphor, despite overlap in
meanings about "superstitious practices." The public demonstrations of
"rapping" or other forms of spirit communication were performances.
As public skepticism grew about the validity of Spiritualist beliefs, staged
séances and other exposés of the arts of Spiritualist imposters became a
staple of the entertainment stage. Some uses of "witchcraft" in relation
to Spiritualism are clearly distinguishable by context from invocations of
Salem's witchcraft episode. The editor of the *Democratic Review*, writing
in 1847 about the current interest in hypnosis and other philosophies that
promised communication (similar to that later widely promoted by Spiritualism), warned readers not to dismiss the ideas out of hand. Without
clear evidence, he said, it was unfair to associate new ideas "in the public
estimation with witchcraft."[71] Others made similar comments about the
connection between the Fox sisters' Spiritualist demonstrations and other
claims that might in an earlier day have simply been called "witchcraft and
necromancy."[72] Perhaps the authors had Salem in mind, but without clear
historical markers of time or place, and in the absence of warnings about
the social consequences for the nation habitually used in connection with
Salem, it is best to consider them outside the metaphorical use of Salem
witchcraft.

The Salem metaphor was used to attack Spiritualism primarily by reminding readers that this was simply the latest "popular delusion." Certainly widespread delusions might endanger society by fostering disruption among fanatical devotees, such as that "witnessed during the Salem

witchcraft."[73] By 1868 a reviewer of Charles Upham's history of the Salem trials reminded his readers that "we may believe that we could never act as the citizens of Salem acted in their superstition and fear" but, he continued, the persistence of interest in "'spiritual circles' made that a hollow boast." And certainly, as any reasonable person knew, Spiritualists were no more than "a company of fanatics" who were as prone was any other fanatics to "wild exultation," and with "less excuse" than could be made for the seventeenth-century Puritans.[74] Looking back at the "fanatical sects" and the "arch imposture" that made "the witchcraft trials of New England...familiar to all," the *Brooklyn Daily Eagle* wondered if such "ignorance and diseases of the brain" would finally halt all human progress.[75] One observer suggested that contemporary followers of these movements had motives similar to those that histories had long attributed to the accusers of witches: "love of notoriety, hope of gain, the prosecution of some private intrigue." This writer said he recalled Salem when he read the descriptions of physical possession reported in histories of other "familiar examples of wide-spread contagious delusions." In 1850 Spiritualist claims of contacting luminaries in death led a Massachusetts orator to jest about such outlandish assertions: he ventured that, were he to believe that he could "get up a conversation with General Washington about fly traps, or with John Adams on the respective merits of hair-dyes...I intend to believe also, unreservedly in the Salem witchcraft!"[76] Thus, practitioners of the "arts or sciences" of mesmerism, clairvoyance, and Spiritualism were "pretenders," but their clients suffered from "self-delusion" in parallel with the accusers and court officials of Salem.[77] A decade after the Fox sisters first came to New York, the *New Englander and Yale Review* suggested that Spiritualism and other practices could be classified as "a sheer delusion, fostered by imposition," the same phenomenon that was once "in vogue among the witches of Salem."[78]

Salem also appeared in critiques that located the geographical origins of the Latter-day Saints in the center of the birthplace of other peculiar American religious notions—a region "famous for queer things."[79] Essex County, Massachusetts, as one newspaper noted, was historically "a credulous place." Indeed, it qualified as the "grand seat of supernatural wonders" in America, since it was the alleged home of a large number of local Spiritualists as well as of "Salem witchcraft and Mormon founder Smith."[80] In fact, during the Sectional Crisis, Southern writers seized on the purported New England origins and associations to Spiritualism, Mormonism, Millerism, and utopian movements in criticizing Northern "fanatics" on the topic of abolition. The South, claimed the *Southern Literary Messenger*, was removed from the wild extremism that could regularly be found in New England. "We know little of its freaks from the days of witch-drowning...the rise and fall of Millerism, the growth of Mormonism or Puritanical Mahomedanism...Spiritualism, [or] Free Loveism." "Why is it," the author asked of New England, "that no other land in the world has troubled mankind with such terrible abominations?"[81]

But before significant numbers of critics settled down in earnest to elaborate their view of Spiritualism as the latest example of "one popular delusion [that] runs into another,"[82] there was a brief honeymoon as most of the public became acquainted with its claims—a short period during which a degree of curiosity and open-mindedness led most skeptics to wait for conclusive evidence of truth or fraud. A correspondent to the *Southern Literary Messenger* in 1850 advised just such a "wait and see" attitude toward spirit communication and provided a rare example of using Salem to support a potentially *progressive* idea. He sternly criticized the occasional "savage customer" who verbally abused the Fox sisters. Such rudeness demonstrated to his satisfaction that, despite the "boasted light of the nineteenth century," the spirit of free inquiry was often aced by "the spirit which hung the witches."[83] Progress, however, not to mention a sense of proper religious ideas and behaviors, remained a chief concern for those who assessed Spiritualism from the opposite perspective. The days of Salem witchcraft brought to mind men who, "creeping cautiously along the narrow limits of the known," could not clearly distinguish between fraud and delusion.[84] The continued interest in spirit communication, claimed the *New Englander and Yale Review* by 1860, would one day be viewed as "the present generation looks upon the Salem witchcraft, as a miserable imposture and delusion."[85]

"Minds not sufficiently enlightened by reason and philosophy," Hannah Adams warned in 1807, could hardly be expected to contribute to the nation's intellectual, economic, or moral progress.[86] Adams expressed the popular wisdom, which had not waned as the century progressed. It could be found in every schoolbook, in the introductory notes to teachers and parents, and embedded in every account of American achievement on every page. The influence of delusions was not rendered acceptable by the reportedly benign nature of the current spirit beliefs. Proof of the argument, as another writer suggested, could be found easily enough: "It will be sufficient to refer to the Salem witchcraft...which is easily explained

if we [consider that it was] an age which was prepared to expect vis-
itations from infernal rather than from celestial spirits."[87] In fact, this
writer predicted that one day Spiritualism itself would be viewed "with
the vague skepticism with which most persons regard the diabolical work-
ings" found in Salem in 1692.[88] Readers of articles about religious innovation were often likewise reminded that "we profess to look down with
lofty pity upon the benighted ignorance that persecuted those who were
accused of witchcraft." But, this essayist concluded, if we but glance about
us "we have our innumerable forms of spiritual fanaticism."[89]

As harsh as the attacks on Spiritualism and other nineteenth-century
religious innovations often were, they were temperate compared with the
attacks on the Latter-day Saints. To many writers, those who claimed to
have contacted Benjamin Franklin or a lost child deserved pity more than
censure. The Saints, however, came to public notice in the 1830s, and
within a decade of their founding they were targets of a relentless print
campaign rivaled only by the anti-Catholic crusade, which it resembled.
The *North American Review* invoked a Revolutionary-era prayer in 1835
that could serve as a brief description of the decades-long anti-Mormon
effort. The Saints, it insisted, like Roman Catholics, would have to "be
brought to reason or ruin."[90]

In everything from anti-Mormon sermons to fiction, Salem witchcraft
became an emblem of this Protestant-based threat. The most virulent
rhetoric against the Latter-day Saints emerged during the same period
when Salem was being used in the sectional debates and the Civil War.
Combined with the tropes familiar from old anti-Catholic campaigns, it
shows the ways Salem could, by midcentury, express perceived threats to
core national values in a variety of crises. In the case of anti-Catholicism
and anti-Mormonism, there was a consistent and pronounced elision in
the definition of both religions within controversial literature. The practices, institutional hierarchy, and social organization of the Latter-day
Saints were most commonly compared to those of Roman Catholicism.
While Salem was commonly invoked to warn of the political and social
consequences both for Mormon communities and for the broader United
States, the concept behind such commentary was that the central founding principles that defined America and Americans would be subsumed
within a Mormon "kingdom" just a surely as they might beneath the pope
and his church. Many contemporaries also considered the Saints' practices
out of place in a republican society. The faithful followed a strong central
leader, and in the nineteenth century they advocated practices easily cast

as superstitious, immoral and foreign. Members aggressively proselytized, and they had their greatest success within the ranks of Protestants, which increased the ire directed toward them. The strong devotion of converts was consistently labeled "fanatical." And most disturbing to many Americans, the Saints called for a "kingdom" that was at the very least only ambiguously situated in heaven rather than on earth.[91] Thus, with teachings labeled "subversive of freedom, morality, and progress," the Latter-day Saints, in the eyes of their opponents, threatened the entire social and political order.[92]

The history of the Church of Jesus Christ of Latter-day Saints, most commonly known as Mormons to those outside the faith, began when Joseph Smith, who lived in the area known from Protestant revivals as New York's "burned-over district," announced that God had revealed to him golden plates that contained the Book of Mormon. For believers, the revelation marked a restoration of true religion after a period of apostasy and provided new scriptures to accompany the Old and New Testaments of the Christian Bible. Smith organized his church in Fayette, New York, in 1831 and actively sought converts. Joseph Smith and his followers traveled from New York to Ohio, Missouri, Illinois, and Iowa before finally establishing their patriarchal kingdom in Utah Territory in 1847. The Saints would reach their promised land without Smith, however: in 1844 he was murdered by a mob in Carthage, Illinois. Unlike religious movements such as Spiritualism, the Mormons developed an institutional structure, complex rituals, and elaborate doctrines that established the church as a major worldwide religion a century later. Long after Spiritualism was gone from the cultural scene, anti-Mormon literature was still recycling not only the arguments but also the language that framed them during the 1840s. Thus the metaphor of Salem witchcraft expressed a desire for limits in American religious practice and warned against transgressing traditional values.[93]

By the late 1840s, it was unusual to read any suggestion of sympathy for Mormons in a non-Mormon newspaper. But the very earliest reports of the Mormons' travails as they sought a home and insisted on the religious liberty promised in the United States had prompted a sympathetic response in many Americans. They used Salem as an example of a community caught up in its own religious fears. In late 1838 reports in the eastern newspapers that Missouri governor Lilburn W. Boggs had issued an extermination order against the then little known religion prompted the *Evangelical Magazine and Gospel Advocate* to ask, How do "such doings comport with the letter and spirit of our inimitable Constitution, the free-dom of the press, and the rights of conscience?" The magazine advocated punishment for Mormons or anyone else who broke local laws; other-wise, to punish religious belief would send the country backward to a time under "the old puritanical laws of New-England."[94] Tolerance for the Latter-day Saints, as for most of the other religious movements that emerged during the first half of the nineteenth century, was relatively short-lived; an active anti-Mormon campaign was soon fully under way. E. D. Howe, an Ohio editor who made a second career out of opposing Mormonism, saw no reason at all for sympathy, since in his opinion the Mormons were not part of a religion but rather fanatical devotees of a sin-gle sinister man. And, Howe insisted, they were excellent proof that once entrapped "there is no turning a fanatic from his folly."[95] This opinion was voiced by others, who either targeted Mormonism alone or included it on a list of dangerous religious ideas that populated the national landscape during the century.

The Presbyterian *Philadelphia Christian Observer* said of Mormons, "if their religious apprehensions may be called faith," then the attraction of it to any sensible nineteenth-century American was "more astound-ing than faith in witchcraft ... which prevailed among many in the seven-teenth century."[96] In the 1850s and 1860s critics assumed that converts were inherently susceptible to "excitements and loss of reason," and this propensity resulted in their becoming "contemptible slaves of a degrad-ing superstition."[97] Indeed, the level of fanaticism found in Mormons, said one commentator in 1853, recalled the "days of witch-drowning."[98] While some seemingly gave the Utah pioneers credit for their "bold and per-ilous daring," they diluted the praise by claiming that it was not courage but the nature of "fanatical enterprises" to persuade such men to follow where they are led. It was part of the "efficacy of religious zeal." Religious excitements interfered with reason, the *Brooklyn Daily Eagle* repeatedly said, and the Puritans were a good example of this.[99] And both in Puritan Massachusetts and elsewhere, "history is replete with wide-spread manias and delusions ... witchcraft for instance."[100]

With a revolution to throw off monarchy and their later battles over disestablishment, Americans certainly were primed to be wary of tyranny in political or religious form. Schoolbooks that educated the rising gen-erations of Americans in appropriate behaviors and beliefs did not single out the Mormon faith as particularly outside the moderate Protestantism they championed until the anti-Mormon literature had done its work for at least a decade. Eventually, most asserted that any claim by the Latter-day Saints to be Christian was dubious and described the church's sway over followers as sinister. One marker of those attitudes is that the formal or full name of the church is rarely used in any schoolbook. Most authors exclusively refer to the church or to its members as "Mormons," which in the nineteenth century was itself a condemnation.

Samuel Goodrich, the prolific author and publisher of every sort of schoolbook, concluded as early as 1850 that the Latter-day Saints were "the worst trouble" facing the western United States. A chapter describing how the Saints "disturbed" other settlers and created a burden by forcing the federal government to send three thousand troops to bring them to "submission" by "crush[ing] their irregularities" concludes by asking children to "describe the conduct of the Mormons."[101] Emma Willard's popular school history in 1868 called the Latter-day Saints "the most extraordinary imposture of the age."[102] Late-century readers found a pervasive sense in schoolbooks that, as for Roman Catholics, "religious freedom does not extend to Mormons."[103] And to some that view obviously extended into the category of political freedom.

Individuals could follow practices that involved "seer stones," attention to astrology, or any number of unusual rituals that Mormonism and other religions could devise, even if neighbors sometimes looked askance. In the end, such habits, even if slandered, could be dismissed as individual peculiarities. But only up to a point. Once the broad application of the familiar terms "deluded" or "fanatical" appeared in print, they signaled an opposition to a particular movement that expressed (or claimed to express) real concern about fitness for the duties of citizenship. In the eyes of opponents and those they influenced with their writings, to become and remain a Mormon was a sign of mental instability. If a convert had been involved in other reviled or ridiculed movements, of course, critics drew more contemporary parallels of irrationality. The *Vermont Gazette* reprinted an item from a Freedonia, New York, newspaper that reported "the Mormonites are doing a pretty fair business in the anti-Masonic party of this town ... fit materials for a fit delusion."[104] That any American could submit to a church that required "unquestioned and unquestioning obedience" in sacred and secular matters was a mystery that tormented opponents.[105]

Kings and popes were useful villains in the abstract, but Joseph Smith was a specific living man. Ridiculing him by omitting the honorifics extended to other public figures or calling him "Joe Smith" and broadcasting scurrilous stories about him and his family as "treasure diggers" had a specific purpose beyond simple insult. Describing Smith's background and character as marked by "ignorance...low cunning...open and shameless vices" and labeling him "the impostor" who ruled over the credulous by means of "pretended revelation" served to emphasize that the author not only considered Joseph Smith unworthy of the courtesy extended to a legitimate religious leader but also questioned the mental competence of his followers.[106] The central position of a leader like Joseph Smith (and later Brigham Young) provided a human target to demonize.[107] Degrading Smith by extension degraded his church and its members as well. Despite his short tenure as Prophet, Smith's reputation as church founder was critical to the religion's origin myth, and as such his reputation continued to be a primary target for critics, in life and in death. Creating "agents of moralized fear" out of figures like Joseph Smith dehumanized them for the express purpose of marking the social boundaries between the normal and the abnormal.[108]

Centralized religious authority that required "obedience" from its members was clearly considered a sign of encroaching tyranny in the United States. Therefore such things were a public, not a private, concern. When Smith was ridiculed with the title "Pope Joseph the First," the abundant anti-Catholic literature and the sentiments it had created were being drawn on to respond to this new and disturbing threat. The 1847 removal of the community to Utah Territory gave opponents writing and watching far from the region "proof" that the Saints intended to build an earthly kingdom with church leaders in both spiritual and secular control, reminiscent of Puritan rule in the manner of "a rude Cromwell." For those who might not immediately associate the English Puritan leader with an American-based threat of theocratic tyranny, "that old New England divine" entered into this imagined drama of tyranny in a republic under Mormon rule. The specter of the Salem trials followed, as the Puritan was pictured "chuckling over his conceit of certain poor women, who had been burned to death in his own town."[109] Just as that "New England divine" found his authority for his witch-hunting in the Bible, so too, critics asserted, did the Mormon leaders attempt to base their spiritual authority and action on scripture. And, readers were reminded, it was New England that was implicated both historically and in the present day, for it "always had some 'God-Smith'" emerging on the public scene.[110] This perception was undoubtedly reinforced by the concurrent use of the example of the Puritan theocracy's descent into witch-hunting in the Sectional Crisis over slavery. If the Mormons thrived, the *Princeton Review* argued during the 1859 campaign, the people of Utah Territory would lose the "principle of individual liberty and responsibility... [that is] so strikingly characteristic of the American mind."[111]

The idea of "foreign" influences on the doctrines of the Latter-day Saints also brought Puritan Salem into the debates in terms familiar from schoolbooks. The coverage of Salem witchcraft in the school histories implied a parallel between foreign autocracy or ideas and wickedness. Puritans who tried and hanged witches followed, after all, "the practice of the courts... regulated" by English "precedents."[112] These new Mormon immigrants, said John Warner Barber in his 1861 United States history text, "have not the first conceptions of their duties to our government, or of their duties as American citizens. They come to Zion, but they do not come to America."[113] *The Southern Literary Messenger* claimed that "the tyranny of fanaticism" was originally imported from England with the Puritans, along with a general population marked by "insanity and knavery." This migration, the writer claimed, alleviated England's religious strife in the seventeenth century just as the current exodus of English Mormon converts to the United States promised to do once again. To properly pull off "a stark imposture" that defined a false religion required uncritical fanatics, and "foreign disciples are generally more fervent and earnest."[114] Thus Brigham Young, the *Brooklyn Daily Eagle* added in a similar argument, "was indebted to his imported converts as much, at least, as to those of our own soil, for the temporary success of his folly."[115] *DeBow's Review* complained (within its ongoing regional war with New England, which finally was erupting into a real war in the spring of 1861) that the lineage of unfortunate elements of the American population from "rigidity of Puritanism to the licentiousness of Mormonism" came from foreign shores.[116] The long history of assigning Puritanism to foreign ideas (which accounted in great part for the excesses at Salem) made it easier to draw rhetorical parallels between them and the Latter-day Saints. By midcentury combining ideas such as foreign origins, theocracies, and tyranny with Puritanism was effective. In all ways, critics of the Latter-day Saints used Puritans to make the case that LDS practices were fundamentally contrary to the American—his prosperity, his reason, and especially his freedom.

The doctrines of the Church of Jesus Christ of Latter-day Saints created not only political but social worries and were persistently described as native to exotic and non-Christian locations. Even more so than Roman

Catholicism, Eastern religions—as American Christians learned from the cradle—"departed most from the pure faith and worship of the one true God."[117] The subtle appeal to racial biases embedded in the arguments further enhanced the essentially "foreign" nature of the Saints' doctrines.[118] Mormon practices such as polygamy were firmly located in "the East," as either "Oriental" or purely "Mohommadan," meaning that in the minds of many Americans extending tolerance was not necessary. In one book an illustration of the Mormon journey west was labeled not a "wagon train" but a "caravan on the prairies." Mormons did not make a journey to Utah; they made a "hejira." And they did not have a religious leader in Smith or Young; "like the Mohamedans, the Mormons have their prophet."[119] Indeed, Mormonism's unique crime in the eyes of its critics was to take the worst religious precedents in American history and mix them with foreign influence. Critics thus continued their campaign to place Mormonism outside the American Christian tradition yet still proclaimed themselves standard bearers of "the ideals of equal rights and government by law."[120]

Polygamy offered the additional opportunity to use "Mohammedism" to highlight the essentially foreign nature of the Latter-day Saints. The framework for antipolygamy attacks was the "convent literature" of the anti-Catholic campaign. If celibacy was considered unnatural or a cover for secret debauchery among the Roman Catholic clergy, plural marriage provoked speculation that Mormon communities were sites of rampant promiscuity. Polygamy, said opponents, was a product of "lusts and superstition."[121] A "degradation" to both men and women, the practice was the same "reward that Mohammed offered to men's lusts."[122] On Judgment Day, two men would surely pay for their sins in life, said the *Ladies' Repository* in 1859: "Mohammed shall suffer for the dupes of the Koran, Joe Smith for the Mormons."[123] Like the Catholic convent, the "Mormon seraglio" loomed large in the oppositional imagination as it served the purpose of working up a moral panic when necessary. Reviving a religious, patriarchal government within the borders of the United States threatened to unleash institutional "fanaticism" across the country. A system that "mixed Puritanism with Mohammedanism" threatened priestly rule: "the kind that burned witches."[124]

When many Protestant Americans looked to Utah, with its centralized church leadership and majority status in the electorate, they likely wondered whether the anti-Mormon writers warning of Puritan Salem might be right. Perhaps it was true, as the *New England Magazine* once said of the Prophet Matthias scandal, that "all the schoolmasters in the universe" could not stave off with mere education the emotional upheavals that came with nineteenth-century religious "enthusiasms."[125] But they could and did provide a cultural context and vocabulary for judging such new spiritual movements in their schoolbooks and in any number of other print sources. In thus marking the boundaries of acceptable religious practices, Americans created a cultural metaphor that would come to have wider social and political applications. Strangely enough, the violent rhetoric opposing anxiety-provoking cultural developments in the United States suggests many feared that neighbors involved in new religious and reform movements risked going not to hell but to Salem. From the 1830s onward, the metaphor would spread beyond public religious controversies to a wide variety of political controversies. One of the most important was the Sectional Crisis of the 1850s and the subsequent Civil War. With that application, the metaphor of the Salem witchcraft trials would truly become established in American discourse.

CHAPTER FOUR

Witch-Burners

The Politics of Sectionalism

On February 16, 1849, Democratic congressman Henry Bedinger of Virginia had had enough. Enough of hearing slavery described in the House of Representatives as a "curse" on Southern culture and morals. More than enough, especially, of Massachusetts congressmen Horace Mann and John Palfrey and their "fanatical abolitionist" friends in the chamber who took every opportunity to make negative comparisons between the North and the South. As Bedinger stood on the floor of the House, he waved Elwood Fisher's recently published pro-slavery speech, which touted the use of statistical data to "prove" that slavery resulted both in more prosperity and in a superior moral climate. As for Massachusetts, he concluded, "she is unquestionably, sir, a great state, and some of her Representatives on this floor seem to know it."[1] But for those members who were unacquainted with the glories of Massachusetts history and culture, he offered an instructional historical episode: "there witches...were, 'in the brave days of old,' burned, literally by the cord!"[2]

Despite Salem's appearance in religious controversies where the perceived excesses of a seventeenth-century theocracy had been a useful cautionary tale since the 1830s, the episode of "witch-hunting" in 1692 Massachusetts Bay Colony still seems an unlikely event to enter the heated debate over slavery. But in the wake of the Mexican-American War that closed the 1840s and the Oregon Treaty, readers of American newspapers, periodicals, pamphlets, and books were exposed to a new level of emotionally charged rhetoric as the struggle for political control of the newly acquired western territories deepened. Southern writers and politicians and their sympathizers invoked Salem witchcraft not merely to defend slavery, but to illustrate the cultural superiority of the society that had been built on slave labor. The finer points of the legality of the 1820 Missouri Compromise had failed to stir any great emotional response in an audience. It was far more effective to speak of the South as having offered a larger contingent of volunteers than the North in the recent Mexican-American War, and of enduring the subsequent "insult" of being asked to "consent to arbitrary and insolent restrictions" by the banning of slavery in that newly acquired land. But most persuasive of all were reminders to constituents or readers that the same men who called slavery a "curse" on the culture of the South were themselves descendants of men who burned "witches," emphasizing that "there are some monstrosities we *never* commit."[3]

Henry Bedinger's 1849 association of Salem witchcraft with "fanatical" abolitionism was not a singular example of hyperbole. It represented an emerging rhetorical strategy designed to counter the cruel "slave master" figure who so dominated Northern discussions of slavery.[4] Southern writers and politicians in the 1850s began aggressively advancing a particular version of the "Puritan" figure toward the same ends.[5] By constructing and promoting a symbolic "Puritan," Southern writers and politicians played their part in the escalation of the emotional climate that historian Avery O. Craven long ago identified as an essential precondition for the Civil War. Political failures, weak men, and missed opportunities were less to blame, he asserted, than were heightened "emotions, cultivated hostilities, and ultimately of hatred between sections. Bloodshed was 'necessary' because men associated their rivals with disliked and dishonorable symbols, and crowned their own interests with moral sanctions.... they were both fighting mythical devils."[6]

The "monstrosity" of "witch-burning" that would become fundamental to the construction of Northern "mythical devils" over the decade of the 1850s was pure invention. No community in the British North American colonies that had hunted and convicted witches ever executed one by burning. Adding "burning" to the narrative of Salem witchcraft was a striking development within the rhetoric of this political conflict and would pepper the commentary on the Northern propensity for brutality and domination of others. The charge clearly originated in contemporary political needs. No historical or literary account had ever claimed such a fate for the convicted at Salem. It was a charge that, through repetition in the slavery debates, become a permanent feature in Americans' popular imagining of the 1692 Salem trials. It would noticeably torment generations of not only colonial historians but those who felt compelled to correct it (primarily in newspaper letters to the editor) every time it appeared in print from that day to this. Its persistence in many popular narratives attests to its efficacy.

The method of legal execution in 1692 Salem, as in most of the United States in the nineteenth century, was hanging. The claim that Puritans burned those convicted of witchcraft intensified the image of injustice and barbarity already attached to the idea of witch hunts, lending the old illustration more horror and thus more rhetorical power. With no parallels in nineteenth-century legal procedure, the idea of witch-burning made Salem seem even more foreign, backward, and brutal. In the nineteenth-century American imagination hanging involved the "rule of law"—the culmination of an orderly legal process where the guilty just might indeed be guilty. "Burning," on the other hand, hinted at extralegal proceedings (or even the Roman Catholic Inquisition) and intensified what Salem's metaphor had invoked so successfully for years: conduct that was dangerously foreign, irrational, and barbaric.[7]

As combatants in the slavery debates recognized when they created sectional types to represent hated political positions, to demonize an opponent is to mark him as outside defined social boundaries. With the "mythical devil" safely outside those boundaries, everyone else is reassured about his own status inside. Simultaneously, defining the parameters of conformity controls both opinion and behavior resembling dissent. The monstrous figures conjured up out of the anxiety-driven imaginations of both sections in the 1850s served to reaffirm their respective social values and demand the appropriate unreflective consensus from their populations. The sectional symbols used in representing the "moral sanctions" that Avery Craven mentioned, or in creating the "agents of moralized fear" that Edward Ingebretsen later defined in American cultural discourse, were successful because they encompassed a broad range of contemporary concerns.[8] For instance, one of the fears that advocates of slavery most frequently expressed in debates and in print was the "threat of amalgamation" or miscegenation that might come with emancipation. But miscegenation was considered a real threat only if they failed to stop the "fanatical abolitionist" in the shape of the "Puritan" from conquering the South. Defining cultural boundaries assures that if unity is not achieved, conformity will do the job just as well.

The charge of brutality had the most potential for affecting public opinion about slavery through emotional appeal, as Harriet Beecher Stowe discovered with *Uncle Tom's Cabin* during this same decade. The brutality of the "slave master" was fundamental to Northern antislavery rhetoric about the South. Adapting this rhetorical strategy, defenders of the slave system suggested that the Salem executions were, if not extralegal, then based on charges that were themselves barbaric within the standards of contemporary public opinion and law. By crafting this response, the charges of "lynching" and the myriad lesser acts of violence that filled the abolitionist oratory and printed sources might be deflected or, at the very least, complicated in the public mind.[9] In this way, defenders of slavery took a historical episode that already existed in the thousands of pages of New England–generated American history and literature as the prime example of New England's "pre-Revolutionary medieval side." Offering the apparition of "burning witches" as a reminder of the cultural legacy of the modern descendant of the Puritan would inoculate—some must have hoped—against the depictions of slavery's inherent violence that poured out of the abolitionist presses of the Northern states.[10]

Although the witch hunt of 1692 might appear to be a weak metaphor for the character and aims of abolitionists, when a Southern congressman or editorial writer called up the seventeenth-century Massachusetts Puritan to stand in first for the abolitionist and finally for the undifferentiated Northerner, he drew on a figure familiar to his audience. For the "Puritan" of Massachusetts Bay Colony was, as we have seen, a fixture in nineteenth-century school histories—North and South—as was Salem witchcraft. Although by 1850 there still was nothing approaching universal common school education in the Southern states, approximately 2,000 private academies served an estimated 70,000 white students.[11] Southern children of necessity used the same schoolbooks as their Northern peers when they read Samuel and Charles Goodrich, Emma Willard, Salma Hale, John Frost, and other authors who told the Salem story in condemnatory terms.[12]

More critical to its appearance in pro-slavery rhetoric, the "Puritan" had another presence particular to Southern letters and imagination that extended back to the 1830s. The popularity of Sir Walter Scott's Waverly novels, as Drew Gilpin Faust and others have argued, nicely dramatized the South's animosity about its increasing sense of cultural and economic domination by the North.[13] Within this imaginary literature, Southerners comforted themselves with visions of their genteel (and even royal) Norman and Cavalier antecedents pitted against Northerners descended from brutish Saxons and Puritans. This fictional refuge, much as for Scott's Highlanders fighting the aggressive Englishmen, allowed some Southerners to retreat into a self-assured fantasy of an innate cultural superiority. The attraction of this 1640s conflict between English Puritans and Royalist Cavaliers also drew on regional myths of Southern colonial settlement. The adoption of the Cavalier as a symbol of gentility and cultural achievement attached new meanings to enduring symbols in the Old South. The same literature also offered an aggressive Puritan type as a traditional foe.

This mythology became central to the creation of a Confederate nationalism in 1860 by intensifying the Southern identification with the Cavalier and narratively relocating the Puritan from England to New England. Once that was accomplished, the besieged Cavalier of the Southern imagination was provided with a critical historical past for Confederate nationalism, one that offered "an interpretative framework in which to view the Civil War as a struggle between great moral-historical principles."[14] It also provided an alternative to the overwhelmingly Northern myth of national origin based in the Puritan settler of Massachusetts—a myth defined for decades by the primarily New England authors and publishing houses of the North.

Still, rhetorical skirmishes before the most vitriolic phase of the Sectional Crisis in the late 1850s rarely laid out so fundamental a dichotomy in cultural development between the two sections. The full potential of the Puritan as a symbol of the North's essentially autocratic and aggressive tendencies, however, was realized only when defenders of slavery placed the model of Puritan-Cavalier conflict firmly on American rather than English soil. Giving the symbolic threat based in English history concrete American connections made danger seem imminent to the Southerners. Salem witchcraft thus became crucial to a Southern rhetoric that already employed Puritan-Cavalier symbolism to express dissatisfaction with social, economic, and cultural development. In addition, the long association of Salem witchcraft in American history books with practices that were essentially foreign completed the idea that the South exemplified "American" virtues founded in the Revolution (albeit within an inherited context of Cavalier gentility) while the North was effectively steeped in European sins of tyranny—or so Southern audiences were encouraged to believe.

By the 1850s, then, defenders of slavery easily refined the older model of Puritan-Cavalier conflict for the current political crisis. By moving the action to the northern region of the United States, they could assign additional negative traits and make the old references to Cromwell and the Puritans of the English Civil War period more explicit and American. The "story" of Salem witchcraft not only was familiar to Southern audiences but was, as we have seen, framed almost exclusively with the sort of provocative language that lent itself to such polemics. Advocates of slavery who wished to associate abolitionists and their goals with "hypocrisy," "delusion," "intolerance," and especially "fanaticism," the popular catchall word tinged with irrationality and violence, had a ready-made example. Each vice could be vividly illustrated by a simple association with long-standing narrative treatments of Salem witchcraft.

Thus, as in the religious controversies where despised religious sects were compared to Puritan Salem's witchcraft episode and described as dangerous "delusions," so too could disturbing political innovations like abolition be joined to witchcraft. In this way Salem became a persistent rhetorical theme within the contemporary political crisis between sections. At least once before in a "sectional" crisis it had been similarly used by Thomas Jefferson. In 1798, describing decidedly regional political tensions in a letter to John Taylor, Jefferson urged patience with New England's Federalist influence. In time, "we shall see the reign of witches pass." Sixty years later, the supporter of slavery could easily meld the image of the Northern-based abolitionist and his moral and religious rationales with the widely circulated image of the Puritan to produce an effective cautionary tale for the current crisis—a tale already deeply embedded in cultural memory. For the American Southern writers or politicians, as well as for those in sympathy with their political position, there were few candidates as apt as the Puritan and the example of his witchcraft trials to promote as a Northern "mythical devil."[15]

Provocative language in Southern publications describing the abolitionist threat emphasized the Northern inheritance from the English Puritans. The association was only heightened as abolitionism tried to use moral suasion to create a sense of a divinely inspired and guided mission in its adherents.[16] Thus William Drayton's 1836 book *The South Vindicated from the Treason and Fanaticism of the Northern Abolitionists* attempted to instill in readers' minds the essential nature of the abolitionists and their ultimate goals. To Drayton, some in the abolition movement were "actuated by honest fanaticism; others are impelled by a sinister ambition, by hatred of the South, or by a natural proneness 'to make trouble,'" but from Ohio in the west to New York in the east, "all are evil—all are mad!"[17] Abolitionist publications, he noted, revealed that "the days of Cromwell were revived, and that his fanatical followers . . . were abroad in the land."[18] Certainly Drayton's warning of Northern political domination relied on a broad depiction of abolitionists as "Northern," but even in 1836 we can see the beginnings of the transformation from English to American that the Puritan symbol would make in political rhetoric over the next decade. Drayton evoked the modern-day Puritan by using a common contemporary description of the New England accent; he said that sermons across all the northern states were notable for being "almost *nasal* with cant."[19]

In the 1840s, popular Southern periodicals helped strengthen the connection between the New England Puritan and the abolitionist. An unsigned editorial comment in the *Southern Literary Messenger* directly linked the two while ridiculing those who would mount a "spirited defense of the character of the people of New England."[20] A decade before territorial questions sharpened both hostilities and metaphors, the writer revealed the true issue of contention—abolitionist "enthusiasm." Others, he noted, had labeled it "fanaticism" or even referred to the "bigotted [*sic*] despotism with which they domineered over all who departed from their stern creed."[21] Contemporary New Englanders had "all the leading traits of their progenitors . . . the same vein of *ultraism* and the same insolent pretension to impose their own dogmas, and their own notions upon others. Take for sample that real fanaticism, that fever, or rather, frenzy of abolitionism."[22]

Another writer, identified only as G, directly connected the Puritans to Salem witchcraft in making the case for New England extremism. "Fanaticism," he noted, "appears to form an essential trait in the New England character." As proof he offered "the old women [who] were burnt as witches." Such a spirit of fanaticism always needed a "discharge," G claimed. "This it has at the present time found in abolitionism."[23] An 1845 reviewer of *Religion in America* in the *Southern Quarterly Review* also attempted to fend off any suggestions that the seventeenth-century English colony of Virginia also had laws against witchcraft on the books by noting that in Virginia they were "mildly," if ever, used.[24] Virginia, he implied, might have been under English law in the 1600s, but in its failure to enthusiastically prosecute witchcraft that colony was well on the road to an American sense of reason. By contrast, the Puritan ancestors of contemporary New England Congregationalists (and by implication the current vocal Massachusetts abolitionists) were still thoroughly English colonials and in their fanaticism were responsible for the "execution of witches." Those, he ominously declared, were "some of the fruits of their principles."[25]

In the 1840s the word "fanaticism" was familiar from religious controversies and rapidly becoming identified with intense reform movements like abolition. Democratic congressman Abraham Venable of North Carolina complained several days after Henry Bedinger's statements in the House of Representatives in 1849 that a new tone, one he heard with an increasingly "sickly sensibility," was entering debates. Slavery had so divided the body that even congressmen were "alluded to as agitators and fanatics" on the floor of the House.[26] But Bedinger's association of Salem witchcraft with abolitionist "fanaticism," and the responses made orally by his Northern colleagues and in print by abolitionists, spurred a whole new set of similar charges in Southern journals and newspapers.

Congressmen Horace Mann and John Palfrey of Massachusetts responded to Bedinger's remarks directly on the floor of the House on February 26, 1849. Mann objected to the turn in the tone of the debates by citing the "torrent of abuse" that Bedinger and several others had heaped on Massachusetts. He asked, "Is a state to have no benefit from a statute of limitations? Is a crime committed by ancestors to be forever imputed to their posterity?"[27] Perhaps, Mann suggested, the Virginian could understand the impetus for Massachusetts's penchant for abolition by considering it an act of atonement for departed victims of other historical wrongs such as the witch trials. John Palfrey mounted a far more aggressive defense of his state's honor. "There has crept of late into this discussion," he observed, "a style of remark.... Gentlemen incline to invite us to the investigation of historical problems," for they "imagine that if they can point out some fault in our ancestors, they do something towards refuting our reasonings."[28] Palfrey, who would later publish his own well-received *History of Massachusetts*, especially objected to Bedinger's "violent hyperbole" and insisted he found no reason for shame in his New England ancestors' actions. In fact, Palfrey turned the attack into an opportunity to advance abolitionism. He mused that being "challenged about the past" reminded him of that "stern but constant ancestry" that continually renewed his antislavery convictions and gave him the courage to press onward in the fight.

As the congressional speeches appeared in print in 1849–50, the introduction of Salem witchcraft also gave fresh energy to a variety of editors and politicians on both sides of the sectional divide. In an obvious reaction to the congressional debate, a February 1849 issue of *National*

Era, a Washington-based abolitionist newspaper coedited by John Greenleaf Whittier, echoed Palfrey's remarks in an article titled "The Reform School in Massachusetts."[29] Whittier praised the idea of "reformation" over punishment and connected lessons learned from the Salem
witchcraft trials directly to the idea of modern progress in penal reform.
Whittier celebrated man's progress by contrasting the new methods used
by the school to the days when crowds were "convulsed with grim merri-
ment . . . [as they] enjoy[ed] the spectacle of an old man enduring the un-
utterable torment of the *peine forte et dure*–pressed slowly to death under
planks—for refusing to plead to an indictment for witchcraft."[30] Likewise,
the arrest of a Wesleyan-Methodist circuit rider in Virginia for antislavery
preaching inspired a report in May that invoked Salem. This article suggested that as long as Virginia had censorship statutes, "let her never talk
of the hanging of witches by Massachusetts a hundred years ago."[31] Nor
was the *National Era* averse to printing speeches of midwestern congressmen whose stand on extending slavery was based less on abolition than
on the rights of "free white laboring men"[32] if they supported the general
cause. Congressman Kinsley Scott Bingham of Michigan objected to admitting California to statehood if it meant establishing "a great slave mart
on the shores of the Pacific." In his view slavery itself was "a living libel
on the Declaration of Independence." Bingham was convinced that one
day slavery would be known, like the "burning of witches," as something
that "an enlightened age condemns."[33]

During most of the nineteenth century there were implicit cultural limits on who could credibly use the metaphor of Salem witchcraft. The call
to reason or order inherent in its use required that the person uttering
this prescriptive metaphor have the authority to call others to reason (or
any other behavior) in public forums and also himself possess the capacity
for "reason." Only then could he dare to define it or demand it from others who were in some manner acting irrationally. For a variety of obvious
reasons, before the twentieth century women, children, and, generally,
African Americans were not assumed to be in this group. For any person in these categories to suggest that white men "come to reason" would
be considered absurd. But two rare examples of the Salem metaphor do
stand out in the black press in a decade when slavery polemics by whites
bristled with appeals to it. Frederick Douglass, a former slave and the
influential editor of an abolitionist newspaper, printed pieces that used
Salem at least twice, and his obvious care in using the metaphor illustrates
the implicit restrictions.

If nineteenth-century African American press's use of the Salem metaphor was limited by propriety, that limitation provided other opportunities. The black press was burdened by none of the conflicts that bedeviled Whittier or the Massachusetts congressmen. It could ignore the defense of Massachusetts's honor to focus directly on the real issue under debate—slavery. Picking up the theme of Salem witchcraft from the white press, Frederick Douglass's Rochester, New York, newspaper the *North Star* found Salem witchcraft useful in its own critique of slavery. "In what respect," Douglass asked in July 1849, as he pondered the issue of slavery in the District of Columbia, was the belief in witchcraft in those faraway days "one whit more absurd, extravagant, foolish, or wicked" than the contemporary belief in slavery? In fact, "dig[ging] up old superstitions" like the episode of witchcraft in Massachusetts was a waste of time. Why not, he argued vigorously, "find full occupation in exposing and combating those that remain?"[34] A letter Douglass printed later that same year described the current popular interest in hypnosis and suggested that perhaps by "the potency of mind upon mind" hypnosis might convince slaveholders to abandon the institution. If not, then at the very least, believers should perhaps experiment in other ways with their "favorite science" by using the contemporary "subject of slavery as well as the Salem witchcraft to illustrate" the powerful influence of one mind upon another.[35]

During that same autumn of 1849, John Greenleaf Whittier continued his efforts to reconcile Massachusetts's witch-hunting past with its abolitionist present. Whittier advanced one of the most novel connections between slavery and Salem witchcraft before abandoning his short-lived attempt to refute or reverse the implications of the metaphor in the pages of the *National Era*. His editorial comment in November 1850 considered the standard Southern argument that slavery, "like the cotton-plant, is confined by natural laws to certain parallels." New England's growing opposition, or so the pro-slavery argument went, was based not on virtue but on economic self-interest. Whittier countered that slavery was in reality a product of "pride and lust and avarice" and had prospered at different times in every latitude from the steppes to the city. Indeed, he said, it had prospered in Massachusetts despite an ordinance banning it in 1649. According to Whittier's view of Massachusetts history, lax enforcement of the law allowed slavery to become established on an "execrable foundation of robbery and wrong." But the "retributive dealings of Providence" set things right. Evidence of divine displeasure with slavery could be found in the first of the accusations of witchcraft in Salem, which

"originated with the Indian Tituba, a slave in the family of the minister."
Is it any wonder, he concluded, that Massachusetts fears the consequences
of the requirements of the Fugitive Slave Act? He left readers to consider
the application of this "instructive fact" that linked God's displeasure with
slavery to community disaster.[36]

Witchcraft also appeared as the subject of one of Whittier's many antislavery poems, which like his editorials, turned the metaphor around to
emphasize the theme of progress and redemption. *Calef in Boston, 1692*,
imagined a meeting between Cotton Mather, the Puritan clergyman most
associated in the popular mind with the Salem trials and their subsequent
defense, and Boston merchant Robert Calef, who just eight years after
the trials published a critique of the procedures used and the men who
conducted them. In Whittier's fantasy, Calef told Mather that while there
were a few eternal verities, belief in witchcraft was not one of them. Instead, such ideas prevented man's intellectual progress:

> Falsehoods which we spurn today
> Were the truths of long ago
> Let the dead boughs fall away,
> Fresher shall the living grow.

In Whittier's poem, Mather remained resistant to the end, but the poet
reminded his readers that ultimately the Boston merchant's struggle to
persuade the minister was validated by God himself as men came to know
the truth:

> The Lord hath blest the seed
> Which that tradesman scattered then
> And the preacher's spectral creed
> Chills no more the blood of men.[37]

Whittier's purpose here extended beyond echoing Congressman Palfrey's demand that men not be asked to pay for the sins of their fathers.
In using Calef as his spokesman, Whittier provided a subtle reminder that
it was not only a Boston man but a merchant (whom he casts as the agent
of progress) who challenged the witchcraft trials in their own day. As the
most passionate of Christian abolitionists, Whittier warned that one day
future generations would view the intransigence of slaveholders and of
Southern congressmen as men now viewed the belief in witchcraft. The
slaveholder, he suggested, was as rigid in his erroneous faith in slavery

as Mather was in his belief in witchcraft. And in concert with Palfrey's comments on the floor of the House of Representatives, the Quaker poet Whittier held out the hope that repentance and reformation could result in moral regeneration for the slaveholder.

This was exactly the sort of blatant moralizing that Southerners like the editor of New Orleans–based *DeBow's Review* grew increasingly tired of hearing over the next few years. In perusing the recently delivered *Edinburgh Review* in 1851, James DeBow found a troubling tone in its reviews of American books. The journal, he complained in an editorial note, increasingly "considers New England the United States, and New England is the land of abolition." Therefore, he acidly observed, it cannot be praised enough. The Southern states, on the other hand, are "tolerated only because they may some day be converted, and turned from the error of their ways, by negro-loving, witch-burning New England, into the paths of redemption and political salvation."[38]

If James DeBow was finding no comfort overseas, he knew he had a consistent political ally of sorts in the *United States Democratic Review*. The Democratic Party organ resisted both militant abolitionists and New England's politicians. In an unsigned article titled "The Conspiracy of Fanaticism," the *Democratic Review* described New England as "more addicted to superstition and fanaticism" than any other section of the country.[39] The *Review* carried the opportunity and the burden of maintaining a bisectional audience throughout the contentious 1850s, and thus it never missed an opening to attack abolitionists, whom Democrats clearly saw as the instigators of the current political crisis. Ironically for a party that rose on the populism of Andrew Jackson, it often showed a fear of "mobs" that would do credit to the most conservative Southern Whig.[40] By 1855 the *Democratic Review* was claiming that the New England "hive is always full and always swarming." Indeed, this writer expected New England, once it had "exhausted all the means of declamation, sedition, and anarchy," to openly combine with a foreign power.[41] For the "infuriated fanatics" of New England, the anonymous author added, there was not much distance between "moral and political treason." In one of its last articles before a party split between Northern and Southern Democrats resulted in its demise, the *Democratic Review* fired a final barrage at the "selfish and rapacious Yankee" who drove the more refined type of Englishman to colonial New York or Virginia in disgust as the Yankee remained in New England to enjoy pursuits such as "the pleasure of burning witches."[42]

These references to "swarms," "hives," and "superstition" echo the familiar nineteenth-century interpretations of Salem witchcraft within the pages of history books, fiction, or the invective of other cultural controversies as dangerous and backward "delusions" that inflamed the population of seventeenth-century Massachusetts, destroyed precious individualism, and resulted in tragedy.[43] And certainly warnings of potential "treason" reinforced the idea promoted in the Southern press about New England's essentially un-American orientation on everything from slavery to homesteading legislation. But while the political rhetoric of the 1840s and 1850s relied on a generalized demonizing of abolitionists and Northerners, a few Southern writers used Salem witchcraft to support the notion that only a complete breakdown of reason explained abolitionism. One contributor to *DeBow's Review* in 1853 argued that all the "delusions of the North"—no matter how "wild and furious the numerous outbreaks of our northern brethren in the way of 'Salem Witchcrafts'... including even 'abolitionism' itself"—were no more than curiosities so long as the consequences were confined to New England.[44]

E. Boyden linked his argument to the ongoing debates over religious innovations that had introduced Salem in controversial literature in the 1830s. Boyden advanced the idea that such episodes of public excitement were a "moral epidemic." Looking to history, he argued, we can see in the "witch mania... [how] honest men... took leave of their senses in pursuing pious and harmless old women to the death, under charges, by modes of trial, and upon evidence such as idiots only could well be supposed capable of listening to for a moment." That history was rife with inexplicable excitements such as "phrenology, mesmerism, clairvoyance, animal electricity... and spiritualism" was a similar concern for "Nella" in the *Southern Literary Messenger.* "Nella" attributed the spread of superstitions like the Salem "witch scare" to "credulity," concluding that "no leaf of American History is so revolting" as the events in 1692 Salem.[45] Southern writers were deeply concerned about this latest Northern delusion and its potential national consequences.

The Salem example thus seemed to many Americans a relevant expression of the threat of the consequences of widespread antislavery sentiment. Like other popular "inexplicable excitements," both abolition and the hunt for witches reflected the mass insanity that resulted when the unscrupulous gained temporary sway over people's reason. Just as concerns about religious demagogues rallying deluded followers provoked outrage in the 1830s and drew comparisons to public support for the Salem witch hunt, so too did the fears about the most vocal of the abolitionists on the public scene in the 1850s.

Advocates of slavery feared that leaders of the abolition movement and their allies in the pulpit would stir up what they called "the tyranny of public opinion." Henry Tuckerman explicitly argued this position using the example of the execution of Quakers and the hunting of witches in an 1851 review of Hawthorne's works for the *Southern Literary Messenger*.[46] Pro-slavery writers had a dual purpose for targeting abolition leaders as the 1850s progressed. By locating abolitionist sentiment in strident moralists colluding with ministers, they appealed to those Northerners whom they believed were as yet uninfected by the abolition "mania." Clearly there was a belief mid-decade that some in the North might yet realize the danger of falling under the "delusion" of abolition through such "professional agitators."

In this way Salem surfaced in response to the immense Southern ire at ministers' using their presumed moral authority to speak out against slavery, petition Congress, or support legal resistance on the grounds of conscience or "higher law." To counter the effects of such influence, opponents reached into the Salem narrative to provide examples of ministers' errors on public topics. Here Cotton Mather, and to a lesser degree Salem minister Samuel Parris, were occasionally useful as object lessons in how ambition could corrupt the clergy when they involved themselves in public politics.[47] In an 1853 review of Bancroft's *History of the United States*, *DeBow's Review* explicitly raised the specter of Salem in conjunction with the dangers of contemporary clerical influence on abolitionist organizations. Cotton Mather, the *DeBow's* reviewer fancifully claimed, was involved in similar politicized activities and earned what he deserved for this violation of his office. He was ever after "hated by many and loved by none...haunted by the gloomy terrors of an evil conscience, and by the innocent blood which he had been instrumental in shedding."[48] With such "a persecuting spirit" as Mather at the head, the 1692 witch hunt proceeded until finally "the spirit of the people began to be roused," priestly influence was overthrown, and the tragedy ended. Undoubtedly, such reviewers and editors were not averse to the "tyranny of public opinion" if it served their own cause. James DeBow's reading of the situation matched the escalating rhetoric, including that of his own journal. A poem about Northern ministers that accompanied his review finished with these lines: "beside the prayer-book on his desk / the bullet mould is seen."[49]

But through the 1850s even moderate non-Southerners had difficulty with abandoning the rule of law for the rule of conscience or "higher law." In 1850 Daniel Webster asked Commodore Robert Field Stockton to comment on extending slavery to California. In his reply, Stockton agreed with Webster that on constitutional grounds slavery could not be outlawed. Further, he believed that it was "the error of fanaticism" to rely on individual conscience in such matters. For conscience was what "burns the supposed heretic at the stake, or hunts down witchcraft."[50] Boston moderate Moses Stuart also objected to imposing a rule of conscience on political questions. "The hangers of witches among us surely had a conscience," he noted. Stuart went on to observe that "when judgment is kept down, and passion set up, men...can manufacture a conscience into any possible convenient shape." As for the issue of a "higher law," "Who has discovered and determined such a law?"[51] Samuel F. B. Morse wrote privately to his brother Sidney that abolition was "a fearful hallucination, not less absurd than...Salem witchcraft," which has "darkened the moral atmosphere of the North."[52] But confronting the antislavery clergyman in the mid-nineteenth century required a delicate hand. The most effective method was to fend off any public presumption of clerical moral authority by casting it as simply inappropriate political meddling—the sort of meddling that might well lead to a repeat of the events in 1692 Salem.

A petition signed by more than three thousand clergymen against the proposed Kansas-Nebraska Act, presented in the United States Senate on March 14, 1854, invoked the memory of Salem when some senators questioned whether moral or political suasion was at work. The petition infuriated some Southern senators for precisely this reason, and they charged the ministers with "usurping spiritual functions for the purposes of agitation."[53]

In May 1854, Massachusetts senator Charles Sumner added more fuel to the fire by expanding the geographical range of religious objections to slavery that were coming into the Senate. When offering petitions from sources that included Quakers in Michigan as well as Baptist clergy and laity in Michigan, Indiana, and New York, Sumner argued that if the Senate could invoke God at will, then certainly the clergy could do so "without just criticism."[54] James M. Mason of Virginia immediately and strenuously objected to the clergy's involvement as a "prostitution of their office to the embrace of political party."[55] Clerical invocations of God in the petition texts and closing salutations, Mason insisted, carried a different authority than that of laymen in the Senate. Democrat Stephen Douglas of Illinois settled for simply categorizing antislavery petitions under clerical endorsement as "treason against the Constitution and the Union."[56] Yet by June 1854 still more petitions were introduced by Sumner and his Massachusetts colleague Julius Rockwell. Because of these petitions, Sumner

became embroiled in a violent two-day debate with Mason that included
Sumner's charge that Senators James Mason and Andrew Pickens Butler
of South Carolina used "Salem as a slur on the state."[57] Butler angrily replied that he wanted to respond to Sumner's latest comments immediately,
for if he took time to answer formally, he might be tempted to act "like a
hyena...scratching at the graves in Massachusetts to take revenge."[58]

By the mid-1850s, except for those embroiled in the public debates,
it seemed that only the New England Society (NESoc) was willing to
publicly address the Salem charge. Salem witchcraft had been a thorn in
the NESoc's collective side for over thirty years. A loosely knit organization with chapters in major cities throughout the nation, the NESoc was
composed of upper-class and upper-middle-class men whose membership
was based on personal or hereditary ties to the region.[59] Largely social in
character, the NESoc held an annual anniversary dinner with orations in
honor of the December 1620 landing at Plymouth. The menus, speeches,
and programs were widely reported on in local newspapers and often
printed independently. Since the central feature of the dinner program
was a celebration of New England's founding and values, Salem provided
a constant provocation for the speakers, who solemnly defended the region against recent uses of the witchcraft trials in public sources. Indeed,
the toasts and orations at the yearly December meetings provide a baro-
metric reading of the anti-Puritan atmosphere in the culture at large.

As early as 1838, Reverend Leonard Bacon devoted a considerable
portion of his remarks before the New York City NESoc to what he perceived as the continual "invective and ridicule against those venerable
men" of colonial New England.[60] "Did these men believe in witchcraft?
Certainly they did." But, he inquired of his audience, should the Puritans
be castigated because they did not throw off the universal "prejudices
and terrors" of their age? By 1847 Charles Boynton, a minister who delivered Cincinnati's annual New England Society address, complained that
the very mention of Salem witchcraft was now "generally supposed to be
the end of all controversy upon New England."[61] Boynton undoubtedly
voiced the frustration of the membership at large when he concluded,
"There are thousands in our own country, whose prominent idea of the
New England Puritans is, that they were a set of misguided fanatics or
prating hypocrites, who sang Psalms on Sunday and hunted witches...
through the week."[62]

Through the 1850s NESoc speakers wrestled with the "problem" of
Salem. The audience at the 1855 New England Society dinner in New
York City listened to a more politically charged program than was usual

for their typically (and determinedly) noncontroversial meetings.[63] The Reverend John Pierpont directly addressed the idea of "higher lawism" and the Fugitive Slave Act by suggesting that the forefathers would be shamed by any descendant who helped send men back into bondage "because so bidden by laws that *men* have made."[64] Oliver Wendell Holmes Sr., on the other hand, defended his native region, if not the actions of its most radical abolition faction. Although he dismissed talk of New England "ultraisms and heresies" as actuating the political decisions of most of the population of the region, Holmes nevertheless stood up for the right of the minority to hold extreme opinions, claiming that "the land that has no enthusiasts, no fanatics, no madmen" is one that suffers from a sort of intellectual death.[65]

But some, like Senator Charles Sumner, reveled in the charge of "fanatic" and never avoided the subject of Salem witchcraft when they found it useful to their own aims. Shortly after his debates with Butler and Mason, Sumner reentered the fray in a September 1854 speech before the delegates at the first Republican state convention in Worcester, Massachusetts. In it he compared the hated Fugitive Slave Act to the Massachusetts witchcraft laws of the seventeenth century. Arguing that "nothing so abhorrent to reason and conscience should be regarded as constitutional and binding," Sumner likened resisting the Fugitive Slave Act to resisting witchcraft prosecution. With sometimes tortured logic and fractured history, he claimed a "parallel between the law against witchcraft and the fugitive act" that was "not yet complete." What was ultimately needed to complete his envisioned historical "parallel" was for Congress to renounce the Fugitive Slave Act and serve as "the successor of that original general court, to lead the penitential march."[66] In a closing designed to hit all the local and national emotional high notes, Sumner said that conscience was of God, but laws were of men. Since it was man's law "which hung witches at Salem—and which affirmed the constitutionality of the Stamp Act," resisting the Fugitive Slave Act was, in effect, both a patriotic and a religious duty.[67]

Wendell Phillips, that most radical of Boston abolitionists, likewise happily donned the "fanatic" mantle before the Pilgrim Society at its annual meeting in December 1855. Linking the past with the most pressing controversy of the moment, the violent struggle over the Kansas Territory then being waged between Free-Soil and pro-slavery settlers, he announced to loud cheers that today the Pilgrims would be "not in Plymouth, but in Kansas."[68] They would ask only, "Is liberty safe? Is man

sacred? They say, sir, I am a fanatic, and so I am."[69] But however irrepressible he often seemed to his enemies, Phillips was less apologetic for
the excesses of history. He claimed that "the Puritans... hung the witches;
George Washington held slaves; and wherever you go up and down history, you find men, not angels."[70]

While Phillips was enthusing in Plymouth, the Southern press continued to expand its Salem-based critique. The *Richmond Examiner* routinely criticized Massachusetts, whose heritage of "Puritan bigotry is not
relaxed in tension since... the hanging of defenseless and toothless old
maidens for 'witchcraft.'"[71] In an 1856 editorial titled "The War Against
the South," the editor of *DeBow's Review* warned that the war between
settler factions in Kansas and the assault on Charles Sumner in the Senate the previous spring no longer allowed Southerners to "beguile" themselves that abolition sentiment was confined to "a few fanatics."[72]

The Kansas situation alerted those on both sides to the potential
spread of violence. And in this context, abolitionist Parker Pillsbury still
carried on the somewhat limited but spirited tradition of attempting to
turn the Salem witchcraft metaphor itself back onto the South. He did
so in a Boston speech in 1859 that connected the "barbarism of slavery"
with beliefs that would in an earlier age be "willing to swing over the gibbet... every homely woman who dared to live a single life, and earn the
reputation of being a witch."[73] Wendell Phillips suggested in his speeches
that the Puritans would have shipped guns to Kansas "in crates marked
Bibles."[74] Meanwhile pro-slavery Judge Samuel D. LeCompte charged a
Kansas grand jury to reject "conscience" as a defense by evoking "the
early witchcraft history of Massachusetts, to prove the impropriety of being regulated by sincerity."[75]

Similar sentiment was expressed by Governor Henry Wise of Virginia
when he declined an invitation to attend the annual New England Society
dinner in New York City in 1857. The *Southern Literary Messenger* was
pleased to print his letter expressing his regrets accompanied by a gleeful
annotation that praised Wise for his ability to "draw in a few strong lines
the character of the Pilgrim fathers more faithfully than the portraiture
has ever been done."[76] Wise extolled Puritan virtues by saying that in all
things their "consciences were on the Lord's side. They were against the
devil and all his witches."[77] In this way Governor Wise took a jab at both
the issue of "higher lawism" and the Puritan figure.

The pro-slavery side, ironically, had a historical example available to
discredit Northern-based abolitionist charges of violence while effectively

attacking the North for its own history of slavery and violence. But it was
an event little known by the 1850s and, in its details, highly problematic.
More to the contemporary point than Salem's witch trials in the Sectional
Crisis were the details of what was called the New York "Negro Plot of
1741."

In eighteenth-century slaveholding New York Colony, during one
dreadful season a crime wave, the always-present fear of slave uprisings,
deceitful witnesses, racism, and anti-Catholicism all culminated in the arrest of 150 slaves and their free black and poor white alleged accomplices
for burglary, arson, and conspiring to start a slave insurrection. When the
frenzy in New York subsided a few months later, seventeen slaves had
been convicted and hanged, several dozen were shipped to Caribbean
colonies, and thirteen had been publicly burned at the stake.[78] In its
outlines of widespread public panic, coerced witnesses, short duration,
and brutality under the cover of law, the 1741 "Negro Plot" resembled
nothing more than the events in Salem only fifty years earlier. This was
not lost on some eighteenth-century observers. New Yorker Cadwalader
Colden, who had publicly urged moderation and care in pursuing the New
York cases, himself received an anonymous letter likening the situation
to Salem's witchcraft trials. But a little more than one hundred years later
the cultural memory of the Negro Plot and the public burnings of the convicted men were neither extensively recorded nor widely remembered in
histories.

Although Daniel Horsmanden, one of the New York justices who
heard the 1741 cases, published an account of the trials that he called a
"standing memorial," his book sat largely unsold because of local "embarrassment" about the hysteria the case generated.[79] In this local un-
easiness with the trials, New York also paralleled seventeenth-century
Massachusetts Bay Colony. William Smith Jr.'s 1757 *History of the Late
Province of New York* was a notable exception to what would be a virtual
erasure of the episode from general and school histories. Writing within a
generation of the trials, from his unique position as the son of the prose-
cutor in the 1741 cases, Smith gave them two full pages. Daniel Horsmanden's book was republished in 1810, and again it found little interest from
book buyers. The publisher's introduction to the new edition declared
that sixty years on readers could only "look back with astonishment" that
such a thing had ever happened at all. In the nineteenth century, Benson J.
Lossing was one of the very few widely read authors of national histories
who included the events in a history text for the general adult and juvenile

markets. Lossing's *Pictorial History of the United States for Schools and Families* provided an overview of the events that by the 1850s few other authors appeared to believe "demanded special attention." In fact, within the narrative itself Lossing drew a direct comparison between 1741 New York and 1692 Salem by calling the trial of the slaves "a regular and horrid conspiracy" and noting that "as in the case of the Salem Witchcraft, an intense panic pervaded all classes, and many innocent persons suffered." But though the book was published when use of the Puritan past as a contemporary national symbol was escalating, the case was cited too seldom to pass into collective memory. It certainly went without significant notice among the adults who dominated the public battle over abolition.[80]

If collective remembering has its purposes and consequences, so too does the equally deliberate act of cultural forgetting. The practical result of New England's role as the prime producer of both schoolbooks and literature for the nation meant that what New England's authors chose to forget stayed forgotten. Thus the desire to dismiss the region's slave-owning and slave-trading past militated for eliminating or minimizing its history in the region.[81]

Therefore the very real public burning of thirteen men in 1741, which might have helped neutralize the increasingly effective image of the brutal Southern slave master with a counterexample from the Northern states, was lost to the defenders of the pro-slavery position. More critically, it was a historical episode that could be framed as judicially sanctioned rather than one that, like local lynching episodes in slave states, could be dismissed as extralegal. Still, the lack of awareness about such episodes as the Negro Plot was not in any sense a political disaster for the advocates of slavery. The audience for these public debates was the *white* public. To bring an imminent threat home to them in the contemporary debates over the institution of slavery, Salem served quite well. Not only was it familiar by the 1850s, but it centered the menace of racial violence where it was most likely to resonate with white audiences: in the fatal consequences of the extremism of other whites. If there was brutality to fear, pro-slavery arguments increasingly insisted, it was in the "Puritan" heritage of the radical New England contingent of abolitionists. It was they, as history clearly documented in the well-known Salem witchcraft cases, who posed a direct threat to innocent white men and women.

Howell Cobb, a Georgia congressman and the author of *A Scriptural Examination of the Institution of Slavery in the United States*, provided a particularly vivid example of this argument within a passage rejecting the claim that Massachusetts abolished slavery out of virtue rather than convenience. "What a pity it was, however, that Massachusetts bestowed such an amount of sympathy upon Negroes, that when afterwards her own citizens (Quakers and witches), stood in need of it, it was all gone! It is so now. It is said, that at this time there are not many Quakers in Massachusetts, fewer witches, and plenty of abolitionists. Happy State!"[82]

The implication in Cobb's argument was that those most at risk in the seventeenth century were the same category of Americans most at risk in the nineteenth: "her own citizens." Citizens who by any contemporary legal or social definition were, like the executed "Quakers and witches," white. The contemporary abolitionists, so carefully defined in pro-slavery print and oratory as the lineal descendants of the Puritans, constituted the direst threat to the average white American. Thus could the illustration of Salem's frenzy of witch-hunting in 1692 not only enter this later battle to communicate the danger of "fanatical" abolitionism but, through skillful use, combine with prevailing national racial fears as well.

Two more antebellum crises offered a final burst of bellicose rhetoric tinged with cultural invocations of Salem—John Brown's 1859 attempt to raid the federal arsenal at Harpers Ferry, Virginia, and incite an armed slave revolt and the campaign for the 1860 presidential election. The ensuing flurry of reaction and commentary over those thirteen months fully exposed not only the level of hate and fear that had developed with the sectional conflict but also the profound ways Salem witchcraft had become intertwined in the expression of those emotions. The persistent theme of the "murders" and "crimes" of Puritans against their "own" was just as persistently equated with the designs of abolitionists against white lives and property in the slave states.

Whether antislavery or pro-slavery, those who paid attention to such things probably expected nothing better of Wendell Phillips than to extravagantly praise John Brown for the "brave act of an old Puritan soul" shortly after the Harpers Ferry raid.[83] And it was completely in character for Phillips to deliberately provoke users of the Puritan image by celebrating Brown on those grounds. Few seemed prepared, however, for the general outpouring of approval in the North for the "spirit" of the raid, if not for the act itself.[84] The day after Brown's execution in Virginia, a North Carolina newspaper warned Virginia governor Henry Wise to burn the gallows, lest some enterprising man remove it and ship it north, since the "Yankees have no objection to mingling money-making with their grief."[85] The idea of memorial services and "mock funerals" rumored to be planned in the North irritated the same editor enough to make him suggest that if Northerners were looking for public entertainment, "it is a pity they haven't a witch or two to drown or burn."[86] Daniel Hundley railed against the "Phillipses and Beechers [who] have spoken about John Brown...beating their drums ecclesiastic in a rage of fanatical zeal!"[87] He, for one, no longer believed that when the old Puritans were "sorely exercised about Quakers, Baptists, and witches...they were not more befogged and befooled than are their descendants today."[88] J. T. Wiswall imagined "swarms of transcendentalists" in New England cheering the impulse that drove "the Kansas gladiator, reeking with the blood of his murders" on to his actions in Virginia. For Wiswall, Brown's actions had their origins in the Northerners' Puritan legacy—an "inability to reason" that resulted in a "thousand kinds of fanaticism" and, of course, the "witch-burnings" that were only the first of these manifestations.[89]

Thus did Congressman Abraham W. Venable of North Carolina, who had complained in relation to the Bedinger-Mann-Palfrey debate in 1849 that men could no longer speak on slavery without being labeled "agitators or fanatics,"[90] come full circle by February 19, 1860. Angered by Horace Mann's comments condemning slavery on the floor of the House of Representatives the previous week, Venable lashed out at the "cant" and "mock sanctity" with which Mann spoke. "Let him blush when he speaks of the sins and crimes of any people on earth...no southern calendar of crime can afford such cases as the Salem murders."[91] But the mark of how much had changed in eleven years was not in Venable's resumption of Bedinger's 1849 charge against Mann, but in the person who came forward to defend New England. It was not Horace Mann who took up the defense of Massachusetts, but New York Republican congressman Charles Henry Van Wyck.

On March 7, 1860, Van Wyck made the first of two responses to Venable, charging that it was Southern Democrats, not Northern Republicans, who were "preaching violence...[and] disunion."[92] It was neither Northern men nor the Republicans who had "unchained the whirlwind of angry passion and bitter invective."[93] In regard to statements made on the floor on February 19, Van Wyck continued, Venable "spoke of Massachusetts burning witches in the ancient times. Does he not know that your own people burn slaves at the stake, and it seems to awaken no horror in your minds?"[94] This roused Reuben Davis of Mississippi to interrupt and call Van Wyck both "a liar and a scoundrel."[95] Although Van Wyck said that Massachusetts had "able sons to defend her reputation," he returned on June 16, 1860, to the subject of Salem in response to Davis's objection. The "rebuke" to Massachusetts for "witch-burning some two hundred years ago" was instructive, Van Wyck argued, as it provoked this compelling question: "How much more, then, are you chargeable with those of your own time?"[96]

Of course Davis and other members of Southern delegations to the House of Representatives had an ideal target in Van Wyck—perhaps better than any of the Massachusetts delegation, given the debate's turn to lynching violence. Surely if the Southerners had been aware of the 1741 New York burnings of thirteen slaves convicted in an alleged conspiracy to revolt, they would have raised it, if only to cloud the issue of "brutality" in the public mind. Given Charles Van Wyck's use of the subject in his speech and his subsequent move to read into the record detailed accounts of lynchings taken from Southern newspapers, he likely did not know about it himself. With the Massachusetts congressmen, the tired (albeit effective) charge of Salem could irritate, but it neither shocked any audience nor raised any contemporary issues. By 1860 the cost of the collective forgetting of the New York Negro Plot of 1741 was the loss of a historically specific Southern congressional rebuttal to New York's Van Wyck.

Defending Northern interests and protecting against a diversion of the debate into the byways of seventeenth-century Massachusetts history, Charles Van Wyck easily dismissed the example of Salem. The Republican position on such things as the Salem witchcraft trials, he said, was simple. The "moral and political world...has its development," and in that process there are always "despotisms and cruelties."[97] But if the modern Southerner wished to spread his "domestic and criminal arrangements... over the common territories," he should expect to answer for the abuses in the system of slavery which was so often defended in Congress as a "great missionary institution."[98]

Historical references filled the leading Southern journals, anticipating a crisis with the upcoming fall elections during the summer of 1860. Many of these references were used to further the claims of what was called a fundamental "racial" difference between *white* Americans of the North and South. Pro-slavery writers insisted it was a fact that the "Puritan" was temperamentally "unfit for rational freedom...[which was] abundantly verified" both historically and in the current crisis.[99] The two sections were "deadly enemies, whose hatred no circumstance of time, place or even interest could soften."[100] Just as "debates" in Congress had degenerated into speeches by men who no longer had faith that they might change one another's minds, the polarization and alienation between sections was reflected in the Southern press as well. The journals of the South reacted to the rise of the Republican Party, the Northern response to the Harpers Ferry raid, and the demise of a national Democratic Party by finally abandoning their attempts to reach across sectional lines. "The Basis of Northern Hostility to the South" in *DeBow's Review* provided a catalog of Northern cultural horrors and signaled that there was no longer even the pretense of believing that the preachers of abolition were "honest fanatics." Rather, there were men who saw in the issue of slavery "a kind of adventitious opportunity."[101] The motives of these men were simply the expression of historical and contemporary "envy and hate." Still, the author claimed, he would have to leave it to the "leisured who study the human psyche" to determine the exact cause of Northern hatred.[102] Even the *Southern Literary Messenger,* whose tone through the 1850s had been generally less inflammatory than that of *DeBow's Review,* hardened its position in the wake of Brown's raid and the advent of the presidential election.

An unsigned article, "The Difference of Race between the Northern and Southern People," repeated the same theme of spelling out fundamental cultural differences between sections. It offered a history of sectional settlement that extended the old Puritan-Cavalier model back in time to an Anglo-Saxon and Norman division. The more tribal, brutish Anglo-Saxons, the author explained, became the English faction that populated New England. Uncontrollable and even uncivilized in England, they "instinctively pursued the same path...squabbling, fighting, singing Psalms, burning witches, and talking about liberty" in the New World.[103] This inability of Northerners to tame their natural "religious fanaticism" had political ramifications that endangered the more genteel Norman-descended Southerners. Those who populated the South were "of royal pedigree" and were responsible for having established "law, order and government over the earth."[104] Such claims were more than overheated rhetoric and grandiose notions of lineage. The claims of a Cavalier heritage were part of an argument that insisted Northerners were fanatics. As Americans they enjoyed "liberty which they do not appreciate" that predisposed them to "anarchy."[105] In this manner, Southern observers warned about the consequences of a Republican victory and the establishment over the entire nation of a "Northern" government.

As the presidential election loomed in the fall of 1860, the Boston-based *Atlantic Monthly* ridiculed Southern fears. The South, it sneered, "seems to have become alarmed at its own scarecrow."[106] And perhaps to the Northern editor it had. But as the journals of the South continued to pour forth editorials and features that emphasized a "Northern mind and character" composed of the "fiercest, wildest elements," literate Southern citizens were bombarded with warnings that a dire peril was on the horizon. And those fears did have a reasonable basis apart from the atmosphere generated by political rhetoric. A Republican administration posed a real danger to slavery despite the language of the Republican Party platform. No one who had listened to William Seward or Charles Sumner over the previous decade could have any doubts about their power in the party or their goals for the disposition of the slavery question.[107] By the time Southerners' worst fears were indeed fulfilled by the election of Republican Abraham Lincoln in November 1860, *De-Bow's Review* would ask, Would it not be "madness, worse than madness, *servility* and *baseness*, for the South to submit to a government which has passed into the hands of the fanatics of the North?" Such a question required little elaboration.[108] Southern use of the Salem metaphor ensured that when citizens read about the recent national election results in *De-Bow's Review* in December 1860, they needed no further explanation of the message: "The North, who, having begun with burning witches, will end by burning us!"[109] The emotions that Avery Craven concluded were an essential precondition for armed conflict were now fully in place. Men did identify "their rivals with disliked and dishonorable symbols."[110] Since those symbols were largely of their own creation, they were able to invest them with traits that they believed not only were antithetical to their own qualities but had the utmost potency for generating hate and fear.

CHAPTER FIVE

Witch-Hunters

The Era of Civil War and Reconstruction

In 1885 former Massachusetts governor John D. Long offered a toast at the New England Society of Pennsylvania's annual dinner that began with a familiar tribute to the "Puritan forefathers." Long's toast, however, ended with words that would have seemed scandalous only a generation before. In remarking that the "Puritan forefathers are now aged men" who "come out rarely—only once or twice a year," Long offered the real subject of his tribute: "the Plymouth Pilgrim ... unlike the Puritan—a distinction which should never be forgotten—their religion was tolerant and large, never marred by persecution."[1] In contrast to the NESoc orators who insisted for most of the nineteenth century that a Pilgrim was a Puritan and that, the issue of Salem witchcraft notwithstanding, the two settler symbols were indivisible, by the 1880s even men like Long acknowledged (or even insisted on) a distinction between the two iconic Massachusetts settler figures.

The language in John Long's toast had become familiar to his audience by the mid-1880s. The Plymouth Pilgrim was a "tolerant" figure who must be "distinguished" from his Massachusetts Bay Colony Puritan neighbor, who could be charged with the "intolerance" and "bigotry" that resulted in "persecution." The war's end in 1865 spurred not only a political reunion but a cultural reconciliation. Reconciliation between sections depended on what David Blight called "a new religion of nationhood" built on a framework of an overtly "racialized reconciliation." The real causes of the war present in the debates of the 1850s were conveniently ignored as the war itself was depoliticized. Within a generation the Civil War and its causes were, in whites' nostalgic memory, little more than a narrative of "two foes struggling nobly for equally honorable notions of liberty."[2] New social and political realities generated by this mind-set required alterations in longtime national symbols as well. The collective memory of the Puritan past was already in tatters from its rhetorical service within the Sectional Crisis and the war. Its previous centrality to the mythology of national founding makes its postbellum transformation an especially good illustration not only of the dynamic power of collective memory to shift to suit new social and political realities, but of how its very use assists in the creation of those new meanings.

The continued use of the Puritan within the invective directed first at abolitionists and finally at the undifferentiated "Northerner" and his government was a vital aspect of the modification of the established meanings of the Salem metaphor in the years immediately before and after the war. The pro-slavery, and later Confederate national, effort to link the Puritan and his "persecution" with "intolerance" of dissent on the issue of slavery was transformed not only by wartime but by peacetime propaganda. The new emphasis was on the dangerous power of just such a "Puritan element" in positions of authority. Whatever troubling pressure the public might create under the spell of a "delusion" paled beside what the government could actually *do* with its power to suppress perceived dissent. The familiar terms "fanaticism" and "delusion," long associated with Salem witchcraft, would appear regularly in the 1860s and well beyond, but they would more often describe the excesses and passion of the persecuting "hunter" than the beliefs or practices that created the "hunted." In particular, Salem's Puritans and their witch hunt would be used to express new anxieties about the power of those running the mechanisms of law and government and their ability to convert "prosecution" into "persecution."

The Puritan as the central representative of a heroic and virtuous national founding thus became a casualty of the war, and by the end of the national Reconstruction in 1877 a shift in collective memory put the Pilgrims of Plymouth Colony into place in the popular imagination as the dominant symbolic New England colonial settlers. This change would be clearly evident in sources as varied as lineage society dinner speeches, schoolbooks, and adult histories, as well as within the metaphorical use of Salem and its Puritans in public controversies.

The "mythical devil" created by the image of the "witch-burning Puritan" in the pro-slavery rhetoric of the 1850s continued to be politically valuable as the Confederate States of America was formed in 1861. Confederate orators, politicians, polemicists, and editors engaged in their own nationalizing process had to quickly establish a sense of identity and cohesion among their citizens. Even while the CSA was forced to defend itself militarily, it simultaneously had to define itself as a nation and cast the United States as an enemy. Confederates involved in the public dialogue chose the most effective route by elaborating on themes that were already widely used during the Sectional Crisis. The project of inculcating a sense of Confederate national identity, of course, never fully matured. As in the effort eighty years earlier by the American Revolutionary generation, creating the affective bonds of Confederate nationalism needed a foundation of "words as well as deeds" and in 1861 relied on many of the same themes and methods of dissemination as Americans had used in the 1790s.[3]

The justification for seceding from the federal union and creating the Confederate States of America in 1860-61 relied on a rhetorical and symbolic structure that stressed "restoration" rather than "revolution." As secession looked to be more than bluster after the election of Abraham Lincoln in November 1860, the idea that union was less important than liberty was regularly argued in the Southern press. The South was not seceding, it was merely returning the nation to the correct founding principles. Secessionists maintained that separation from the union was "a continuation of the struggle of 1776." Therefore they defined the action not as a revolution or rebellion but as a simple (and even patriotic) "fulfillment of American nationalism."[4] Any number of commentators who addressed the public through print in the crucial year 1860-61 stressed what they claimed were the original intentions of the "fathers" to create only a "temporary bond" in the 1790s. The same Revolutionary "fathers" in this formulation "expended their blood and treasure not for the sake of the Union, but for Independence."[5] The Northern states and their "foaming maniacs" who, inspired by the "Massachusetts fanaticism" called abolition, departed from the values established by the founding generation and thus destroyed the national union. The election of 1860 signaled that "the union of our forefathers is already gone" and, as such, secessionists were keeping faith with the American Revolution.[6]

The argument for guardianship of the republic also rested on the familiar claim of possessing the virtue necessary to guide the nation to its fulfillment. Senator Andrew Pickens Butler of South Carolina said during the debates of the 1850s that only the Southerners had remained faithful to "the true American character."[7] Such appeals to the notion that Southern colonists had possessed appropriate virtue during the Revolution also provided an opportunity to note the absence of disqualifying vice. If a Southern slave society was degenerate and unredeemable, D. J. McLord argued in *DeBow's Review,* it could at least say of its Revolutionary generation that, unlike the North, it produced "no Arnolds."[8] Claiming that military victory was assured for the Confederacy based on the character of its leading men, George Fitzhugh used Benedict Arnold as his prime example of the character differences between the two nations. "Yankees have little self-reliance or personal courage, are submissive and easily drilled, and make better common soldiers; but they have few men qualified to make officers. Benedict Arnold was the best officer the North has produced."[9] Fitzhugh thus neatly established a tradition of Southern independence and virtue while firmly locating the greatest national crime on the enemy in one vivid and familiar image.

The early decades of the nineteenth century had seen Americans ground the mythos of Revolutionary virtue in their colonial experience. This too was recast in the Confederate nationalizing effort, with a new origin in the Southern colonies. Drawing on themes fully developed during the decades of sectional tension, Confederates were ready with an alternative to the Massachusetts settler figure—the Cavalier. The Cavalier-Puritan model of conflict used during the 1850s could continue to define the contemporary enemy in familiar language even while it contributed to a symbolic founding-generation underpinning for Confederate nationalism. As in the prewar rhetoric, the emphasis was on the essential racial characteristics of the Cavalier and the Puritan. The heritage of the specific groups, went the argument, lent each section of the former union a specific temperament and an ideology reflected in its orientation toward social and political organization.

George Fitzhugh, J. Quitman Moore, and Frank A. Alfriend, three of the most vocal proponents of this theory, repeatedly located national virtue in the English Cavalier origins of Southern colonists. It was the Cavalier as the traditional "advocate of rational liberty," not the Puritan, they argued, who was the proper model for a republican citizen. The only heritage of the Puritan colonist, Moore asserted, was what promoted the creation of a "religious fanatic and a political agitator and a reformer."[10] Such men, as any number of editorials or articles had stressed from the 1830s through the crisis of the 1850s, took rigid moral positions that were disruptive to society. "Rational liberty," by contrast, said George Fitzhugh, was rooted in orthodoxy and conservative order. The English Cavalier and the French Huguenot, Fitzhugh similarly claimed in 1861, had "no disposition to interfere improperly in the judgments and convictions of other people."[11] Of the three men, Frank Alfriend in particular refined the link between the fulfillment of the Revolution and the conservative goals of the newly formed Confederate States of America by defining the Cavalier heritage in opposition to the Puritan heritage. Alfriend claimed that the Confederate nation's Cavalier legacy provided a natural inclination to administer "regulated liberty." The South, he said, honored the original intentions of the Revolutionary generation within its social hierarchies and political ideology. Unlike the Northern states, the South had long understood that promoting an "aristocracy—socially, at least, while admitting the prevalence of Democracy in our political constitution" was the only path to a peaceful and orderly republic. And by "aristocracy," Alfriend was careful to clarify, he meant no "invidious distinction between classes of our citizens" but rather safety from the "control of the ignorant and fanatical mobs." Alfriend located the problems with "Northern civilization" in a familiar place: "that Puritan element."[12]

To best serve both nationalist and wartime ends, however, the new Confederate national identity needed to be fully disseminated. As Americans did in the aftermath of the Revolution, builders of Confederate nationalism in the wake of secession recognized the value of print for inculcating a new rendition of national founding and its desirable cardinal values. In particular, they had the nineteenth-century Americans' faith in the ability of the common schoolbook to best effect that goal. In anticipation of a sectional split, calls for a "native" literature at all levels circulated several years before the crisis provoked by the election of 1860. In 1856, the *American Publishers' Circular* reprinted an article from the *New Orleans Picayune* that addressed what "may be assumed to represent, in a degree, the sentiment of the South upon a subject of especial interest to our readers."[13] The author advocated establishing Southern publishing companies and vigorously promoting schoolbooks written in the South for the South. The consequences of failing to do this were obvious: in the event of secession the South would be left with schoolbooks from the North. And those books, the article continued, were "written with a view to arraying children against their parents" because they were "hostile" to a slaveholding society.[14] In the fall of 1861, with separation a reality, the *Southern Literary Messenger*'s editor made a similar plea to its readers for the development of a complete Southern literature, since "a nation cannot live upon bread alone."[15]

Many Southerners had long complained that Northern authors had in essence seduced Southerners into a belief in a national past full of error and deception. Certainly when the schoolbook authors in particular were not targeting slavery as a specific evil, they had long drawn unflattering comparisons between Virginia's early settlers and those of Massachusetts. In 1850 J. W. Morgan made an impassioned plea for a native juvenile Southern literature. "Lessons learned in youth are formative and enduring," and wise parents, he stressed, were selective about what their sons read. "The department of school books" was so completely dominated by Northern authors that many children were taught that their own fathers were "a heartless, cruel, bloody-minded set of robbers, kidnappers, and slavery-whippers." It was in the schoolbook that "Northern cunning and ingenuity had exercised its utmost power." Schoolbooks, with their overwhelming Northern orientation to the nation's history, functioned as the "most efficient mode of corrupting the minds of Southern youth." Morgan pleaded for any of the "men among us who are well-suited to the work" to provide books that "Southern parents and teachers can with safety and good conscience place before their children."[16] In making the case for just how dire the situation was, Morgan reminded his readers that the available schoolbooks were

> filled with praise and glorification of the first settlers of the New England and Northern States generally, as a set of incorruptible patriots, irreproachable moralists...on the other hand, the individuals, who organized society in the Southern States, are pictured as a race of immoral reprobates...[while] the institution of slavery...[is] made the occasion of much violent invective, there is but a slight effort at rebuke, and a large amount of apology is offered, for the amusements of burning witches...formerly so very popular in New England...such is the state of the histories.[17]

But the dissemination of information in the Confederacy was hampered by the lack of an infrastructure for producing books and was constantly disrupted by the conditions of warfare. *DeBow's* contributors recognized this even as they called for more Southern books. Dr. Samuel Cartwright warned the periodical's readers in 1862 that despite idealistic goals, the Confederacy was not "sufficiently supplied with book agencies and other facilities for the extensive distribution and diffusion among themselves of the works of their own writers."[18] But as the war raged over the next four years, even established publications like *DeBow's Review,* based in New Orleans, had significant breaks in publication because it was hard to obtain the most basic supplies like ink and paper. Nevertheless many authors tried to answer the call, and a few "Dixie Readers," "Dixie Spellers," and similar schoolroom titles either appeared in print or were promised in advertisements during the short life of the Confederacy. In the adult market, more books and any number of established or new newspapers and periodicals continued to appear despite short runs or interruptions. But along with a low general literacy rate and few production facilities, distribution of printed material was severely hindered not only by the war but by a barely organized Confederate postal system.[19]

Some of those who answered the Confederate call for native publications did so in a decidedly polemical vein, and here Salem witchcraft filled a familiar role. "A South Carolinian" offered *The Confederate* in 1863. A wartime diatribe meant to reinforce nationalist sentiment, one of its targets was the insidious cultural effect that generations of schoolbooks by Northerners had had on the South. Throughout its hundred-odd pages, it rains invective on "the Yankee race, true descendants of their false and fanatical progenitors, the bigoted Pilgrim Fathers...[who] have caused the severance of that union between the States which can never be renewed."[20] The author stressed his intention to deliberately and interchangeably "use the words, Puritan, Pilgrim Fathers, and Yankee in common...[as they] signify the same worthless crew." By way of introduction, he invited readers to "look a little into their antecedents and see what record they have left...written in the tears of their helpless and hapless victims." Victims who were defined in this wartime polemic, as they were in the earlier Sectional Crisis rhetoric, included Massachusetts's white Quakers and its Puritan townspeople.[21]

The Confederate lingered in particular over Salem witchcraft, for it originated in a time when, "at a loss how further to annoy and harass humanity, the Puritans happily fell upon the notable device of witchcraft." The discovery of witchcraft "afforded a glorious field for the display of Puritan intolerance, bigotry, malignity, and cruelty, and for a considerable time they flourished and luxuriated in it without stint or limit." No one else on this continent, the author claimed, using the image refined in the Sectional Crisis of the 1850s, "ever burned witches." For this crime alone, "let these bigoted, fanatical, mischief-making, would-be enlighteners, instructors, exemplars, and reformers of the moral, political and religious world, be branded, like Cain for their crimes, and held up to the lasting scorn and derision of the world."[22]

This wartime complaint emphasized all the most dramatic elements of the ongoing Southern representation of the "Puritan apotheosis" that infected American schoolbooks published in the North over the nineteenth century. The average citizen, the author asserted, was unaware of how extensively and subtly both regional and national identity had been shaped by decades of Northern intellectual influence. He joined the chorus of those who called the Confederate nation not only to arms but to letters: "For more than half a century, Southern apathy has permitted our country to be deluged with northern books and northern papers. Our schoolbooks, our histories, our journals, even our almanacs, have been printed, published by Northern men in Northern cities." The goals of such devious men, he said, were evident not only in their success in dominating the market, but in their control of the narrative of national founding in their publications, where they boldly transformed "the vices and crimes of their forefathers into virtues and heroic actions."[23]

The inclusion of Salem witchcraft in this 1863 publication was far from surprising, for its repeated use as a symbol in the prewar rhetoric made it a convenient and meaningful symbol to define the vices of Northerners in opposition to the virtues of Southerners. But the most critical aspect of the use of Salem by 1863 was the perceptible shift from its primary focus of association. Rather than detailing the consequences of popular "delusions" or "fanaticism" within the community itself, writers increasingly stressed the "intolerance" or "bigotry" of leaders with the power to "instruct" as the root of both the 1692 witch hunt and policy making in the Union government. Older associations of Salem witchcraft with "delusions" and "fanaticism" provided a useful foundation for claims of "congenital intolerance" among Northerners. This intolerance was again seen as a racial trait derived from the colonizing generation, who were "men of small minds, fanatical, and to a considerable extent, tinctured with insanity; this last feature has been the prolific source of the countless 'isms' which have afflicted that region, and those settled by its descendants, from the days of witchism."[24]

But however useful such language was for articulating a belief in the enemy's irrationality, others were beginning to move away from an emphasis on irrationality as a foundation for abolition fervor. The editor of the *Richmond Enquirer* insisted on defining the conflict as one based on a mere difference of opinion between the two nations. Congenital Yankee "intolerance" for the views of others was at the heart of their opposition to the institution in the South. Shortly after the creation of the Confederate States of America, the *Enquirer* told its readers that "the Confederacy may pride itself, as making us a distinct people from the Yankee nation," in part because of the absence of "that diabolical spirit of intolerance" that marked the Yankee.[25] By investing the now familiar Salem metaphor with new meanings, pro-slavery arguments could be further dignified by shifting some of the terms of debate. Like the editor of the *Enquirer,* some noted Salem's lack of "tolerance" for dissenting behaviors, which were then conveniently labeled "witchcraft" and prosecuted as crimes, and they claimed that a parallel could be drawn with an equal "intolerance" by contemporary Puritan descendants on the issue of slavery. It was an emphasis that would be more fully realized after the war, as whites reconciled and redefined the terms of their shared American identity. But the wartime shift from an explicit discussion of the morality of the institution of slavery to a more abstract realm of "tolerance" for differing opinions could also be used to appeal to those in the Union still not fully committed to the war, to those who were ambivalent about slavery, or to outright racists.

The opposition Union press and average citizens found this new casting of Salem to be a boon within any appeal for a "moderate" position based on "tolerance" for differing "opinions" about slavery. By casting abolition as "radical," the abolitionist was a "fanatic," not a reasonable, "tolerant" man. Those who held Free-Soil opinions, or even those completely indifferent to the fate of the enslaved, were provided with a veneer of morality in expressing their own views that matched the stance of their abolition-minded neighbors. In addition, the "moderate" course provided a platform for direct challenge to the federal government's policies toward the Confederacy. Critics of the Lincoln administration were well aware of the care needed when condemning either the government or those abolitionists with close ties to the administration in wartime. A thin line always separates accepted dissent from charges of treason. By shifting the terms of morality within the argument over slavery and employing the associations already understood in the Salem example, the Union use of Salem's witch hunt shows the fundamental transformation it would undergo during the war years. This transformation was possible because it continued to work within the understood meanings of the metaphor to censure extremism even as it shifted to address new cultural anxieties about the power of government.

As secession began, the *New York Herald* and the New York–based *Harper's Monthly* had brief but telling flirtations with this new emphasis within the Salem metaphor. Between January 1861 and the Confederates' firing on Fort Sumter in South Carolina in April, both of them printed articles that attempted to rally public support for moderation or appeasement by the Lincoln administration toward the seceding states. With little time between the crisis and the onset of war, the campaign was extremely short. Nonetheless, the effort by these Northern publications is interesting because they adopted previously *Southern*-based images of the abolitionists as Puritan and emphasized both their "intolerance" and their presumed power.

Harper's Monthly contributed only one extended reference to Salem witchcraft in the three months before the war, but it is significant in its timing and content. The March 1861 issue reminded readers that "Puritans ... were a grim, gloomy, severe race of men."[26] The idea that Puritans were "severe" would come as no news to any American reader in 1861. But the anonymous writer went on to describe New England's founders using language that over the next two decades would largely displace older explanations of the causes and justification for any perceived "fanaticism" by the historical Puritans. Puritans would always "be more tenacious of their own views than tolerant of those of others; and the liberty they would defend at all hazards would be the liberty of thinking as they did." To the old defense that the Puritan was a product of his times, the author had a ready answer: "Our reply is that every sinner can be excused by the same plea ... what are the times but people? And what are faulty times but tyrannical persons?" Yet despite his dismissal of the Puritans' own historical context, the *Harper's* editor made a plea for his own place in his own cultural moment: "This whole matter seems to us only a hideous nightmare as we look at it in our lights of to-day." Thus he also relied on the old assumption that Salem witchcraft was a relic of an ignorant, unenlightened age even as he dismissed it as causal. The ultimate result of the Puritans' tenacity of opinion (and by implication of the radical abolitionists') was "the shame of the witchcraft massacres." Curiously, the lesson to be drawn from Salem, and presumably used to achieve a bloodless resolution of the current national political crisis, was "toleration." In the end, the essential battle between the sections was not about slavery (which was all but erased as a moral question, as were the enslaved, whose humanity was erased as well) but about abstract ideas. We must compromise on the Southerner's insistence on maintaining slavery, he advised, in order to properly "respect the rights of others just as firmly as we insist upon our own." Only "toleration" for the slaveholders' viewpoint would avoid the threatened "massacres" of civil war.[27]

The *New York Herald's* pro-Southern stance in the early months of 1861 reflected editor James Bennett's own sentiments about slavery.[28] The paper had opposed Lincoln's election and advocated compromise on slavery by confining it to the states where it existed. Bennett and his staff never missed an opportunity to ridicule both the president and New England with a single evocative image. Since Lincoln had instituted a ban on liquor in the White House, it asked, did he realize that his high-level staff members were imbibing on a train trip? The *Herald* thought he might want this brought to his attention, "knowing as we do that the President is as prim a Puritan as ever sat under Cotton Mather's preaching."[29]

As the secession movement began, the *Herald*, as a daily, had more opportunity to work the historical warning of Salem witchcraft into its portrait of extremist New England abolitionists. It alleged that abolition extremists were the driving force in the Lincoln administration in the first four months of 1861. Indeed, the *Herald* began the year with an editorial stretching over two issues, titled "The Story of Puritanism—Real Origin of Southern Secession." This series, the editor promised in the first installment, would deliver the details on "the fierce controversy which has sprung from the propagandism of the Puritan sect of New England."[30] There is, the editorial asserted (with a pointed choice of terms), a long tradition of "glorifying New England and its Puritans at the expense of the rest of the people of the *confederacy*, and glossing over the indubitable facts of history which tell a very different tale."[31] Reminding readers that there was an argument for the Union's being made up of a "confederation of states," the *Herald* attempted to remove the onus from the term that within a month would formally name the nation formed by the seceding Southern states. The editorial described Massachusetts as a haven for "self complacent divines," "flattering orators," and "mutual admiration anniversaries."[32] As for philosophy, Massachusetts, with its Puritan past and present, possessed "one idea that penetrates and pervades them ... that they have a right to regulate the whole political, moral and religious world, and that God has appointed them as supervisors over the conduct of their fellow men to control even their domestic affairs."[33]

The *Herald* series sketched a bizarre portrait of a Massachusetts devastated by the closing of the Atlantic slave trade. The state then turned "with a holy horror" on Southern slaveholders, "as they are intolerant of the prosperity which it gives the South."[34] Under the cover of abolition, the writer argued, Massachusetts's present-day Puritans sought only economic and political power over others. Puritanism itself was part of a mentality that once had "claimed an exclusive patent from Heaven for religious persecution—a Divine right to do wrong."[35] Indeed, the state of Massachusetts was, the *Herald* concluded, the sole cause of Southern secession. Its abolitionist activities constituted a fraud "on a par with their sincerity touching religious persecution in days of old . . . innocent men and women of the best character were put to death as witches by this intolerable fanatical despotism."[36]

The *Herald* kept up this drumbeat on February 3, 1861, when it attacked both Henry Ward Beecher and Wendell Phillips for implying that within the Puritan tradition lies "the germ of which everything that is good in the country has sprung." It was typical of such "narrow minded Puritanism," the editor thundered, that Virginians Jefferson, Madison, and Washington were not mentioned. After invoking the Virginia trinity, he closed with a flourish by resurrecting Massachusetts's own contribution to American history and ideas: "It was not the witch burning, persecuting sectarianism of Massachusetts that modeled the constitution, but the liberal ideas of Virginia." Massachusetts, he averred, "has always arrogated too much credit to herself."[37]

Going into the secession crisis, Bennett and his *Herald* were indeed unapologetically "prosouthern, proslavery, [and] anti-Republican." New Yorker George Templeton Strong, on hearing of the firing on Fort Sumter in April 1861, cynically predicted an about-face for Bennett and the *Herald*: "It takes naturally to eating dirt and its own words (the same thing)."[38] The very next day, as Lincoln called for volunteers to put down the uprising, the *Herald* decided that when the shooting started, prudence demanded that the more vitriolic censure should end. But the *New York Herald* did not undergo a complete conversion, despite the advent of war or Lincoln's sending an intermediary to appeal directly to Bennett. Rather, supporting the United States was good for business.[39] Still, small doses of the old vitriol occasionally surfaced. For example, New England and its abolitionists drew the *Herald*'s ire and the label of "fanaticism" for "intrigues" and "machinations" in the fall of 1861. Laying the blame for the war itself and for the "cry of mourning [which] will arise from untold bereft families" squarely at the door of New England abolitionists and their allies, the *Herald* argued that it was only their "fanaticism" that had caused the South to be "goaded into overt acts of treason."[40]

The newspaper did its part to chastise the Lincoln administration for appeasing the "fanatical" Puritan faction, and it inveighed against the abolitionist "war of propagandism."[41] In minor skirmishes in its pages from 1861 to 1865, the *Herald* continued its own war against the Massachusetts Puritans of the 1860s, even while it backed down from its overtly pro-Southern position. Indeed, through its persistent use of the Puritan as the symbol of Massachusetts and abolitionism, and Salem witchcraft as the symbol for Puritan excess–all joined in their natural "persecuting" spirit–the widely read New York daily helped disseminate more broadly the new meanings of the Salem metaphor. And so, nationally, Salem would come signify the "intolerant" elite whose power allowed them to "persecute."

That such language circulated quickly and widely was evident in a variety of print sources large and small. A Philadelphia Presbyterian weekly, the *Christian Recorder*—one of many journals that reprinted a letter from an English reporter who had toured the South just after secession–provides one example. William Howard Russell, who had reported on the Crimean War for the *London Times*, related that South Carolinians he spoke to detested "New England and the populations of the Northern States, whom they regard as tainted beyond cure with the venom of 'Puritanism.'" South Carolinians informed Russell that "the State of South Carolina was founded by gentlemen. It was not established by witch-burning Puritans, by cruel, persecuting fanatics, who implanted in the North the standard of Torquemada, and breathed into the nostrils of their newly-born colonies all the ferocity, blood-thirstiness, and rabid intolerance of the Inquisition." The vehemence with which such opinions were delivered clearly alarmed the English-born Russell. He maintained that it was difficult to preserve a "decent neutrality" when faced with their "violence."[42]

C. Chauncey Burr, whose newspaper the *Old Guard* was a Copperhead catalog of abolitionist-inspired horrors, enthusiastically drew on the Salem metaphor and combined it with the equally provocative imagery of the Roman Catholic Inquisition to condemn the current policies of the United States. "The Puritan War" detailed the sympathy that "the friends of the constitution and liberty in the North" had as they, like the Confederate nation, were "deluged with blood" in this war. Calling on the memory of the "Revolutionary fathers," he charged "Puritanism" with destroying liberty itself as it promoted "consolidationism, centralism" and destroyed "localism and the eternal right of self-government."[43] Burr found ample interpretive power in the full range of words that had over many decades been associated with Salem. "Intolerant fanaticism!" was his blunt evaluation of the Lincoln administration. Chauncey Burr claimed he had moved his office between New Jersey and New York several times to save himself from "Mr. Lincoln's dungeons and his reign of terror" and raged that "Puritanism has always been a political religion."[44] But even as Burr freely compared the Lincoln administration to the Inquisition for terrorizing dissenters, he paradoxically praised colonial Roman Catholics as he went after his real nemesis in the current crisis. It was the Puritans, he argued, who had a history of "drowning the Baptists, whipping the Quakers, boring holes through their tongues with red-hot irons, and driving women naked through the streets of Boston. All this because they would not adopt the Puritan sectarianism, [as] the Catholic 'slave'-holders of Maryland were laying the deep foundations of religious toleration and liberty."[45]

But in Chauncey Burr's persistent assignment of "intolerance" to the North and his praise for what he deemed the contrasting "openness" of Southern culture, he joined a chorus that aimed to marginalize abolitionists in the North as dangerous and powerful extremists. He did this by linking Salem with the power to repress dissent rather than with the danger of popular delusions.

Criticisms of what were perceived to be the powerful, radical elements of society were not, of course, confined to the public press. Individuals wrote essays, poems, and treatises for private and public distribution, their themes and language permeated by the now familiar illustration of Salem. But most also shifted the metaphor from the danger posed by popular delusions that bred public disorder and focused on the threat to the nation's stability from those who had extremist ideas and the power to enforce them. One enterprising journalist offered an erratically published newspaper called the *Banner of Liberty* that promised on its masthead to promote the Union while exposing such extremism as "Priestcraft." The newspaper, published in nine issues from 1848 to 1866, came out of Middletown, New York, but proximity to New England did little to dull its hostility to Massachusetts. Priestcraft, it claimed, was introduced into America by the Puritans, "whose narrow-brained and silly dogmas were enforced by...burning or drowning obnoxious persons under the pretense of the clergy and their dupes that they were witches!"[46] Just when Puritanism had appeared to be finally dead, the anonymous editor wrote, what should occur but that "another generation should arise in place of that which had won liberty at such cost."[47] Once in power, these ungrateful descendants obviously reverted to the Puritan type and celebrated the "triumph of fanaticism and ignorance in electing the nondescript Lincoln as President." To such writers, the American extremist was a Puritan; Boston was his home, fanaticism the wellspring of his ideas, and the persecution of others his goal.[48]

The theme of Puritan intolerance likewise informed public opposition to politicians' war policies. As James McPherson has revealed, the cries of Free-Soil, Democratic, and Copperhead public figures about New England's power in the early 1860s had some basis in political reality. By 1862 "a unique combination of history and geography had given New England–born radicals extraordinary power in Congress, especially the Senate." Those in opposition to the Lincoln administration worried about the influence of this group of men as well as their ultimate goals. The administration's using wartime as an excuse to confiscate property, institute broad new taxes, suspend writs of habeas corpus, and abolish slavery in some areas through the Emancipation Proclamation all seemed to them the actions of a despotic government. The growing power of the federal government during and after the war fueled new concerns within a significant portion of the American population of every region and every political stripe. Clement L. Vallandigham spoke the thoughts of many wary citizens in the Union when he repeatedly claimed that the country was ruled by a despot and predicted that the war would end in the "enslavement of the white race by debt and taxes and arbitrary power." It was "the heartless, speculative Yankees" who crushed the Midwest and who led the charge to war.[49] Again, the New England extremist was at the heart of this endeavor and provided, as in pro-slavery rhetoric, the greatest threat "to his own kind."

Ohio congressman Samuel Sullivan Cox was likewise involved in the vigorous campaign to expose what he termed federal "Puritan" treachery and treason. The Emancipation Proclamation provided an opportunity for him to address a New York audience of over three hundred in January 1863. Cox inveighed at length against "narrow, arrogant, selfish Puritan policy" in Washington. In his pointed critique of the Lincoln administration's war policies, he concluded that the influence of "New England intolerant fanaticism made compromise impossible." Cox called for a return to a national "policy . . . which declared no war for conquest—no anti-slavery crusade." But with "the bigots of New England" influencing policy, he saw no such hope on the horizon. As a "western man," Cox continued, he didn't intend to stand idly by as Puritanism, "the reptile which has been boring into the mound which is the Constitution," destroyed the nation. It was, he said, "wild utterances of New England Puritanism, in press and pulpit" that continued the war.[50] By 1863 the shift to the Puritans who would crush "dissent" and continue their "radical" political agenda against the will of the majority was becoming the dominant theme in appeals to the memory of the Puritan past.

The appeal to Salem witchcraft as a specific exemplar of the violent consequences of "Puritan rule" had one further use as the war ended, before it quickly dropped out of print debates about sectional differences. Several former Confederates used Salem within Southern-based periodicals to describe their fears about how "fanatical" Northerners would act in victory. George Fitzhugh provided the most detailed of these few references. In "The Impending Fate of the Country," Fitzhugh blended old images with new language as he meditated on "history and experience . . . and the lessons which [Salem witchcraft] teaches." Worried about the radical "rationalism" inherent in the philosophy of Northerners who enjoyed what history taught was always dangerous—"undue and prolonged ascendancy" in any society—Fitzhugh suggested "looking to the blood" to find the likely future for the South under continued Northern rule. It was not a comforting image. As Fitzhugh explained, "Among the New England people (who rule the North with a rod of iron) . . . we find the former fanatics, radicals, and destructive by inheritance, just the same people now as . . . the witch-burners and Quaker hangers two centuries ago . . . the Puritan fathers were sincere, earnest, conscientious men, but bigoted, fanatical, intolerant, narrow-minded, and cruel in the extreme."[50]

Surveying the postwar political landscape from this vantage point, Fitzhugh predicted more "civil war and military despotism."[51] George Fitzhugh had long been one of the most articulate of the Southerners who promoted the Cavalier-Puritan model of American colonial settlement, and it was perhaps fitting that he (at this moment and in pages of *DeBow's Review*) made one of the last impassioned appeals to the memory of Salem "witch-burning" and incorporated the new emphasis on the Puritan's "intolerance" and "bigotry" that would define the collective memory of Puritans in the postwar decades.[52]

As a society uses the past as a point of common reference, artifacts of cultural memory like the Salem metaphor change to serve new interpretations when social and political needs change. In this case the very use of Salem witchcraft as an effective political metaphor helped change the context within which it operated. The Southern incarnation of the old schoolbook icon the Puritan as the "demon" of the North in the Sectional Crisis and Civil War, and its subsequent appearance in the Northern press, completed what had been started by a half-century's evolution of Salem as a symbol of backwardness, superstition, and fanaticism: it drove the Puritan into a decidedly secondary role as the colonial repository of American national virtues. The process was neither complete nor uncontested, but even the staunchest promoters of the Puritan image were compelled to recognize that their tainted symbol had limited utility as the colonial originator of national virtues. The rise of the Pilgrim of Plymouth in the decades following the Civil War solved this vexing cultural problem and, in the case of New England "nationalists" and their societies, also allowed them to preserve their own regional centrality in the national narrative.[53]

The 1620 English Pilgrim of Plymouth Colony made a second, albeit symbolic, migration to the shores of America in 1866. Benjamin Scott, an English Congregational minister, delivered a historic oration before the Friends' Institute in London, where he insisted that to label the Pilgrim of Plymouth Colony a Puritan was as "unreasonable as it is unhistorical." In advancing his case for the "fundamental and irreconcilable" differences between the pioneering groups of English settlers, he considered at length the divergent origins and philosophies of the inhabitants of New England's two early colonies. The seventeenth-century Massachusetts Bay Colony Puritans, he argued, had their origins in a reformation movement within the Church of England. As such, their aims were "to purify the State Church in their own image, to impose conformity, and to persecute" those who resisted. By contrast, Scott argued, the Pilgrims emerged out of John Robinson's separatist tradition and were invested with a truer congregational spirit. Wanting only to be left alone to perfect their relationship with God, he said, the Pilgrims left others alone as well. The proof of their philosophy, Scott offered, was in the Pilgrims' willingness to shelter rather than persecute Massachusetts Bay Colony exiles. In providing such a refuge, the Pilgrims lived their principles and thus were the true "founders of religious and civil liberty in America." There were no equivalents of the Quaker executions or witch hangings in Plymouth to mar the usefulness of the Pilgrim image.[54]

The idea that the Pilgrims were responsible for religious and civil liberty could easily be passed over as simply a moment of denominational chauvinism of the sort commonly advanced by ministers for a variety of reasons. But by 1866 the "rediscovery" of the Pilgrim solved an uncomfortable cultural problem by providing an alternative and noncontroversial symbol of New England's (and by extension the nation's) founding. In a political context where not only former Confederates reviled the region and the symbols associated with it, even the Democrats were once again focusing on New England as the origin of postwar political problems. "Hell for a New Englander," said one Democrat in the *New York World* in 1867, "was a place where everybody had to mind his own business." Post-bellum white Americans bent on reconciliation were eager to embrace the idea that there were two strands to the traditional story of the nation's founding—one moderate and tolerant, one relentless and coercive.[55]

Benjamin Scott emphasized the autonomy of the Plymouth colonists but also stressed their separatist beliefs and their nonconformity. Promoting the idea that true persecution was incompatible with the beliefs of the Plymouth settlers allowed reconciliation-minded descendants to express their newfound emphasis in public discourse about laying to rest the "differences" that caused the war in the interests of reunification. This idea of tolerance over differences of opinion became the postbellum Pilgrim's salient characteristic. The old conflation of Pilgrim and Puritan in collective memory served these ends well, as elements of the old commemorative narrative provided ample material to selectively and appropriately assign qualities to the newly individualized symbols. Just as postwar racialized reconciliation rested entirely on not discussing the true issues that led to the Civil War (and failing to address its consequences for freed slaves), so too did this mutable conflated artifact of collective memory. The distinction between the settler groups was offered not as a new narrative of founding, but as a "clarification" of an old story based on new historical research and insights. It did not require repudiating the Puritan but allowed a separation alleged to be in the interests of historical accuracy. And either could be used depending on the qualities the speaker wanted to emphasize. The effort to separate the historical Puritan and Pilgrim by arguing for historical accuracy itself relied on a narrative of progress. The Pilgrim thus was given a sentimental narrative that not only suited the spirit of reconciliation but reflected it.

The Pilgrim was regularly portrayed as the yeoman settler of New England. Simple in his habits and in his beliefs in congregational democracy, he did not need to be defended against charges of extremism. The Pilgrim was cast as a figure of a pastoral nostalgia with little ideology beyond his "separatism"—which, in many narratives, was defined to include separation both from the king's church and from that of the rigid Puritans in the neighboring Massachusetts Bay Colony. Abraham Lincoln's 1863 proclamation establishing a national Thanksgiving holiday also helped confirm the primacy of the tabula rasa Pilgrims in the American mind by linking Plymouth's harvest feast with the new holiday. Best of all, the Pilgrims could be effectively promoted by regional partisans as the true "first" permanent settlers.[56]

In his new incarnation, the Puritan served as the repository for the less democratic and more repressive impulses of the seventeenth-century Englishman and a counterbalance to the tolerant, democratic, and (it was implied) individualistic Pilgrim. The more widespread attraction of the Pilgrim for late nineteenth-century Americans rested, according to Wesley Frank Craven, on the symbol's ability to represent "the people themselves." "Have we not seen in them, what we like to think we are—men of faith and men of courage, men who are free and men who are tolerant?"[57] Certainly the rhetoric that defined the Puritans as domineering, powerful, and judgmental hinted at an elite status. By the last decades of the nineteenth century, Puritans had been recognized, Michael Kammen concluded, "as the mixed blessing that they in fact were." As the Pilgrims' ascendancy got under way in earnest, attacks against New England's Puritan past became so common that, according to one contemporary New Englander, "all of our local historians are engaged in defending somebody." White Americans, tired of war and sectional strife, clearly wanted emblems of "intense faith, imagination, and courage," not those that evoked charges of intolerance.[58]

The 250th anniversary of the landing at Plymouth in 1870 offers an unusually good moment to observe a cultural transition in the making, as the increasingly problematic Massachusetts Bay Colony Puritan gave way to the Plymouth Pilgrim as the symbolic Massachusetts settler. By witnessing and seizing that moment for a transformation of the Puritan icon, the promoters of national reconciliation could, in yet another small way, put to rest the rancor of the recent war by relocating the memory of founding firmly in Plymouth Colony. A number of ceremonies and special church services marked the occasion, but the ceremonies at Plymouth, Massachusetts, itself show how broadly the discomfort with the Puritan figure had spread and how well poised the Plymouth descendants were to take advantage of the moment.[59]

Robert C. Winthrop, scion of the founding Massachusetts Bay Colony Puritan family and longtime New York New England Society member, offered the main oration at the anniversary ceremonies in Plymouth. That times had changed even for New England's champions in their own homes was evident in Winthrop's comments on Puritans, Pilgrims, and even Virginia. Back in 1839 Winthrop himself had boldly declared to those attending the New York NESoc dinner that America was the product of New England values, saying: "I fear not to be charged with New England bigotry or Puritan fanaticism" for drawing a comparison with Virginia. Jamestown, he asserted, was founded upon "the greediness of Corporations or the ambition of Kings," while New England's more admirable motives were the "intelligent and virtuous industry of a free people."[60] Forty years and one civil war later, Robert Winthrop's message was substantially different as he bowed to Jamestown's status as "elder sister" of the colonies. Winthrop, undoubtedly laboring under the double yoke of family loyalty and hoary NESoc traditions, also claimed to be unwilling to separate the two symbols of Massachusetts colonial settlement despite the prevailing fashion. Yet he conjured up the specter of Salem to distinguish the two, even if he did not intend to do so. His listeners would have quickly grasped Winthrop's reference to "the charges of intolerance, bigotry, superstition, and persecution, which there seems to have been a special delight in some quarters, of late years, in arraying against our New England Fathers and founders." These charges, Winthrop insisted, "apply without a doubt more directly to other Colonies than to that whose landing we this day commemorate." Intentionally or not, in evoking the memory of the Massachusetts Bay Colony's founders in contrast to Plymouth's, Winthrop himself lent support to the separation of the symbols as he tied his own Puritan forebears to a legacy of "intolerance."[61]

In no sense did the 1870 Plymouth celebration overtly vilify or reject the Puritan. Within Robert Winthrop's oratory and other speeches and toasts, the Puritan was given his due as a founder even within what was officially Plymouth's day. But there was a new note of criticism and certainly a new language of distinction between Massachusetts Bay Colony and Plymouth Colony. Massachusetts congressman William Everett's verse tribute to Plymouth outlines that reality most clearly:

> We know the fun you love so well at Puritans to poke,
> Your witches and your Quakers and every threadbare joke.
> Go read your history, school-boys; learn on one glorious page,
> The Pilgrim towers untainted above that iron age.
> From stains of mightiest heroes the Pilgrims' hands are clean,
> In Plymouth's free and peaceful streets no bigot's stake was seen;

The sons of other saints may wince and pale beneath your mock,
Harmless the fool-born jesting flows back from Plymouth Rock.[62]

The very performance of such a poem at a "Forefathers' Day" celebration indeed marked a "sea change in attitudes," but it would be wrong
to see Everett's poem as simply a "humorous dismissal" of the old issues.
In the prewar decades promoters of the memory of the Puritan past, like
New England Society members, never reacted with humor to assaults on
the Puritans over the witchcraft issue. The poem at Plymouth in 1870 reflected a new context for the collective memory of the Massachusetts past
in the national imagination. As such, it reminded audiences of the "clean"
history of the Pilgrims recently raised to prominent view and, in a sense,
of surrender on the continued unqualified defense of the Puritan image.
Undoubtedly, Everett's Plymouth audience found reason to "wince and
pale" at what had been done in recent decades to local and national memory of the Puritans. Although given his due in the poem for surviving in an
"iron age," the Puritan was nevertheless tainted by his nineteenth-century
incarnation. In fact, even as Everett made reference to the Puritan as one
of the "mightiest heroes," he admitted that his hands were "stained," and
by whose blood was clear to all. The Puritan as founder had suffered his
greatest rout through the continual invocation of Salem witchcraft, whose
metaphorical life included false assertions that victims had been burned
at the "bigot's stake." Yet Everett sent another clear signal to his audience about the endurance of New England and its symbols. The white
South came out of the Civil War with a comforting motto that claimed it
could "rise again." William Everett in 1870 delivered less a commemorative oration than a eulogy, but he nonetheless finished on a note of triumph. Despite the brutal "fool-born jesting" directed at the Puritan, by
transferring its allegiance to the Pilgrim, white New England might ensure
its continuing cultural ascendancy in the nation's collective memory.[63]

With a virtual, albeit symbolic, "surrender" of the Puritan ascendancy
in favor of that of the Pilgrim at the 1870 anniversary, the closed world of
the New England Societies seems the most likely place to find a continued
nurturing of the dual symbol and a defense of the Puritan himself in the
closing decades of the century. The various NESoc chapters, however, not
only reflected the attitude of the larger society, they helped shape it. The
Civil War was an extremely difficult time for the New England Societies.
The strongest group, in New York City, had an established membership
and an elevated status among the elite local men's clubs; it weathered the

storm out of sheer will, despite New York's divisive conflicts during the war and, of course, the suspension of oratory after 1859 as "inexpedient." Likely for these reasons, the membership of the New York NESoc shows the reconciliationist vision most clearly.

At New York's annual "Forefathers' Day" dinner in 1870, which also marked the 250th anniversary of the Plymouth landing, Ralph Waldo Emerson was called on to resume the tradition of after-dinner oratory that had been abandoned in favor of more collegial annual dinners after John Brown's Harpers Ferry raid in 1859.[64] The irony of Emerson's selection in this context (he had said that Brown was "the saint whose martyrdom will make the gallows glorious like the cross") would be more startling if not for the overwhelming atmosphere of reconciliation and the ability of Emerson, like others in those decades, to invest the Plymouth Pilgrim with the admirable qualities of the colonial New Englander, which were in wide circulation as alleged historical correctives to the old myths.[65]

The aging Emerson rendered his judgment on both the Pilgrims and the Puritans. Their history of persecution and intolerance, Emerson said, left the Puritans "more enamored with death than of life."[66] But Emerson found a worthy subject in the Pilgrims, who had of late been the beneficiaries of "careful study." Who best exemplified the nation's finest principles? "The Pilgrims, not the Puritans," for the Pilgrims "did not persecute."[67] Thus the Pilgrim not only was a more tolerant, enlightened settler but provided relief from the damaged Puritan icon. Certainly popular usage continued to conflate the two (as it does to this day), but the new public emphasis on distinguishing the two settler figures affected even the New England Society members themselves.[68]

The New York NESoc membership exemplified the men who nationally embraced a "sectional reunion forged out of business enterprise and a Reconstruction that sustained white supremacy." Their hosting Atlanta editor Henry W. Grady's "New South" speech in 1886, and their reaction to it, shows how far this racialized reconciliationist impulse based on shared interests had permeated twenty years after the war ended. Grady, whom David Blight described as one of the most "adept manipulators of reconciliationist Civil War memory and master promoters of nostalgia," had the right Northern audience for his message of a "common ground."[69] Grady openly declared that "the South has nothing to take back" and that each of the Confederate dead died a "patriot's death." The *New York Times* reported that this stance received "loud applause" from the New York audience. Henry Grady put the onus for reunion on his audience, asking if "New England...will permit the prejudice of war to remain in the hearts of the conquerors, when it has died in the hearts of the conquered?"[70] According to the *Times*, "there was a general and resounding shout of 'no.'"[71]

Henry Grady's message spoke explicitly about the benefits of the "fullness of reconciliation" and claimed a "New South" where, in a parallel to John Winthrop's "City on a Hill" speech in 1630, he described how postbellum Southerners had "planted the schoolhouse on the hilltop and made it free to white and black." Most important to his audience, Grady's South was a region that now "put business above politics."[72] The New York NESoc audience was both eager for investment opportunities in the rebuilding South and willing to overlook "Jim Crow" segregation to engage in a mutually beneficial arrangement between sections.[73] Stressing "shared concern with property rights and the political power of lower-class citizens," Grady's rhetoric, like that of other New South boosters reaching across the postwar divide, could encompass Northern race-based fears of immigration as it also encompassed Southern anxieties about freedmen. These Northern-based men of business to whom Grady spoke in 1886 were men whose cross-sectional economic and social ties were attuned to the requirements of racialized national Reconstruction. They not only easily made the transition to a reconciliationist vision, they clearly helped construct it.[74]

But the NESoc members, of course, had an equal vested regional interest in the symbol of the Plymouth Colony Pilgrim, and it was there that they found an easy organizational refuge. This accommodation of the reconciliationist view was predicted by Oliver Wendell Holmes Sr. as early as 1855 when abolitionism threatened the peace of the annual NESoc dinners in New York. Although he called slavery "the detested social arrangement of our neighbors" and said he found a "manly logic" in abolition, he plainly stated before the assemblage that if the situation ever called for a choice between alliance with the black or the white Southerner, "the great family instinct" would settle the matter in favor of race.[75]

In other NESoc chapters that survived, the Puritans received less uncritical veneration in oratory than was common before the war. In fact, perceived attacks on the symbolic and historical Puritan no longer occasioned reflexive, unqualified defense. For example, at the 1886 meeting in St. Louis, the chapter heard its president, James Richardson, traditionally refute charges of Puritan "narrow mindedness" in his remarks. He was followed by member George Leighton, who did not challenge the criticism but joined in by reminding all that there was indeed much about the Puritan that "amuses" from "the high vantage ground of the nineteenth-century."[76] By 1893 old irritants became the subject of jokes in Philadelphia, as one speaker said: "When we make an unassailable position in politics or statesmanship, they say to us, 'Well, we, we quite don't know about you—you hanged the witches!'" The telling commentary on the remark is found in the record of the dinner program. Instead of the earnest and concurring response about the unfairness of such characterizations that greeted a similar complaint by Charles Boynton at the Cincinnati dinner of 1847, nearly fifty years later such comments (according to the newspaper report of the dinner) provoked only laughter from the members.[77]

While the Pilgrim fulfilled the cultural desire to remember the war and the nation's past within a sentimental, nostalgic framework, the Puritan was once again an easy historical source of cautions about deviating from agreed-on cultural norms. New preoccupations could be articulated by referring to the Puritan's "persecuting" nature. Salem once again provided the ultimate expression of the Puritan's dangerous power to wield the law in his own interest. The linkage of Salem witchcraft to power found reinforcement in print as new books and articles treating at length the distinction between the Puritan and the superior Plymouth colonist proliferated in the last decades of the century.[78] Separate histories of Salem witchcraft began to appear as well, and schoolbooks offered updated narratives of national founding buttressing the new commemorative narrative of Plymouth Colony that underpinned American nationalism.

In the juvenile market schoolbooks played their familiar role as the primary vehicle for creating nationalist sentiment, and by the turn of the century they reflected the new emphasis on the Pilgrim founding. The increase in public schools and compulsory attendance laws exposed more children to the basic narrative of the common schoolbook. As high school and even college became a middle-class goal, more advanced texts appeared. That most Americans believed in education as ardently as their early-century ancestors was evident above all in the continuing Southern battle over the content of history books. The United Daughters of the Confederacy and the United Confederate Veterans in particular lobbied every school board in the former Confederate states to "select and designate such proper and truthful history of the United States, to be used in both public and private schools of the South and to put the seal of their condemnation upon such as are not truthful histories."[79] Whatever the influence of the common schoolbook compared with the first half of the century—there were far more competitors offering factual and fictional tales from American history than in 1830—clearly adults thought that the proper narrative orientation to national history remained important.

Although many of the early nineteenth-century schoolbooks measured new editions in double digits right into the twentieth century, many new authors with a new orientation toward the study of history and the nature of "useful knowledge" emerged in the last two decades of the nineteenth century. Unlike the early national textbooks whose narrative memory of Salem slipped into public controversies, the later textbooks reversed the process. Largely owing to the burst of new textbooks starting in the mid-1870s, postbellum schoolbooks included narratives about the original founding settlers that were first developed and circulated within postwar political discourse.

Schoolbooks still carried moral overtones in their narratives, but pedagogical styles had changed. An emphasis on civics—the structure of the political system, terms of treaties, and major national events and figures—showed the maturation of the political nation over the century and mirrored the decline of morality as the most essential characteristic of the citizen. But even with a new emphasis on civics lessons rather than morality, descriptions of settler generations in colonial Virginia and Massachusetts still carried freighted language about character, goals, and legacy. One of the most interesting transformations was in the treatment of colonial Massachusetts. No longer was the Pilgrim invariably a sort of "advance man" for the Puritan. Newer schoolbooks included much more extensive descriptions of Plymouth than of Massachusetts Bay Colony, and often more about Plymouth's founding. Some popular authors (most notably Edward Eggleston, John Fiske, and John Bach McMaster) either left out Salem witchcraft entirely or reduced the coverage to a few lines, favoring late seventeenth-century political developments like the 1692 royal charter.[80] Most valorized the Pilgrim of Plymouth by specifically awarding him credit for introducing "civil and religious liberty" to American shores. In their chapter questions many asked something that had never appeared in antebellum books: "What was the difference between the Puritans and the Pilgrims?"[81]

This separation of the Pilgrims and the Puritans mirrored the other narratives that were reshaping collective memory of national founding based in the British colonies. And unlike the schoolbooks of the early nineteenth century, current texts received rather than created the narratives of New England colonial founding. By the time a substantial body of new schoolbook titles started to appear in the 1870s and 1880s, the "new" narrative of Salem had been established in the adult world of print and politics and filtered down into the schoolbook. This reversed the path by which Salem had become ensconced within the American imagination, but through its simple presentation and its repetition it nicely distilled the themes of Pilgrim "tolerance" and Puritan "intolerance."

In the postbellum schoolbook narratives, the Pilgrims were the "separatists" who did not discriminate against others or oppress them but merely wanted "a home where they could educate their children and worship God as they pleased."[82] The Plymouth narrative in the new textbooks provided a collective past that was progressive in its separate democratic and tolerant spirit. The Puritans might have had "little self-governing republics" worthy of emulation, but they "were not free from the intolerance of the times," and in comparisons with the colony at Plymouth thus suffered even more in the simple narratives created for the average schoolbook than in the adult histories.[83]

Schoolbook Puritan intolerance was usually situated in two related and telling events, the persecutions of Roger Williams and of Anne Hutchinson. In both examples the Puritans are once again the greatest threat to others in their own community, always valuing ideology over the greater virtue of tolerance, and using the law to enforce conformity. Williams and Hutchinson, who often did not appear at all in the antebellum books, were given new prominence in the late nineteenth-century schoolbook narrative precisely to perform this role as victims of official religious intolerance. The two Puritan dissenters were more suitable illustrations of the progressive nature of the United States from its very beginnings to the present day (which schoolbooks still took as their guiding principle). Roger Williams and Anne Hutchinson were presented as Puritans who dissented from orthodoxy in ways that fit more modern Protestant doctrines, making them more sympathetic figures than their "persecuting" leaders, who also chased down witches. Williams in particular, who "dissented heartily from the intolerance of the people of Massachusetts,"[84] was universally hailed as "one of the noblest men of his time."[85] His banishment for his beliefs, which in turn provided the foundation for the religious tolerance of his new colony in Rhode Island, gave the story a redemptive arc and made him an admirable proto-American, in contrast to the backward colonial Puritans who oppressed him.

Salem witchcraft had a far less prominent place in the postbellum schoolbooks as their narratives demoted the Puritans to fewer pages and

to a less direct influence on future national values. The change, however, still gave Salem witchcraft some useful interpretive power in relation to Puritan extremism in thought and practice. The "strange delusion" of witchcraft in 1692 often now served as a defining characteristic
of Puritan religious beliefs or of the dangers of church-state union. Salem
was simply dismissed as inexplicable (or even completely ignored) unless
considered within the context of a host of "very strict principles" held
by the Puritan colony that modern readers "should now consider ridiculous or repulsive."[86] That the episodes with Roger Williams and Anne
Hutchinson predated Salem helped this general argument, reinforcing the
idea that the Puritans were overbearing and somewhat irrational as they
clung to Old World ideas that some contemporaries were discarding. The
seventeenth-century Massachusetts Bay Colony's witch-hunting was now
more often framed as a civics lesson about the evils that occur when "of-
fence against religion [is] treated as a civil crime."[87] The schoolbooks of
the late nineteenth century no longer treated Salem primarily as a communitywide "delusion" whose consequences were dangerous public disorder, but offered a cautionary tale about "intolerant" or "bigoted" men
in power who had the ability to "persecute" those they "disagreed" with.
It was the personifying of such "witch-hunters" in the last quarter of the
nineteenth century that fatally imprinted Cotton Mather in the popular
imagination as the central villain in the 1692 witchcraft trials.

In an 1869 review of Salem-related publications, William Frederick
Poole bitterly objected to historical accounts of the Salem trials that
were full of fanciful speculation and what he considered character assassination. Most troubling to him was that these erroneous and biased accounts obviously "have obtained a lodgment in all the minor and school
histories."[88] In 1869, however, very few school histories singled out Cotton Mather for special blame. Most schoolbooks in circulation were from
earlier in the century, and if any minister was mentioned, it was just as
likely to be the Salem Village minister Samuel Parris as the more famous
Mather. Even when one or both appeared, they were minor elements in
narratives that warned of communitywide backwardness, delusions, or fanaticism. They were seen more as men trapped in their times than as catalysts. In his 1869 review Poole addressed the book that more rightly could
have been charged with validating the tactic of creating a historical per-
sonage to serve as the "witch-hunter" in popular and school histories.

Writing at the end of a decade in which the historical Puritan and the
1692 witchcraft trials were a common feature of the most vitriolic political rhetoric, William Poole was certainly correct in stating that Salem's

episode of witch-hunting was "receiving more attention to-day than at any former period." As "the last great exhibition of a superstition," witchcraft demonstrated, much to Poole's chagrin, extraordinary staying power. "Every incident connected with it," he complained, "has been preserved."[89] Poole's primary target in this piece was popular historian Charles Upham. A Unitarian minister, Salem native, and politician, in 1831 Upham had published a shorter history called *Lectures on Witchcraft.* The 1867 work was a massive undertaking that reflected his own background, his thirty years of public lectures on the topic, and the predilection for accounts of Salem to provide moral lessons for future generations. Upham's was among the first of the separate histories of Salem that would be published, and it was a great success.

Charles Upham relied on Thomas Hutchinson's and Robert Calef's work as his foundation and emphasized the idea of lying, cunning accusers while continuing to promote the lesson so familiar to any reader of schoolbooks and general histories: a story of "people given over to the power of contagious passion" who were eventually "swept by desolation and plunged into ruin." He mapped the physical locations of the accusers and accused and found in the witchcraft trials a history of local conflicts.[90] But despite his emphasis on community upheaval and dishonest accusers, Upham also helped shift the responsibility for the episode to Boston minister Cotton Mather.[91]

Charles Upham singled out Mather in pointedly modern terms as crucial to the escalation of the trials: "There is some ground for suspicion that he was instrumental in originating the fanaticism in Salem; at any rate, he took a leading part in fomenting it." And as for Mather's documented cautions to the authorities about procedure in the matter of spectral evidence? In this, Charles Upham says, Mather was merely acting like "other ambit[ious] and grasping politicians."[92] Before Upham's history (and before the Civil War years in particular), Mather tended to be named in tandem with Samuel Parris (as the local and provincial figures who could have stopped the trials but did not) or within discussions of a general category of "ministers" who were to blame. The popularity of Upham's history of the trials (already in print two years by the time of Poole's review), William Poole claimed, taught Americans that "nineteen innocent persons were hanged, and one was pressed to death, to gratify the vanity, ambition, and stolid credulity of Mr. Cotton Mather."[93]

As long ago as 1700 Robert Calef, in *More Wonders of the Invisible World,* had certainly identified Mather as particularly culpable for the course of the witch hunt, but over the next century the popular view of the trials had been shaped more by succeeding authors' selecting elements from his narrative to suit their own cultural contexts. The elements of Calef's narrative that showed the consequences of community support for "popular delusions" or "fanaticism," of course, spoke to their own controversies and fears, most particularly over the danger that popular movements might erupt into dangerous "mobs" or "disorder." The anxieties of the postbellum decades brought later authors and commentators back to the Salem narrative. Upham's focus on Mather as a powerful leader who could turn the machinery of government against dissenting citizens clearly suited the anxieties of the postbellum American.

The emphasis on Cotton Mather reached its zenith in nineteenth-century scholarship with the 1886 publication of Brooks Adams's *Emancipation of Massachusetts*. Adams cast Mather as the despot in the witchcraft episode, since it was simply "not credible that an educated and sane man could ever have honestly believed in the absurd stuff which he produced as evidence of the supernatural."[94] Samuel Parris also came in for his usual share of criticism as the minister at the epicenter of the original cases; Adams claimed he set out to investigate the idea of possession "with a frightful relish" and in general "behaved like a madman."[95] But in Adams's evaluation, Mather was at fault for not controlling lesser ministers like Parris. It was Calef's book, Adams concludes, that exposed Mather as it "shook to its centre the moral despotism which the pastors still kept almost unimpaired over the minds of their congregations."[96] Calef, in Brooks Adams's opinion, was owed a "debt of gratitude and honor...never yet repaid."[97] Both the amateur Upham and the scholar Adams came to the same conclusion: the witchcraft episode ended as the people challenged the despotic power of an intolerant religion. The Puritan leadership and religion sought unfailingly to crush the democratic impulse that the more admirable Plymouth Pilgrims fostered. Because of the influence of both men, in most of the late nineteenth-century popular and scholarly accounts the face of the intolerant despot, the "witch-hunter," was Cotton Mather's.[98]

When Salem's witch hunt emerged in the 1830s as a cultural metaphor, it reflected the way Americans saw the colonial past as a prologue, a resource to be selectively mined for materials to valorize the nation even as it repudiated the British colonial past. The course of Salem witchcraft in Americans' collective memory over the century ran from a cautionary tale about the community's potential to become a "mob" to a warning about the danger to the community from the unchecked power of those in authority. In its various transformations it delineated the changing terms of both the symbolic foundations of American nationalism and the anxieties of contemporary social and political life. By the 1890s, postwar political and social realities left Salem witchcraft in American memory, but it was clearly in decline as an active metaphor in public controversies. Its diminished role in public discourse, however, was merely another stage in its life cycle: latent, perhaps, at least compared with its vital presence in public debates in the previous decades, but still present in memory. Salem's 1692 witchcraft trials were always ready for metaphoric duty within political controversies. As Perry Miller once said of witchcraft beliefs in the seventeenth century, "The formula, with its neatly boxed heads of argument and application, with its rhetorical tags already minted, was ready to be wheeled into action as a loaded fieldpiece."[99]

The Crucible of Memory

In 1919, Prohibition brought the metaphor of Salem witchcraft back from its late nineteenth-century decline into frequent use in American public discourse.[1] "Witch-burning" Puritans had sporadically livened up the prose of opponents of any laws to prohibit alcohol in the decades before a law was federally enacted. As the *Washington Post* noted in 1885, Georgia's citizens appeared to be taken up with the "holier than thou sentiment which hanged Quakers and burned witches in New England." Drys, others claimed, were descendants of the people who "carried flint and tinder at the witch-burning in Salem" or, in general, those in the present day who were even "more stupid, bigoted and fanatical than the Puritans."[2] When Prohibition was finally enacted, the active assistance of religious "fanatics" who helped government enforcement agents "persecute" drinkers seemed to many critics to recall how far the "meddling zeal of Puritanic cranks who feel the old witch-finding urge" might go if they were not checked.[3]

The resurrection of the metaphor of Salem in public opposition to Prohibition shows not only its durability in the American imagination but the way previous uses shaped its latest iteration. As Salem appeared over the twentieth century in a variety of social and political controversies, those controversies would share certain characteristics that drew on earlier meanings associated with the metaphor. Each was marked by a religious or moral undertone or issue that animated a particularly passionate segment of the community—one whose opponents would be alarmed by the implications of their adversaries' underlying beliefs. In this way, the use of Salem resembled the earliest incarnations of the metaphor as a warning about the dangers of public passions, fanaticism, and even backward beliefs that threatened national progress. Each controversy would also involve disputes about the use of government enforcement powers that echoed postbellum anxiety about the limits of power. In this way, both the community and the government could be implicated in dangerous "fanatical" excess and become "witch-hunters."

American newspapers and their readers (in particular) found Salem a suitable historical precedent in the Prohibition controversy and returned the reference to widespread use. The passionate involvement of citizens in reporting violations of the law and the enthusiastic pursuit of complaints by enforcement agents at the local and federal level brought regular allusions in the press to 1692 Salem. In 1928 the *Chicago Daily Tribune* suggested that "citizens of undisputed morals" who supported the law and those who enforced it might find modern penalties insufficient and would "be glad to have their attention called to a method of punishment used in the witch trials at Salem." After all, as the *Tribune* editor reasoned, it was apparent that "the fury of Salem is the fury of prohibition."[4] Letters to newspapers by the general public and speeches by politicians and public figures often went so far as to define liquor-law violations as patriotic civil disobedience. In effect, they were an active "protest against the revival of witch-burning tendencies in this Republic."[5] When Prohibition was repealed in 1933, Henry Morton Robinson praised the event the following summer in the *North American Review* as the end of "Puritanism," which had "pinned the American people to the mat for three long centuries."[6]

During the 1920s, journalist H. L. Mencken raised blaming the Puritans for every antimodern impulse in the United States to an art, most notably in his commentary on two subjects that captured both the attention and the concern of Americans—national Prohibition and the Scopes trial. Mencken understood that the moral and the political joined in metaphorical uses of the Puritan past. The genius of "organized Puritanism," he said, "was the device of summoning the massive forces of the law to help in a private feud." Where questions of public policy crossed religious beliefs with legislation, he said, Puritans were always "ferocious and uncompromising." It was Mencken, naturally, who memorably defined the inner nature of the "Puritan" for twentieth-century Americans: "The haunting fear that someone, somewhere, may be happy."[7]

Like Prohibition during the same decade, the 1925 trial of Tennessee high school biology teacher John Scopes for teaching evolution provided critics with a moral crusade within a political framework. Press coverage characterized the events, popularly known as the "Monkey Trial," as rationality (in the form of modern science) on trial against a particularly backward or superstitious religious worldview.[8] Editorial writers, scientists, and even clergymen worried that a guilty verdict for Scopes might stunt American scientific knowledge and the material progress of the nation. Failing to accurately teach how the physical world worked, some warned, would inevitably lead to a society in which Americans would again be "drowning witches in Salem."[9] Clarence Darrow, for the defense, framed the case in equally simple terms. He claimed that the charges came out of "plain religious ignorance and bigotry as any that justified the Spanish Inquisition or the hanging of the witches in New England."[10]

But the central political crisis of the twentieth century that drew on the collective memory of Salem witchcraft as a cautionary tale—the "red scare"–and revived "witch-hunting" as a metaphor did not have the overt moral claims found in the prohibition and evolution issues but did adopt a distinctly moral tone. The campaign to root out "subversives," particularly from 1938 into the 1950s, also combined the language of morality (delusions, fanaticism, and irrationality) with warnings about government power against the citizen. With agents of federal, state, and even local governments perceived as so single-mindedly devoted to rooting out Communist ideology from cultural institutions and pursuing rumors of espionage, many complained that protections of the law were routinely ignored. In this way, by the early 1950s the "red scare" rose to the status of another "fanatical" moral cause in the minds of many Americans. That perception, along with the more recent emphasis on the Puritan as the symbol of the aggressive brandishing of power, melded the oldest and newest associations with Salem into an explosion of references to "witch hunts." The issues of the 1950s are still alive today, and some of the individuals and events of that decade are still a matter of active controversy. What is clear, however, is how Salem entered into that controversy in the early fifties, the way it was used, and how Arthur Miller's stage play *The Crucible* fit into both this crisis and the memory of the Salem trials.

Republican Senator Joseph McCarthy of Wisconsin arrived on the national scene with a speech he made in Wheeling, West Virginia, on February 9, 1950. He claimed to have a list of State Department employees who he said were known members of the American Communist Party. He rode an ongoing congressional preoccupation to become nationally identified as an aggressive hunter of subversives in government. On reelection to the Senate in 1952, with his new crusade as the cornerstone of his campaign, he took over the chairmanship of a minor Senate subcommittee with investigative powers. From this position he conducted his own investigations into subversives in government service. Most notably, he took on the U.S. Army in televised hearings in the spring of 1954. This choice of target, along with his style, alienated many of his most ardent supporters in and out of Washington. By December 1954 his conduct was condemned by a vote of the Senate and he slid into relative obscurity, dying only three years later.[11]

It is ironic that such a brief stay in the political limelight resulted in such a close association of McCarthy with anti-Communism. The investigations and hearings in Congress began long before his appearance and continued for a significant time afterward. "McCarthyism," however, became another metaphor for the aggressive government pursuit of alleged subversion represented by Salem's witch hunt during the same few years. That "McCarthyism" failed to completely replace Salem's witch hunt even in relation to the red scare shows the term's cultural limitations and Salem's comparative flexibility.

"McCarthyism" could not encompass much more than simple anxiety that agents of the government might use their temporary investigative or political power against citizens. Even temporary power can ruin individual lives, but in the end the Senate condemned Joseph McCarthy, the Republican administration did its best to isolate him, and he was marginalized by his own political party. If anything, the trajectory of Senator McCarthy's career could serve as another metaphor in support of the American political system. While Salem's "witch hunt" reminds us that government power can always be used recklessly, Joseph McCarthy's fall reassures us that, even when it is wrong or controlled by the unscrupulous, the system is ultimately self-correcting. The greatest bar to adopting "McCarthyism" as the same broad warning as Salem, however, is not only that the man himself remains in living memory but that his reputation is still in flux.[12]

In the long run, Arthur Miller did more than anyone else to associate Salem witchcraft with the midcentury "red scares." In fact, as well known as McCarthy was in early 1953, his own public role in congressional investigations started after the play opened. Historians have noted (and those who try to teach 1692 Salem have bemoaned) that Miller's Broadway drama *The Crucible* has "probably influenced Americans' understanding of 1692 more than anything any historian has ever written."[13] But the same could be said for the nineteenth century regarding the effect of Nathaniel Hawthorne's *House of the Seven Gables*, Samuel Goodrich's popular, often fanciful, and always dramatic elementary-level histories, or the pro-slavery articles describing "Puritan murders" in such periodicals as *DeBow's Review*. There is nothing new about popular narratives' shaping the memory of Salem.

In January 1953 Arthur Miller was a relative latecomer to the practice of publicly linking Salem and the national anti-Communist campaign. *New York Times* critic Brooks Atkinson wrote in his review of the opening night performance, "Neither Mr. Miller nor his audiences are unaware of certain similarities between the perversions of justice then and today."[14] Audiences should indeed have been well primed to make the connections. Journalists, social critics, writers of "letters to the editor," and political opponents of the investigations had been explicitly doing so for more than a decade by the time Joseph McCarthy and Arthur Miller became associated with the collective memory of Salem's witch hunt. In the period immediately before 1953, a crucial year for both men, George Marshall's "Salem, 1950" appeared in "*Masses and Mainstream,*" and groups as disparate (and unlikely) as college fraternities, professional wrestlers, and optometrists passed resolutions at their national conventions lauding the government's vigorous pursuit of subversives. Although the fraternity men hoped there would be "no witch hunts," the optometrists said they did not believe there had been or would be any "witch hunts" connected with congressional investigations. (The professional wrestlers apparently did not comment publicly on the historical parallel.)[15]

Other contemporary contributions to the literature on Salem's trials influenced the continuation of the memory in less directly political ways. In late 1949, Marion L. Starkey's *The Devil in Massachusetts* was published. The best-selling work of historical fiction (which had much in common with Miller's play in its very contemporary interpretation of the participants' motives and behavior), was even favorably reviewed in two of the leading scholarly historical journals in 1950. One reviewer, colonial historian Edmund S. Morgan, said Starkey made the fears of the devil's presence in 1692 Salem "quite as real and plausible as those aroused by Communist infiltration today."[16] Morgan offered a different perspective than many writers about where fear was located in 1950, but his authoritative recommendation of the book as sound history and the explicit link between Salem and Washington helped provide the context within which Atkinson expected the audience of *The Crucible* to be evaluating the stage play.

At the center of the play's plot is a vindictive young woman who cynically uses the community's fears about witchcraft to attack a faithless married former lover and his family.[17] That the two main characters have the same names as well-known historical figures from 1692 Salem reinforced the sense of historical authenticity. The generic themes of "lying girls," sanctimonious, rigid ministers and officials, and hypocritical witnesses can find their twins in one or another historical or fictional treatment over the two centuries since the trials themselves. Miller succeeded in shaping Americans' latest memory of Salem witchcraft into a narrative he created because of his skill in reimagining scenes and presenting motives that resonated with contemporary sensibilities in the midst of the political crisis he was commenting on. Ultimately, for the audience viewing *The Crucible,* the ritual of 1692 courtroom scenes with the panel of judges who insist on confession, the lack of defense attorneys, and witnesses who offer testimony that is often years old and unverifiable resembled the televised congressional hearings more than any real or televised modern American courtroom. That Miller also embedded a familiar moral lesson about Salem in line with long-established narratives made his drama more influential. It not only articulated contemporary social and political anxieties through a particular collective memory, it integrated them with its previous meanings.

Whatever the dramatic merits of *The Crucible,* in the age of mass communication the play's setting gave propulsive force to the association of Salem with the 1950s "red scare." Half a century later, it is still widely read in high school and college literature courses and is one of the most popular plays for revivals and for production by amateur theatrical companies. Its narrative distortions thus have influenced American collective memory about the 1692 trials and so the subsequent use of the Salem metaphor.

The most recent widespread and sustained use of the metaphor of Salem witchcraft since the "red scare" of the 1950s came with the impeachment of President William Clinton in 1998. On the surface, the Clinton case was another partisan political drama in which the charges of an equally partisan "witch hunt" were sure to fly. But the specifics of the Clinton impeachment case brought together the moral and the political in a way that resulted in the sort of complex and vibrant use of Salem's metaphor not seen since the antislavery debates. It also shows the influence of *The Crucible* on late-century collective memory. The impeachment case emerged out of a perjury charge related to Clinton's testimony about an affair with White House intern Monica Lewinsky in a deposition taken in a separate civil suit related to a sexual harassment complaint. The combination of moral issues and the questions raised about the parameters of government power within the investigation inspired Americans to find parallels to Salem's Puritans and their witchcraft trials through the entire ordeal of what some called "our Salem of 1998."[18]

The most intriguing issue that emerged in this latest eruption of the metaphor within the Clinton impeachment controversy was not that Salem appeared in a case that created a major public debate on moral and political issues, but the different perspectives displayed by the press and the public. For those who sought to report on the case or to shape public opinion through commentary in print and electronic media, the route ran directly from 1692 Salem through the drama *The Crucible*. The media perhaps reflexively defaulted to a recent well-known popular culture representation because its narrative contained the sexual elements that both the original colonial event and the subsequent metaphorical use did not. Whatever the reason, in the press, *The Crucible* rather than either the history or the memory of Salem was most frequently the narrative-framing device of choice.

In the coverage of the investigation and the impeachment proceedings, reporters and professional commentators often strained to make parallels that used Salem as a "hook," but that quickly reverted to the 1953 drama in its specific references. In the wake of his report to the House Judiciary Committee, independent counsel Kenneth Starr was interviewed on television, which one media reviewer described as an attempt to show the public that Starr was not "some scary-vindictive super prude out of *The Crucible*."[19] Another described Starr as looking like "the cartoon of a dour-faced Puritan."[20] Kenneth Starr himself was even considered by some to be a victim of a "witch hunt" in the press, although the *Times*'s columnist Frank Rich somewhat less sympathetically considered that Starr's own actions got him "branded as a Puritanical witch-hunter."[21] One critic advised those baffled by the case to "take another look at Arthur Miller's 'The Crucible.'"[22] And a public relations expert, with an eye toward public perceptions about the players in the case, advised that the primary witness for the adultery charge get a "makeover."

With a better hairstyle and some attention to makeup, he said, the woman would look "somewhat more sympathetic than ... a finger-pointing harpy out of a dinner-theater production of 'The Crucible.'"[23]

The allusions to Salem witchcraft and to *The Crucible* brought renewed attention to the 1953 drama, and Arthur Miller himself was sought as an "expert" commentator on the similarities between the Clinton case and the 1692 witchcraft trials—a role he assumed with obvious pleasure. Miller, who had added the sexual dimension to the dynamics of the Salem narrative in his drama, resumed his attention to that theme in his commentary on the impeachment case. His essay for the *New York Times* in October 1998, "Salem Revisited," further connected the past and present episodes by claiming that both trials were driven by men "spooked by women's horrifying sexuality awakened by the super stud Devil."[24] Miller's commentary was emblematic of where the concerns of the wider American public and the moral arbiters of the newsroom, the political stump, and the pulpit diverged. One news magazine's headline, "America's 'Puritan' Press: Journalists Wonder Why the Public Isn't Outraged, Too," explicitly labeled what was troubling the press and commentators like Miller even while it failed to identify both what the public found troubling about the Clinton case and how people connected it to Salem's witch hunt.[25]

The public's route from Salem's witchcraft trials to the Clinton impeachment case could more accurately be said to run through decades of "Letters to the Editor" rather than the press's preferred route through *The Crucible*. Although reporters and commentators frequently mentioned the drama, members of the American public who were interviewed or who continued in this most recent crisis to write to newspapers seldom referred to it at all. Whatever level of disapproval they expressed for Clinton's violation of their own standards of morality, their concern was clearly about perceived excesses in the investigation. In this members of the public might not have made any clearer direct association with the historical event of 1692 in their analogies than did the press or the politicians who commented on the issue, but they did make a more direct connection with the long-standing cultural memory of Salem and the historical use of it as a metaphor. For the American public in 1998, the issue was once again the potential for prosecution to become persecution.

A reporter in a "prosperous largely Republican and now fed-up pocket of America" in New Jersey found far less support than she expected for the impeachment trial of a Democratic president. Many voters there voiced their concern for an unseemly zeal in the government prosecutors' pursuing a lie about private sexual matters to such lengths. One man who was donating to a defense fund for Clinton summed up the reported position of many Americans, who condemned the man's private morals yet found the penalty of impeachment too extreme and the investigatory powers too broad. Others interviewed during the process frequently told reporters that they too felt the need to in some way "stand up against an ugly witch hunt."[26] A number of Floridians who wrote to their local newspaper expressed the same concern about the relentless nature of the investigation: "What Bill Clinton has done is shameful, but this is surely a witch hunt!" And, "I wasn't present at the Salem witch trials, but accounts of those trials sound eerily like our present-day impeachment trial."[27]

What no one commented on was the irony of raising Salem in relation to Clinton's situation and the way it reflected the public's own fear of vulnerability. Clearly, in the public mind the most frightening issue at stake was the perception of unchecked power. If the president of the United States was not safe from excesses by government prosecutors, what chance would an average citizen have? As twenty-six men in Massachusetts Bay Colony, petitioning on behalf of neighbors charged with witchcraft, asked in 1692, in such a state of affairs, "Who can think himself safe?" Some Americans in 1998 asked themselves the same question— and through their letters to the editor and statements in newspaper interviews, they asked it of those claiming political or cultural authority. The "outrage" journalists could not seem to find in 1998 was present, but it was not where they expected to find it. It was in the political, not the moral, realm. The American people were not simply viewing the impeachment crisis as a contemporary event but were filtering their understanding of the legal processes and the motives of those with the power to enforce the law through the collective memory of Salem. As they did, they expressed their own sense of appropriate social and political boundaries.

The long, strange career of the Salem "witches" as an American cultural metaphor is an artifact of an equally long-held and complex collective memory of the trials of 1692. Always linked to cultural anxieties, the metaphor has meanings that shift to suit contemporary realities. But from a narrative created to give meaning to the recent community ordeal after the trauma of the trials themselves through its evolution into a useful prescriptive metaphor, the memory of Salem has always held at its core meanings meant to mark the boundaries of generally accepted beliefs and behaviors. Perhaps Salem's ultimate meaning as a rhetorical weapon in any era or in any controversy can best be expressed by borrowing a useful quotation from a Puritan. In warning religious dissenter Anne Hutchinson to cease her heretical preaching in seventeenth-century Massachusetts Bay Colony, John Winthrop reminded her, "Your conscience you must keep, else it must be kept for you."[28] In raising the specter of Salem witchcraft in later centuries, Americans warned each other that there were limits both to liberty and to power.

Notes

Introduction

1. Some of the more recent and best analyses from a variety of perspectives include Mary Beth Norton, *In the Devil's Snare: The Salem Witchcraft Crisis of 1692* (New York: Vintage Books, 2002); Paul S. Boyer and Stephen Nissenbaum, *Salem Possessed: The Social Origins of Witchcraft* (Cambridge, MA: Harvard University Press, 1974); Jane Kamensky, *Governing the Tongue: The Politics of Speech in Early New England* (New York: Oxford University Press, 1997); Carol F. Karlsen, *The Devil in the Shape of a Woman: Witchcraft in Colonial New England* (New York.: W. W. Norton, 1987); John Demos, *Entertaining Satan: Witchcraft and the Culture of Early New England* (New York: Oxford University Press, 1982); and Elizabeth Reis, *Damned Women: Sinners and Witches in Puritan New England* (Ithaca, NY: Cornell University Press, 1997).

2. For the best and most complete analysis of these narrative additions and their consequences, see Bernard Rosenthal, *Salem Story: Reading the Witch Trials of 1692* (New York: Cambridge University Press, 1993). In the concluding chapter of *Salem Story,* Rosenthal briefly considers Salem as a cultural metaphor, particularly in relation to the child sex abuse frenzy of the 1980s and 1990s. Philip Gould likewise considers the use of Salem as a metaphor in a specific time and place. While Gould also demonstrates how post-Revolutionary political anxieties are illuminated by using Salem as a metaphor in the Unitarian-Congregationalist battles in Boston in the early national period, I argue that such fears (and uses) predate his and are considered more broadly. See Philip Gould, "New England Witch-Hunting and the Politics of Reason in the Early Republic," *New England Quarterly* 68 (1995): 58–82. For considerations of Salem witchcraft as a plot device within American imaginary literature, see especially David Levin, *Forms of Uncertainty: Essays in Historical Criticism* (Charlottesville: University Press of Virginia, 1992); Lawrence Buell, *New England Literary Culture: From Revolution through Renaissance* (New York: Cambridge University Press, 1986); and Richard Slotkin,

Regeneration through Violence: The Mythology of the American Frontier, 1600–1860 (New York: HarperPerennial, 1996).

3. "Civil Liberties Union Praises Quiz Inquiry," *New York Times*, November 6, 1959. George Marshall, "Salem, 1950," *Masses and Mainstream* 3 (July 1950): 62–63. Hoover quotation: "How to Hunt Spies," editorial, *New York Times*, July 28, 1950. Also quoted in a news story in the same edition: "President Pledges Action on Traitors," *New York Times*, July 28, 1950. Hoover was fond of using the formula to express not what the agency was capable of but what "citizens" might do if "attempting to conduct their own investigations"; see, for instance, "F.B.I. Head Alerts Nation on Security," *New York Times*, February 28, 1951.

4. Benedict Anderson, *Imagined Communities: Reflections on the Origin and Spread of Nationalism,* new ed. (New York: Verso, 2006), 64. In fact, the term "American" can be questionable in itself, since it neglects the many nations in North and South America that are equally entitled to that designation. I use it here because I am considering a very nationalistic process that constantly relies on the cultural memory of Salem in defining specifically stated "American" values as internally understood.

5. Alon Confino, "Collective Memory and Cultural History: Problems of Method," *American Historical Review* 102 (December 1997): 1386n and 1399.

6. Barry Schwartz, *Abraham Lincoln and the Forge of National Memory* (Chicago: University of Chicago Press, 2000), 302.

7. This is in stark contrast to the largest field of memory studies, which centers on the Holocaust. The historians of the United States are later entrants into the field, and books include David Blight, *Race and Reunion: The Civil War in American Memory* (Cambridge, MA: Belknap Press, 2001); Marita Sturken, *Tangled Memories: The Vietnam War, the AIDS Epidemic, and the Politics of Remembering* (Berkeley: University of California Press, 1997); and Jerry Lembcke, *The Spitting Image: Myth, Memory, and the Legacy of Vietnam* (New York: New York University Press, 1998). These works show an evolving interest by American scholars in trauma and its cultural memory. The foundational works that shape the broader subfield of collective memory are Maurice Halbwachs, *The Collective Memory,* ed. and trans. Edward A. Cosner (Chicago: University of Chicago Press, 1992), and Pierre Nora, "General Introduction: Between Memory and History," in *Realms of Memory: The Constructions of the French Past*, vol. 1, *Conflicts and Divisions*, ed. Lawrence D. Kritzman, trans. Arthur Goldhammer (New York: Columbia University Press, 1997). The issue of trauma and collective memory has a vast literature, and a useful guide to the historiography can be found in Nancy Wood, *Vectors of Memory: Legacies of Trauma in Postwar Europe* (New York: Berg, 1999). The issues of suppressing and creating memory in relation to traumatic national events are represented well in Henry Russo, *The Vichy Syndrome: History and Memory in France since 1944,* trans. Arthur Goldhammer (Cambridge, MA: Harvard University Press, 1991), and Edward T. Linenthal, *The Unfinished*

Bombing: Oklahoma City in American Memory (New York: Oxford University Press, 2001).

8. A selection of excellent studies of American memory in this vein includes Robert S. Tilton, *Pocahontas: The Evolution of an American Narrative* (New York: Cambridge University Press, 1994); Michael Frisch, "American History and the Structures of Collective Memory: A Modest Exercise in Empirical Iconography," *Journal of American History* 75 (March 1989): 1130–55; Karal Ann Marling, *George Washington Slept Here* (Cambridge, MA: Harvard University Press, 1988); John Mack Farragher, *Daniel Boone: His Life and Legend* (New York: Owl Books, 1992); Merrill Peterson, *Lincoln in American Memory* (New York: Oxford University Press, 1994); John Seelye, *Memory's Nation: The Place of Plymouth Rock* (Chapel Hill: University of North Carolina Press, 1998); Wilbur Zelinsky, *Nation into State: The Shifting Symbolic Foundations of American Nationalism* (Chapel Hill: University of North Carolina Press, 1988); and David Thelen, "Memory and American History," *Journal of American History* 75 (1989): 1117–29. For brief mention of the memory of Salem witchcraft in historical and cultural studies, see Frank Wesley Craven, *The Legend of the Founding Fathers* (New York: New York University Press, 1956); Michael Kammen, *Mystic Chords of Memory: The Transformation of Tradition in American Culture* (New York: Vintage, 1993); Ann Uhry Abrams, *The Pilgrims and Pocahontas: Rival Myths of American Origin* (Boulder, CO: Westview Press, 1999); and David Lowenthal, *The Past Is a Foreign Country* (Cambridge: Cambridge University Press, 1988).

9. Slotkin, *Regeneration through Violence*, 313. John Mack Farragher's study of Daniel Boone works within such assumptions.

10. Edward Ingebretsen, *At Stake: Monsters and the Rhetoric of Fear in Public Culture* (Chicago: University of Chicago Press, 2001), 1–10, quotations on 4 and 44. Sociologists have been in the forefront of the study of social deviance and collective memory and have reached similar conclusions about the function of categories of deviance maintaining the boundaries of normative ideology and actions. The classic sociological study of Salem's 1692 society and deviance is Kai Erikson, *Wayward Puritans: A Study in the Sociology of Deviance* (New York: Wiley, 1966). On the seemingly universal tendency to classify groups into normal and deviant categories and the ways this is played out in collective memory, See especially Eviatar Zerubavel, *The Fine Line* (New York: Free Press, 1991); Gary Alan Fine, *Difficult Reputations: The Evil, the Inept, and the Controversial* (Chicago: University of Chicago Press, 2001); and Lembcke, *Spitting Image*.

11. Cynthia Ozick, *Metaphor and Memory: Essays* (New York: Alfred A. Knopf, 1989), 280.

12. My consideration of how Salem functions as a metaphor is informed by the work of George Lakoff and Mark Johnson. Lakoff and Johnson challenge the idea of metaphors as "ornamentation" and instead see them as embedding "the most fundamental values in a culture" to shape response and ensure social continuity.

As such, they argue, metaphors not only structure our entire conceptual system but "govern our everyday functioning." Lakoff and Johnson, *Metaphors We Live By* (Chicago: University of Chicago Press, 2003), 3-6. See also Max Black, *Models and Metaphors* (Ithaca, NY: Cornell University Press, 1962), 44–47.

13. While I find collective and cultural memory to be interchangeable within both formal and informal expressions, public memory seems to me to be more suited to memorialization projects with formal commemorative ritual. James Young has more recently introduced the term "collected memory" to describe what he sees as a process that actually is fragmented and highly individualized even within a social context. James E. Young, *The Texture of Memory: Holocaust Memorials and Meaning* (New Haven, CT: Yale University Press, 1994). In this book I have chosen to use the more traditional categories to reflect the nature of the process I am describing. Authors and orators are attempting to craft persuasive language that resonates with the most broadly distributed and understood moral narratives about the witchcraft trials. Young's concept, it seems to me, has more interpretive value for those events (like the Holocaust or September 11) in the age of instant mass communication where narratives are created in larger numbers and put in circulation quickly and widely, and where there is the opportunity to participate in a "virtual" way through such media as television or the Internet.

14. Merrill D. Peterson, *The Jefferson Image in the American Mind* (New York: Oxford University Press, 1970), xiii.

15. Ruth Miller Elson, *Guardians of Tradition: American Schoolbooks of the Nineteenth Century* (Lincoln: University of Nebraska Press, 1964).

Chapter One

1. John Hale, *A Modest Enquiry into the Nature of Witchcraft, and How Persons Guilty of that Crime may be Convicted: And the means used for their Discovery Discussed, both Negatively and Affirmatively, according to Scripture and Experience* (Boston: B. Green and J. Allen for Benjamin Eliot under the Town House, 1702), 24. According to Hale's title page, the account was actually written in 1697.

2. Cotton Mather, *Wonders of the Invisible World, Being an Account of the Tryals of Several Witches Lately Executed in New England: And of several remarkable Curiosities therein Occurring* (London: John Dunton, 1693), 16.

3. My own narrative is drawn from the extant legal records, contemporary accounts of the trials, and the many histories written over the past three hundred years. Direct quotations are cited individually. The original spelling and capitalization have been retained in passages taken from seventeenth-century documents. The first full scholarly edition of all the extant records relating to the trials was used as the authoritative source unless otherwise noted: Bernard Rosenthal, Gretchen Adams, Margo Burns, Peter Grund, Risto Hiltunen, Leena Kahlas-Tarkka,

Merja Kytö, Matti Peikola, Matti Rissanen and Richard Trask, eds., *Records of the Salem Witch-Hunt* (New York: Cambridge University Press, 2008). Hereafter *RSWH*, referenced by the edition's document numbers.

4. Deodat Lawson, *Christ's Fidelity the only Shield Against Satan's Malignity, Asserted in a Sermon Deliver'd at Salem-Village the 24th of March, 1692, Being Lecture-day there, and a time of Publick Examination, of some Suspected for Witchcraft,* 2nd ed. (London: R. Tookey, 1704). As authors would note in later accounts of the trials to make points about the essential "foreignness" of the charge of witchcraft, some of the most prominent jurists of seventeenth-century England were publicly debating the validity of witchcraft charges. Joseph Glanvil's *Saducismus Triumphatus,* published in 1681 in London, is the publication most commonly referred to as supporting the idea. For an overview of religious ideas operating in New England in the same period as both the English debates and the Salem cases, see David D. Hall, *Worlds of Wonder, Days of Judgment: Popular Religious Belief in Early New England* (Cambridge, MA: Harvard University Press, 1989), and for an analysis of the issues related to gender and Puritan theology, see Elizabeth Reis, *Damned Women: Sinners and Witches in Puritan New England* (Ithaca, NY: Cornell University Press, 1997).

5. Tituba is often portrayed in later histories and literature as of African descent. The contemporary accounts all describe her as Indian. For her origins and the issue of her "transformation" by historians, See Bernard Rosenthal, *Salem Story: Reading the Witch Trials of 1692* (New York: Cambridge University Press, 1993), chap. 1; Elaine Breslaw, *Tituba, Reluctant Witch of Salem: Devilish Indians and Puritan Fantasies* (New York: New York University Press, 1996); and Chadwick Hansen, "The Metamorphosis of Tituba, or Why American Intellectuals Can't Tell an Indian Witch from a Negro," *New England Quarterly* 47 (March 1974): 3–12.

6. Examination of Tituba, March 2, 1692. Salem Selections, Massachusetts Box, Essex County, New York Public Library. New York, New York.

7. In his examination by the court on August 29, 1692, William Barker Sr. testified to having seen about one hundred witches at a meeting in the area. "Examination of William Barker, Sr.," *RSWH*, doc. 525. Susannah Post's examination revealed that she saw two hundred at one meeting and claimed knowledge of five hundred witches in the colony. See "Examination of Susannah Post," *RSWH*, doc. 519. On the issue of the belief in a widespread conspiracy by Satan against the churches themselves as motivation for the acceleration of the witch hunt, see Benjamin C. Ray, "Satan's War against the Covenant in Salem Village, 1692," *New England Quarterly* 80 (March 2007): 69–95.

8. "Warrant for the Apprehension of Sarah Good, and Officer's Return," *RSWH*, doc. 1.

9. Rosenthal traces this addition to the Salem narrative to Upham's 1867 book, *Salem Story* (10–15). Rosenthal did not use the common school histories in his

consideration of the development of Salem narratives. He is correct in saying Upham's volumes appear to give it a particular credibility that establishes it in "serious" adult market histories after that point, but it was an idea widely distributed in print for the juvenile market since the first decade of the century, which might well be where Upham himself learned it. Mary Beth Norton considered a passage in John Hale's account of the trials, which also might be considered a contemporary fear of the role of folk magic in the Salem episode (frowned on, at best, by ministers like Hale), but both Hale and Norton effectively dismiss it as unrelated to the initiation or intensification of the 1692 events. Mary Beth Norton, *In the Devil's Snare: The Salem Witchcraft Crisis of 1692* (New York: Vintage Books, 2002), 23–24.

10. Bernard Rosenthal, "General Introduction," *RSWH*, 3.

11. "Petition of Israel Porter, et al. for Rebecca Nurse," *RSWH,* doc. 254. Bernard Rosenthal also discusses this dynamic specifically in his "General Introduction," *RSWH*, 13–14.

12. Thomas Brattle also makes a contemporary claim for the preferential treatment of some in his famous letter. See "Letter of Thomas Brattle," in George Lincoln Burr, *Narratives of the Witchcraft Cases, 1648–1706,* available online at: http://etext.lib.virginia.edu/salem/witchcraft/ (accessed April 5, 2004). The text of the Brattle letter was first printed in Thomas Brattle, "Copy of a MS. Letter... Written by Thomas Brattle, F.R.S. and Communicated to the Society by Thomas Brattle, Esq. of Cambridge," *Collections of the Massachusetts Historical Society* (1798), 61-80. For more on the Englishes, see Norton, *In the Devil's Snare*, 238–39.

13. The numbers vary according to later histories, but recently translated letters from a Dutch New Yorker who was in Boston during most of the crisis give us a figure of two hundred. Evan Haefeli, "Dutch New York and the Salem Witch Trials: Some New Evidence," *Proceedings of the American Antiquarian Society* 110 (October 2003): 303.

14. Hale, *Modest Enquiry*, 27.

15. "Return of Several Ministers" was included in Increase Mather, *Cases of Conscience Concerning Evil Spirits Personating Men; Witchcrafts, Infallible Proofs of Guilt in Such Are Accused with That Crime* (Boston: Benjamin Harris, 1693), 74. For a discussion of the dating of some of the publications, see Mary Rhinelander McCarl, "Spreading the News," *Essex Institute Historical Collections* 129 (January 1993): 54–58. For the most recent argument about the role of spectral evidence in English courts (in both the home country and the colonies) and its role in the Salem episode, see Norton, *In the Devil's Snare,* esp. 31–42 and 213–17.

16. For example, see Sarah Osburn's March 1, 1692, examination where the afflicted make claims in court about her alleged actions during the examination: "Examinations and Mittimus of Sarah Good, Sarah Osburn, & Tituba Recorded by John Hathorne," *RSWH*, doc. 4.

17. "Cotton Mather to John Richard," in Kenneth Silverman, *Selected Letters of Cotton Mather* (Baton Rouge: Louisiana State University Press, 1971), 35–40.

18. John and William Bly both testified that Bridget Bishop used "poppits" (puppets) to torment people and that they had personally seen these seven years earlier. See "Testimony of John Bly, Sr. and William Bly," *RSWH*, doc. 280.

19. "Letter of William Phips to the Privy Council, October 12, 1692," *RSWH*, doc. 693. Original, Colonial Office 5/857, British National Archives, London, 88. This can also be found in a modernized, edited form in Burr, *Narratives of the Witchcraft Cases*, 197. Phips apparently also sent a letter to New York ministers asking for their advice on witchcraft investigations and spectral evidence in trials. They agreed that Satan could indeed assume the guise of an innocent to torment victims. For a discussion of Phips's whereabouts during those critical months, see Norton, *In the Devil's Snare*, 287–88.

20. Norton, *In the Devil's Snare*, 304.

21. "Petition of Twenty-Six Andover Men Concerning Townspeople Accused of Witchcraft," *RSWH*, doc. 696.

22. Richard Godbeer, *Escaping Salem: The Other Witch Hunt of 1692*, New Narratives in American History (New York: Oxford University Press, 2005), 129.

23. We can, of course (and historians have long done so), find in the personal letters and diaries of the ministers involved a sense of their impressions of the public temper from their own complaints about it. Here I am concerned with determining how individuals within the wider community, especially accused witches (or their families), expressed their own opinions about events even in the limited way available in petitions and noting at what point in the event time line their language changed.

24. George Lee Haskins, *Law and Authority in Early Massachusetts: A Study in Tradition and Design* (New York: Macmillan, 1960), 197. On Puritan law and the nonuse of attorneys, as well as the role and function of petitioning, see also Cornelia Hughes Dayton, *Women Before the Bar: Gender, Law, and Society in Connecticut, 1639–1789* (Chapel Hill: University of North Carolina Press, 1995), and David Thomas Konig, *Law and Society in Puritan Massachusetts: Essex County, 1629–1692* (Chapel Hill: University of North Carolina Press, 1979).

25. I calculated the number of petitions from those found and verified within *RSWH*. From October through December 1692 there are twelve, for 1693 there is one, and the largest group is sixty from 1694 to 1750. It is unknown how many have been lost in the intervening centuries.

26. The portions of the text in brackets have been reconstructed from fragments and are included within the transcription found in "Petition of Twenty-Six Andover Men Concerning Townspeople Accused of Witchcraft," *RSWH*, doc. 696.

27. "Act to Reverse the Attainders of George Burroughs and Others for Witchcraft," *RSWH*, doc. 931.

28. "Petition of Abigail Faulkner Sr. for a Pardon," *RSWH*, doc. 711.

29. "Petition of Abigail Faulkner," *RSWH*, doc. 875. The 1703 petition by Francis Faulkner on behalf of his wife Abigail and others speaks of the "invalidity of the aforesaid Evidence and the great wrong which (through Errors &

mistakes in those tryalls) was then done." See "Petition of Francis Faulkner et al. to Clear the Records of Rebecca Nurse, Mary Esty, Abigail Faulkner Sr., Mary Parker, John Procter, Elizabeth Procter, Elizabeth How, Samuel Wardwell, & Sarah Wardwell," *RSWH*, doc. 876.

30. "Petition of Abraham Foster for Restitution for Anne Foster," *RSWH*, doc. 905; "Petition of Francis Johnson for Restitution for Elizabeth Johnson Jr.," *RSWH*, doc. 914; and "Petition of Samuel Nurse for Restitution for Rebecca Nurse," *RSWH*, doc. 921.

31. Cotton Mather noted in his diary the next day that his sleep the previous night had been "afflicted...with discouraging thoughts as if unavoidable Marks, of the Divine Displeasure must overtake my Family, for my not appearing with Vigor enough to stop the proceedings of the Judges when the Inextricable Storm from the Invisible World assaulted the Countrey." Cotton Mather, *Diary of Cotton Mather*, 2 vols. (Boston: Massachusetts Historical Society, 1911–12), 1:216.

32. "Petition of Ministers from Essex County," *RSWH*, doc. 878.

33. "Memorandum for Bill to Acquit Abigail Faulkner Sr. & Others," *RSWH*, doc. 880.

34. "Act to Reverse the Attainders of George Burroughs and Others for Witchcraft," *RSWH*, doc. 931.

35. The best and most straightforward time line of Salem's witch hunt from the first accusations in early 1692 to the last reversal of conviction in 2001 (which the acting governor of Massachusetts, Jane Swift, signed in a tasteless ceremony specifically scheduled for Halloween) can be found in the encyclopedic chronological study by Marilynne K. Roach, *The Salem Witch Trials: A Day-by-Day Chronicle of a Community under Siege* (Lanham, MD: Taylor, 2002).

36. Petition of Reverend William Milborne. The arrest warrant can be found in the National Archives, London, UK. Colonial Office 5/785: 336–37. I am using the printed copy from the *New England Historical and Genealogical Register and Antiquarian Journal* 27 (1873): 55.

37. "Letter of William Phips to the Privy Council, October 12, 1692," *RSWH*, doc. 693.

38. Deodat Lawson published *A Brief and True Narrative* in the first months of the episode and so, one assumes, never came under Phips's edict. The first edition (1692) was more reportage than reflective consideration of what was going on in Salem through the first week in April. The 1693 London edition provides a post-trial updating of the introduction that indicates he was well aware of the ongoing controversies over spectral evidence. But Lawson does not validate the skepticism about the issue. Instead he attempts to explain the irregularities that were by 1693 a matter of public discussion: "Satan did seem to Spin a finer Thred of Spiritual Wickedness than in ordinary methods of Witchcraft...[the judges] were inclined to admit the validity of such a sort of Evidence as was not so clearly and directly demonstrable to Human Senses." Deodat Lawson, *A Brief and True Narrative Of*

some Remarkable Passages Relating to Sundry Persons Afflicted by Witchcraft, at Salem Village Which happened from the Nineteenth of March, to the Fifth of April, 1692 (London: John Dunton, 1693).

39. McCarl, "Spreading the News," 39–61. McCarl connects printer Harris with "clandestine" political publications in London giving him, before his emigration, experience in "politically dangerous" situations. It is hard to know how, despite public opinion, printing for the government in Massachusetts Bay Colony was truly as dangerous as his activities in London in the 1680s, but he would be skilled at misrepresenting imprint information. Mather's account went through at least three printings in London in the first year of its publication, attesting to the interest in the trials in the capital. Ibid., 59.

40. As Bernard Rosenthal effectively argues, one comment by Increase Mather is consistently misunderstood. In his autobiography Mather says of the trials: "I doubt that innocent Blood was Shed." Rosenthal determined both from the context and from other diary entries that Mather meant "doubt" in the older sense of the word: "dread" or "fear," which changes the reading of the line dramatically. See Rosenthal, *Salem Story*, 250n60.

41. Quoted in Burr, *Narratives of the Witchcraft Cases*, 215.

42. Perry Miller, *The New England Mind: From Colony to Province* (Cambridge, MA: Harvard University Press, 1953), 204.

43. One final "official" narrative was completed but not published in the 1690s. John Hale's *Modest Enquiry into the Nature of Witchcraft* was not published until after his death in 1702. The minister at Beverley, just north of Salem, during the outbreak, Hale was described by Robert Calef as "very forward" in the initial stages of the witchcraft pursuit. Whatever his enthusiasm for finding the alleged witch conspiracy in the early months of 1692, by 1697 he had clearly reconsidered the entire episode. Describing the mood in the colony, Hale said, "it left in the minds of men a sad remembrance of that sorrowful time; and a Doubt whether some Innocent Persons might not Suffer, and some guilty Persons Escape." While paying his respects to the judges and juries as having "Integrity, with a zeal of God against Sin," he admitted that it was yet "unresolved" whether the courts nevertheless had used methods that were "insufficient and unsafe." Hale's statement might have been a bombshell if lobbed into the public awareness immediately after the trials, but by 1697 when he was writing, others had already expressed doubts, if not remorse. By 1702, when it was published, it could only support the arguments of Robert Calef's *More Wonders of the Invisible World* (written in 1697 as well), published in 1700.

44. Mather, *Wonders of the Invisible World*, 2, 16–19.

45. Quoted in Roach, *Salem Witch Trials*, 320.

46. Samuel Willard, "A Brief Account of a Strange and Unusual Providence of God," in *Useful Instructions for a Professing people in Times of Great Security and Degeneracy* (Cambridge, 1673), reprinted in *Groton Witchcraft Times*, ed. Samuel

A. Green (Groton, MA, 1883), 15. See also McCarl, "Spreading the News," 54–58.

47. Willard, *Some Miscellany Observations on Our Present Debates respecting Witchcrafts, in a Dialogue between S. & B.* (Philadelphia, 1692), 7, 15.

48. George Lincoln Burr, "Letter of Thomas Brattle," http://etext.lib.virginia.edu/salem/witchcraft/ (accessed May 16, 2006). Brattle's letter therefore had no effect on the opinion of the general public toward the trials, and what precise effect it had within the highest circles of Massachusetts Bay Colony as it was privately circulated during the last weeks of the witchcraft trials is unknown. No known public statement was made by him or anyone else of influence at a time when questioning procedure might have saved lives, but circulating manuscripts and letters like this makes it clear that some influential portion of the community was in discussion about the irregularities of the court. The first printing of Thomas Brattle's letter was after the Revolution. Rosenthal, *Salem Story*, 189.

49. Perry Miller expanded on Morison's comment when he quoted it by saying that Mather "tried to make those killings legitimate when he knew they were murders." For that alone, Miller concluded, "the right can was tied to the proper tail." Miller, *New England Mind*, 204.

50. For a discussion of the reception of Calef's book in Massachusetts, see McCarl, "Spreading the News," 39–61. The book appeared shortly afterward in Massachusetts Bay Colony with a Salem imprint. Quoted passages are taken from that edition. Robert Calef, *More Wonders of the Invisible World* (Salem, MA: William Carlton, 1700). The book had an enduring popularity in the United States with new editions appearing at least five times by 1870 (in 1796, 1823, 1828, 1861, and 1866). One question that has never been seriously addressed, however, is how Calef got the court transcripts from which he quotes so extensively. Calef's role as a public voice for families can be seen as the sort of "vernacular memory" that John Bodnar has defined as in opposition to the Mathers and other ministers who wrote an "official" version, see John E. Bodnar, *Remaking America: Public Memory, Commemoration, and Patriotism in the Twentieth Century* (Princeton, NJ: Princeton University Press, 1992), 20.

51. Robert Calef, *More Wonders*, 298–99. The rebuttal to Calef is attributed to Obadiah Gill (one of the seven signatories to the work), but the bulk of the text is a letter written by Cotton Mather, and its overall argument is generally believed to be his. In fact, the work is quite often is found in catalogs with Mather as sole author: this quotation is taken from Obadiah Gill and Cotton Mather, *Some Few Remarks upon a Scandalous Book Against the Government and Ministry of New England* (Boston: Printed by T. Green, 1701), 50. Perry Miller, *The New England Mind*, 2:196. Certainly the primary appeal for later readers of both Brattle's letter and Calef's book is the authors' seemingly "modern" orientation. In the excerpts from Brattle's letter in later publications, the difference between his prose and that found in Hale or Mather is significant, but I maintain that the overall attraction is

that both men appear to be closer to the secular sensibilities of the later writers and their readers because of their conclusions about the trials in general, if not in the particulars. See also Reis, *Damned Women*, 164–67. Reis argues that one important theological development resulting from the Salem episode was a change in the Puritan understanding of how Satan worked on earth. "The concept of evil changed as a result of the witchcraft trials. . . . People no longer thought of the devil as a physical entity; his powers were relegated to the realm of the merely spiritual . . . who tempted sinners and physically presided over hell, rather than one who preyed on people and possessed souls in the immediate, living world." Reis, *Damned Women*, 164. This is in answer to Perry Miller's famous statement that the intellectual history of New England up to 1720 can be written as though no such thing ever happened. "It had no effect on the ecclesiastical or political situation, it does not figure in the institutional or ideological development." Miller, *New England Mind*, 191. I would add that it has profound consequences for the political as well, both in its contemporary moment and in subsequent generations by its postmortem life as a metaphor.

52. Yael Zerubavel, "The Death of Memory and the Memory of Death: Masada and the Holocaust as Historical Metaphors," *Representations* 45 (Winter 1944): 73, 92.

53. Daniel Neal, *The History of New-England containing an impartial account of the civil and ecclesiastical affairs of the country to the year of our Lord, 1700* (London: J. Clark, R. Ford, and R. Cruttenden, 1720), 44; [Thomas] Salmon, Modern History, or The Present State of all Nations, vol. 31 (London: J. Roberts, 1738), 229; George Chalmers, "Continuation of Chalmers Political Annals," Collections of the New-York Historical Society for the year 1868 (New York: New-York Historical Society, 1868), 110. In 1831 a reviewer of another history would take a swipe at Chalmers for writing this as "a lame apology for the royal cause." *North American Review* 32 (January 1831): 179. Isaac Backus, *A Church History of New England* (Providence, RI: John Carter, 1784), 5.

54. William Douglass, *A summary, historical and political, of the first planting, progressive improvements, and present state of the British settlements in North-America* (Boston: Rogers and Fowle, 1749), 364, 449. Miller, *New England Mind*, 362.

55. Mr. [Nathaniel] Gardner, "Another Dialogue between the Clergyman and Layman," *New England Courant*, January 22, 1722. According to Leo LeMay, this article was one of three parodies of Cotton Mather's recently published work, *Sentiments on the Small Pox Inoculated* (Boston: S. Kneeland for Edwards, 1721). See http://www.english.udel.edu/lemay/franklin/citizen.html (accessed December 21, 2004). Mather wrote in his own diary about Gardner's several attacks, "Something must be done towards the Suppressing and Rebuking of those wicked Pamphlets, that are continually published among us, to lessen and blacken the Ministers, and poison the People." Mather, *Diary*, 2:674. Mather had earlier made a

similar complaint about the Franklin brothers' "vile paper" in virtually the same words and called their efforts on this and other subjects "a Wickedness never parallel'd any where upon the Face of the Earth!" Ibid., 2:663.

56. Miller, *New England Mind*, 357, 360–62. It should be noted that while Mather appears to be ahead of his time and Douglass distressingly backward for a physician, Mather's support of the procedure is based on reading one account, although he had medical "practitioner" Zabdiel Boylston publicly in his corner. Douglass's objection is that inoculation has not been proved either safe or useful in preventing disease. Once Douglass was convinced of the efficacy of the process he became a supporter (and a vocal one) during the 1730 epidemic. The ultimate irony would be that though Benjamin Franklin later became convinced of the importance of inoculation, he would himself lose a child to smallpox in 1736.

57. For analyses of the First Great Awakening that discuss the social implications and concerns raised by the revivals, See especially Alan Heimert, *Religion and the American Mind: From the Great Awakening to the Revolution* (Cambridge, MA: Harvard University Press, 1966). Heimert argues that there was the seed of a democratic and even revolutionary leveling in the movement. For a different view, See Butler, *Awash in a Sea of Faith: Christianizing the American People* (Cambridge, MA: Harvard University Press, 1990). By contrast, during the Second Great Awakening of the early nineteenth century, the differences in both print culture and public debates about revivals would provide a different social context, and Salem witchcraft would appear as a metaphor.

58. Thomas Hutchinson, *The History of the Colony and Province of Massachusetts-Bay*, vol. 2, ed. Lawrence Shaw Mayo (Cambridge, MA: Harvard University Press, 1936), 25, 62, and passim. For an extended evaluation of Hutchinson and the writing of his history of the colony, see also Bernard Bailyn, *The Ordeal of Thomas Hutchinson* (Cambridge, MA: Harvard University Press, 1974), and Edmund Morgan, *The Stamp Act Crisis* (Chapel Hill: University of North Carolina Press, 1953).

59. Unsigned letter to the editor, *Pennsylvania Gazette*, December 8, 1768. The inclusion of the three Quakers executed in Massachusetts Bay Colony in 1659–60 would appear intermittently with Salem witchcraft and, unlike Salem witchcraft, seldom appeared alone as a historical illustration.

60. John Leacock, *The First Book of the American Chronicles of the Times, 1774-75,* ed. with an introduction and notes by Carla Mulford (Newark: University of Delaware Press, 1987), quotations on 63, 12, 20. Alexander King, "Journal of Alexander King" (typescript), Connecticut Historical Society, book N5, July 26, 1776, 9. King was a physician, a patriot, and a prominent citizen of Suffield who served as a local selectman and state representative before and during the Revolution. As a selectman, King would have been involved in overseeing the duties of the committeemen assigned to his town. We can take his comment as a reflection of their enthusiasm for their duties. Biographical information, pers. comm.

Lester Smith, curator, Alexander King House, Suffield Historical Society, Suffield, CT.

61. Daniel Leonard, *Massachusettensis, or A Series of Letters, Containing A Faithful State of Many Important and Striking Facts which Laid the Foundation of the Present Troubles in the Province of the Massachusetts-Bay* (London: J. Matthews, 1776). Also printed in Boston newspapers in 1774, the *New Hampshire Gazette, and Historical Chronicle*, December 12, 1774, with slightly different orthography and editing. Italics in the original. John Adams, "Novanglus, or A History of the Dispute with America, from its Origin, in 1754, to the Present Time," in *The Works of John Adams, Second President of the United States*, vol. 4, ed. Charles Francis Adams (Boston: Charles C. Little and James Brown, 1851), viii. John Adams, *Diary and Autobiography of John Adams*, ed. Lyman H. Butterfield (Cambridge, MA: Harvard University Press, 1961), entry for March 5, 1775. As an educated man and a resident of the colony, Adams in particular had multiple ways he could have learned about Salem. Adams, *Diary*, Thursday August [7 or 14] and 1766 Wednesday August [6 or 13], 1766.

62. A good reason to doubt the local existence of a strong oral tradition about the trials might be that by the late eighteenth century no one could conclusively say where the gallows had been located in 1692. John Symonds, when he was nearly one hundred years old, reportedly told his physician that he had been born just before the first hangings and that the woman nursing his mother once told him that she saw the executions from a window in the Symonds house. Antiquarians in the early nineteenth century found that the traditional site of "Gallows Hill" could not be seen from the location of the Symonds house. John Adams's helpful diary has an entry related to this site as well. In August 1766, while visiting family in Salem, Adams records being taken for a walk after dinner to see "Witchcraft Hill." This notation led later searchers back to the traditional site of "Gallows Hill," while other efforts, such as amateur excavations in the early nineteenth century, led some to favor other Salem locations. For a very concise but exhaustive overview of the various claims, see Marilynne K. Roach, *Gallows and Graves: The Search to Locate the Death and Burial Sites of the People Executed for Witchcraft in 1692* (Watertown, MA: Sassafras Grove Press, 1997).

Chapter Two

1. Nathaniel Hawthorne, *The House of the Seven Gables* (New York: Modern Library, 2001), 16. Hawthorne found that combining history and fiction can have some unwelcome repercussions when a letter writer complained that the book had made his grandfather "infamous." As Hawthorne wrote to his publisher, James Fields, "Who would have dreamed that there were once Pyncheons in Salem!" Explaining that he had "pacified" the man with a "gentlemanly letter," he thought

the matter closed. More letters about the same issue, though, led him to again complain to Fields about "these Pyncheon jackasses." James T. Fields, *Yesterdays with Authors* (Boston: Houghton Mifflin, 1926), 58, 60.

2. Nathaniel Hawthorne to Elizabeth (Hawthorne) Manning, quoted in James R. Mellow, *Nathaniel Hawthorne in His Times* (Baltimore: Johns Hopkins University Press, 1980), 73–75 passim. He also suggested to Elizabeth that the two of them collaborate on the history assignment, since writing history was "so much less difficult" than writing standard magazine articles. Nathaniel Hawthorne to Elizabeth Manning Hawthorne, letter dated July 1837, quoted in John A. Garraty and Mark C. Carnes, eds. *American National Biography* (New York: Oxford University Press), 9:265. For an evaluation of this ongoing relationship with Goodrich as well as Hawthorne's lifelong financial woes, see also Lawrence Buell, *New England Literary Culture: From Revolution through Renaissance* (New York: Cambridge University Press, 1986). For a discussion about how Hawthorne's personal difficulties related to both his personal and his commercial connections and the effect they had on his literary reputation, see Jane Tompkins, *Sensational Designs: The Cultural Work of American Fiction, 1790–1860* (New York: Oxford University Press, 1999), 32–37.

3. Sarah Purcell in particular details this process from the end of the Revolution until about 1820, focusing on the use of Revolutionary history and symbols. See Sarah Purcell, *Sealed with Blood: War, Sacrifice, and Memory in Revolutionary America* (Philadelphia: University of Pennsylvania Press, 2002), 3. Likewise, Lauren Berlant detailed and defined the process of creating a "collective consciousness" with the specific intent of creating, in a national context, a "national subjectivity" that she defined as the sum of a culture's "icons, its metaphors, its heroes, its rituals, and its narratives," which make up a "collective consciousness." Lauren Berlant, *The Anatomy of National Fantasy* (Chicago: University of Chicago Press, 1991), 20. Jeremy Belknap was a clergyman, a historian, and a founder of the Massachusetts Historical Society. Gordon Wood, *The Radicalism of the American Revolution* (New York: Vintage, 1991), 213.

4. The idea of a relentlessly forward-living culture is one that I think is obvious in the economic, political, and geographic expansionism of the next few decades. I am, of course, working from Michael Kammen's discussion about a "visionary polity." On the tension between embracing the past and rejecting it in the antebellum decades, see especially Michael Kammen, *Mystic Chords of Memory: The Transformation of Tradition in American Culture* (New York: Vintage, 1993) 11, 35. On post-Revolutionary attempts to define a new social as well as political order, see also Caroll Smith-Rosenberg, "Dis-Covering the Subject of the 'Great Constitutional Discussion,' 1786–1789," *Journal of American History* 79 (1992): 841–73; Benedict Anderson, *Imagined Communities: Reflections on the Origin and Spread of Nationalism,* new ed. (New York: Verso, 2006), 64; and Wood, *Radicalism of the American Revolution,* 229–32.

5. On popular politics following the Revolution, much of the best work not only examines the role of class, race, and gender within popular politics but looks at how the celebration of the political nation helped define both the citizen and the political role of the noncitizen. Some of the best studies include David Waldstreicher, *In the Midst of Perpetual Fetes: The Makings of American Nationalism* (Chapel Hill: University of North Carolina Press, 1996); Len Travers, *Celebrating the Fourth: Independence Day and the Rites of Nationalism in the Early Republic* (Amherst: University of Massachusetts Press, 1997); Simon P. Newman, *Parades and the Politics of the Street: Festive Culture in the Early Republic* (Philadelphia: University of Pennsylvania Press, 1997); Sean Wilentz, *Chants Democratic: New York City and the Rise of the American Working Class, 1788–1850* (New York: Oxford University Press, 1984); Gary B. Nash, *Forging Freedom: The Formation of Philadelphia's Black Community, 1720–1840* (Cambridge, MA: Harvard University Press, 1988); and Catherine Allgor, *Parlor Politics: In Which the Ladies of Washington Help Build a City and a Government* (Charlottesville: University Press of Virginia, 2000). On the role of the press, see also Jeffrey L. Pasley, *The Tyranny of Printers: Newspaper Politics in the Early American Republic* (Charlottesville: University Press of Virginia, 2001); Charles E. Clark, *The Public Prints: The Newspaper in Anglo-American Culture, 1665–1740* (New York: Oxford University Press, 2001); Richard D. Brown, *Knowledge Is Power: The Diffusion of Information in Early America, 1700–1865* (New York: Oxford University Press, 1989); and Michael Warner, *The Letters of the Republic: Publication and the Public Sphere in Eighteenth-Century America* (Cambridge, MA: Harvard University Press, 1990). For the classic discussion of the newspaper as an instrument of nationalism within a creole population in North America, see Anderson, *Imagined Communities*, 203.

6. Simon Newman also comments on his use of "American" to refer to both the contemporary self-designator and the process of creating an American nationalism, which I follow. See Newman, *Parades and Politics*, 199. For the role of rhetoric in shaping expectations and the difficulty of inculcating appropriate republican virtues widely, see also Wood, *Radicalism of the American Revolution*; Joyce Appleby, *Capitalism and a New Social Order: The Republican Vision of the 1790s* (New York: New York University Press, 1984); and Wilbur Zelinsky, *Nation into State: The Shifting Symbolic Foundations of American Nationalism* (Chapel Hill: University of North Carolina Press, 1988). David Waldstreicher also considers the "didactic aspects of celebrations" that include spectatorship as well as participation. See Waldstreicher, *In the Midst of Perpetual Fetes*, 73. Effective symbols could transform ideology into action that had political and social consequences. See especially Caroline Winterer, "From Royal to Republican: The Classical Image in Early America," *Journal of American History* 91, no. 4 (March 2005): 1264–90.

7. Purcell, *Sealed with Blood*, 3, 2, 5, 7. Simon Newman addressed this within his own discussion of the need for "ordinary" people to feel that participation was

available to them and that the rites were commonplace rather than extraordinary. Newman, *Parades and Politics,* 11-43. See also Waldstreicher, *In the Midst of Perpetual Fetes,* 53–56 and 73–77; Smith-Rosenberg, "Dis-Covering the Subject," 841–73; Catherine Albanese, *Sons of the Fathers: The Civil Religion of the American Revolution* (Philadelphia: Temple University Press, 1976); and Kammen, *Mystic Chords of Memory,* 101-9.

8. Gordon Wood describes virtue as something absolutely required in a republic. Gordon S. Wood, *Creation of the American Republic, 1776–1787* (Chapel Hill: University of North Carolina Press, 1998), 420.

9. For the role of the villain as a political symbol in the case of Arnold, see also Gary Alan Fine with Lori J. Ducharme, "Benedict Arnold and the Commemoration of Treason," in *Difficult Reputations: Collective Memories of the Evil, Inept, and Controversial,* ed. Gary Alan Fine (Chicago: University of Chicago Press, 2001), 36, 32. Certainly there are often, as there are in every society, active efforts by some factions to promote a particular collective memory narrative designed to obscure other possible interpretations of the past. For some specific examples of this in an American context, see especially Michael Schudson, *Watergate in American Memory: How we Remember, Forget, and Reconstruct the Past* (New York: Basic Books, 1992), 52–53; Marita Sturken, *Tangled Memories: The Vietnam War, the AIDS Epidemic, and the Politics of Remembering* (Berkeley: University of California Press, 1997), 7–9: and Gaines M. Foster, *Ghosts of the Confederacy: Defeat, the Lost Cause and the Emergence of the New South* (New York: Oxford University Press, 1987). An excellent case study within a non–United States context is, of course, the recasting of the Vichy regime as the work of only a few malefactors within a larger national collective memory of widespread and heroic resistance in Henry Rousso, *The Vichy Syndrome: History and Memory in France since 1944,* trans. Arthur Goldhammer (Cambridge, MA: Harvard University Press, 1991), 5–10 and 60–97.

10. Charles Royster, "'The Nature of Treason': Revolutionary Virtue and American Reactions to Benedict Arnold," *William and Mary Quarterly,* 3rd ser. 36 (April 1979): 186. On Benedict Arnold's reputation and the issue of the utility of the one-dimensional, irredeemable villain in American culture in particular, see Gary Alan Fine, *Difficult Reputations: The Evil, the Inept, and the Controversial* (Chicago: University of Chicago Press, 2001). Recent studies that have considered the use of collective memory in creating marginalized symbols also include Jerry Lembcke, *The Spitting Image: Myth, Memory, and the Legacy of Vietnam* (New York: New York University Press, 1998); Karen Halttunen, *Murder Most Foul: The Killer and the Gothic Imagination* (Cambridge, MA: Harvard University Press, 1998); and Edward Ingebretsen, *At Stake: Monsters and the Rhetoric of Fear in Public Culture* (Chicago: University of Chicago Press, 2003).

11. Ingebretsen, *At Stake,* 1–10, quotes from 4 and 8. Ingebretsen is particularly useful on the issue of dehumanizing "social monsters" toward cultural-political

ends. My discussion here is obviously limited to the political utility of such cultural "monsters," who are most effective in a one-dimensional form in rhetoric; hence my use of Ingebretsen's categories of "sacred" and "taboo" and the creation of such "monsters" in public discourse. For the role of the more complex symbol and the dichotomy between the related concepts of the "sacred and profane," see especially Mircea Eliade, *The Sacred and the Profane: The Nature of Religion* (New York: Harcourt, 1968); Jonathan Z. Smith, *To Take Place: Toward Theory in Ritual* (Chicago: University of Chicago Press, 1992); and Jonathan Smith, *Imagining Religion: From Babylon to Jonestown* (Chicago: University of Chicago Press, 1988).

12. Gary Alan Fine describes the need to destroy the reputation of the defined villain so that he is "irredeemable" in order to have maximum utility. Fine, *Difficult Reputations,* 34–35. A generally approved heroic model within political rhetoric provides more latitude for interpretation. The case of Joan of Arc is a good example. While one end of the political spectrum in France venerates her for her piety, the opposition approves of her presumed dedication to justice. They may disagree on the terms of her goodness, but both agree on the critical issue–her cultural importance as a symbol for emulation. See especially Michael Winock, "Joan of Arc," in *Realms of Memory: The Construction of the French Past,* ed. Pierre Nora and Lawrence D. Kritzman, trans. Arthur Goldhammer (New York: Columbia University Press, 1992), 433–82.

13. Purcell, *Sealed with Blood,* 6. Sarah Purcell also discusses the usefulness of Ernest Renan's definition of nationalism to understanding the American process of defining within the terms of a "mythic past." For Renan's argument, see Ernest Renan, "Qu'est-ce qu'une nation?" in *Nationalism,* ed. John Hutchinson and Anthony D. Smith (New York: Oxford University Press, 1994), 17. On origins myths and nationalism, see also Anderson, *Imagined Communities,* and Hayden White, *Metahistory: The Historical Imagination in Nineteenth-Century Europe* (Baltimore: Johns Hopkins University, 1973).

14. Joseph Story, "A Discourse Pronounced at the Request of the Essex Historical Society, September 18, 1828," in *Commemoration of the First Settlement of Salem, Massachusetts* (Boston: Hilliard, Gray, Little, and Wilkins, 1828), 60–61.

15. Albrecht Koschnik, "Young Federalists, Masculinity, and Partisanship during the War of 1812," in *Beyond the Founders: New Approaches to the Political History of the Early American Republic,* ed. Jeffrey L. Pasley and David Waldstreicher (Chapel Hill: University of North Carolina Press, 2004), 166.

16. New Englanders were indeed well situated to pursue this goal through a cultural inclination to preserve records of the past. For efforts in the region before 1815, see, for example, David Van Tassel, *Recording America's Past: An Interpretation of the Development of Historical Studies in America, 1607–1884* (Chicago: University of Chicago Press, 1960), esp. part 3, and Frank Wesley Craven, *The Legend of the Founding Fathers* (New York: New York University Press, 1956), 1-55. Stephen Nissenbaum provides the best evaluation of this process and its

effectiveness. Even if, as he suggests, the pastoral vision of New England that was relentlessly promoted was never quite a reality, it was nonetheless so much an article of faith that even most New Englanders believed it, despite all evidence to the contrary. Stephen Nissenbaum, "New England as Region and Nation," in *All Over the Map: Rethinking American Regions,* ed. Edward Ayers, Patricia Nelson Limerick, Stephen Nissenbaum, and Peter Onuf (Baltimore: Johns Hopkins University Press, 1996), 38–61. The phrase "errand in the wilderness" comes from Perry Miller, "Errand into the Wilderness," *William and Mary Quarterly,* 3rd ser., 9 (January 1953): 3–32. For recent discussions on the origins and concept of an American "exceptionalism," see Michael Kammen, "The Problem of American Exceptionalism: A Reconsideration," *American Quarterly* 45, no. 1 (March 1993): 1–43, and John M. Murrin, "The Jeffersonian Triumph and American Exceptionalism," *Journal of the Early Republic* 20 (Spring 2000): 1–25.

17. Wood, *Creation of the American Republic,* 418. This is obvious in the concurrent rise of Daniel Boone as a contemporary hero in 1784, when John Filson's biography of Boone was published, emphasizing the same qualities.

18. Richard Slotkin, *Regeneration through Violence: The Mythology of the American Frontier, 1600–1860* (New York: HarperPerennial, 1996), 310, 269.

19. John Seelye, *Memory's Nation: The Place of Plymouth Rock* (Chapel Hill: University of North Carolina Press, 1998), 157.

20. Isaac Allerton, *History of the Pilgrims, or A Grandfather's Story of the First Settlers of New England* (Boston, 1831), 1.

21. As Lawrence Buell and Michael Kammen have concluded, I believe it is obvious that the Puritan was the dominant cultural figure before at least 1870. For "the prevalence of the Puritans" in imaginary literature in the first half of the nineteenth century, see Seelye, *Memory's Nation,* 157, and Buell, *New England Literary Culture,* 193-260. This is in contrast with most who have studied the invention of the symbolic "Pilgrims" and "Puritans" from the perspective of Plymouth. But all admit that the two are conflated until some point (it varies) between 1850 and 1900. John Seelye in his compendious study of Plymouth Rock and the role of the Pilgrim figure does see the conflation and some of the ways the Puritan figure is dominant. Michael Kammen refers to the regional symbolic settler as "blended" after 1820. Kammen, *Mystic Chords of Memory,* 64. Joseph Conforti argues that the Pilgrim was always the primary figure and that the Puritan was "Pilgrimized" to hide his unpleasant historical presence in the New England narrative. Joseph Conforti, *Imagining New England: Explorations of Regional Identity from the Pilgrims to the Mid-Twentieth Century* (Chapel Hill: University of North Carolina Press, 2001). Ann Uhry Abrams, primarily concentrating on the iconography related to both groups, gives yet another date and reason. Ann Uhry Abrams, *The Pilgrims and Pocahontas: Rival Myths of American Origin* (Boulder, CO: Westview Press, 1999), 180.

22. M[arcius] Wilson [*sic*], "Review of American Common School Histories," *Biblical Repository and Classical Review* 59 July 1845: 517. The author of this

article is actually Marcius Willson, one of the most popular of the schoolbook authors. This is a print version of a speech that he gave before a group of educators, mainly to promote his own new history. Willson said that the eight most popular authors nationally were Salma Hale, John Frost, Samuel Goodrich, Charles Goodrich, Emma Willard, John Olney, William Grimshaw, and Noah Webster. His conclusions seem to be based more on his own sense of his competition than on any real investigation. Many thanks to Peter Knupfer for verifying Willson's identity from his own research. For an example of the numbers involved in editions of just one popular school history, Charles Goodrich's *History of the United States* went into at least forty-four editions.

23. Ruth Miller Elson, *Guardians of Tradition: American Schoolbooks of the Nineteenth Century* (Lincoln: University of Nebraska Press, 1964), 340.

24. Benjamin Rush, "Thoughts upon the Mode of Education Proper in a Republic," in *The Selected Writings of Benjamin Rush,* ed. Dagobart D. Runes (New York: Philosophical Library, 1947), 92 and 91. Rush's ideas are very similar to Noah Webster's on this issue.

25. Noah Webster, *A Grammatical Institute of the English Language* (Hartford, CT: Huntington and Hopkins, 1784), 14; Carl F. Kaestle, *Pillars of the Republic, 1780–1860* (New York: Hill and Wang, 1983), 5. On the value of education to a republican form of government, see also Jonathan Messerli, "The Columbian Complex: The Impulse to National Consolidation," *History of Education Quarterly* 7 (Winter 1967): 421; David B. Tyack, "Forming the National Character: Paradox in the Educational Thought of the Revolutionary Generation," *Harvard Educational Review* 36 (Winter 1966): 29-41; and Noah Webster, "The Education of Youth," in *A Collection of Essays and Fugitive Writings on Moral, Historical, Political, and Literary Subjects* (Boston, 1794).

26. David D. Hall, "Readers and Writers in Early New England," in *The Colonial Book in the Atlantic World,* vol. 1, ed. Hugh Amory and David D. Hall (New York: American Antiquarian Society and Cambridge University Press, 2000), 121; Kammen, *Mystic Chords of Memory,* 70.

27. Noah Webster, *A Grammatical Institute of the English Language,* pt. 1 (New York: E. Ducykinck, 1904), iii.

28. This work was an expansion of his original schoolroom book *Geography Made Easy: Being an Abridgment of the "American Universal Geography" first published in 1784.* The prefatory notes in Morse's various editions, and especially his copious correspondence housed at Sterling Library, Yale University, provide a useful view of the reception of his books, readers' expectations, and the attitude of both Morse and his correspondents, who range from merchants and surveyors taking issue with details of local geography to historian Jeremy Belknap. See especially Jedidiah Morse to Jeremy Belknap, January 18, 1788; and, William Poole to Jedidiah Morse, September 21, 1792, Morse Family Papers, Special Collections, Sterling Memorial Library, Yale University. For the idea of the way identity was constructed using cartography, literature, and other cultural artifacts in England, a

process similar to what occurred later in the United States, see Richard Helgerson, *Forms of Nationhood: The Elizabethan Writing of England* (Chicago: University of Chicago Press, 1992).

29. Elson, *Guardians of Tradition*, 9. See also William J. Gilmore, *Reading Becomes a Necessity of Life: Material and Cultural Life in Rural New England, 1780–1835* (Knoxville: University of Tennessee Press, 1989). On the importance of education in early national America and the nationalist orientation of schoolbooks, see also Waldstreicher, *In the Midst of Perpetual Fetes*, and, Melvin C. Yazawa, "Creating a Republican Citizenry," in *The American Revolution: Its Character and Limits*, ed. Jack P. Greene (New York: New York University Press, 1987), and Van Tassel, *Recording America's Past*, 90. Ruth Elson also notes that by 1860 there were only twelve public school systems nationally, with six in New England and six private concerns run by churches. Elson, *Guardians of Tradition*, 5. On education and whites in the southern states, see also John McCardell, *The Idea of a Southern Nation: Southern Nationalism, 1830–1860* (New York: W. W. Norton, 1979), 179. Benedict Anderson also briefly mentions the role of schools in inculcating nationalism. Anderson, *Imagined Communities*, 113.

30. Daniel Fenning, *The Universal Spelling Book* (Baltimore: William Warner, 1802), 157. For a complete discussion of this method and its origins, see especially Elson, *Guardians of Tradition*, 8–11; Frances FitzGerald, *America Revised: History Schoolbooks in the Twentieth Century* (New York: Vintage Books, 1980), 18-19; John Nietz, *Old Textbooks: Spelling, Grammar, Reading, Arithmetic, Geography, American History, Civil Government, Physiology, Penmanship, Art, Music, as Taught in the Common Schools from Colonial Days to 1900* (Pittsburgh: University of Pittsburgh, 1961), 234; Charles Carpenter, *History of American Schoolbooks* (Philadelphia: University of Pennsylvania, 1963); and Daniel H. Calhoun, "Eyes for the Jacksonian World: William C. Woodbridge and Emma Willard," *Journal of the Early Republic* 4 (Spring 1984): 1–26.

31. Quotations in order: Hannah Adams, *An Abridgement of the History of New England* (Boston: Etheridge and Bliss, 1807), 183; Jesse Olney, *A History of the United States: On a New Plan, Adapted to the Capacity of Youth* (New Haven, CT: Durrie and Peck, 1836), 69; Samuel G. Goodrich, *Peter Parley's Pictorial History of North and South America* (Hartford, CT: House and Brown, 1848); and, A. B. Berard, *School History of the United States*, rev. ed. (Philadelphia: Cowperthwait, 1867), 34. See also Joseph Emerson, *Questions and Supplement to Goodrich's "History of the United States"* (Boston: Richardson and Lord, 1829), 100.

32. For a general discussion of the shift in authorship, see Elson, *Guardians of Tradition*, 9; Buell, *New England Literary Culture*, 41–42; George H. Callcott, "History Enters the Schools," *American Quarterly* 11 (Winter 1959): 473; and Rolla M. Tryon, *The Social Sciences as School Subjects* (New York: Ginn, 1935), 121. A few authors, most notably Samuel Goodrich, published a variety of American histories for different grade levels. I have reviewed eighty of the pre-1860

histories (including within that category geographies and readers with historical selections) for content relating to colonial British North America and more specifically Salem witchcraft. I will be treating them as belonging to one evolving group rather than as books specific to a decade. The practice of "compiling" from previous books and the multiple editions of the same book for decades provides a similarity across the history texts that remains until well after the Civil War.

33. Benson J. Lossing, *A Pictorial History of the United States for Schools and Families* (New York: F. J. Huntington-Mason Brothers, 1854), iii.

34. For examples of this in introductory passages, see Adams, *Abridgement of the History of New England*, 3, and Charles A. Goodrich, *A History of the United States of America, on a Plan Adapted to the Capacity of Youths*, 35th ed. (Boston: Richardson, Lord, and Holbrook, 1832), 3. In regard to this method of assembly, see Elson, *Guardians of Tradition*, 10.

35. Elson, *Guardians of Tradition*, vii. Frances Fitzgerald finds much of the same orientation in the schoolbooks of the late nineteenth and early twentieth centuries. She does, however, claim that the way textbooks "now hint at a certain level of unpleasantness in American history" is recent. It is not. Nineteenth-century schoolbooks page for page feature more death, disaster, and condemnation of historical actors than any contemporary volumes. They are now, however, less likely to claim that misfortune is either divinely directed or a result of weak character. Fitzgerald, *America Revised*, 9.

36. Elson, *Guardians of Tradition*, 174. Elson says that in nineteenth-century textbooks "the roots of American civilization are not Southern." This same orientation toward the narrative of colonial founding can be found in the annual orations of the New England Society. See especially Robert C. Winthrop, "Address," in *New England Society Orations: Orations, Sermons, and Poems Delivered Before the New England Society in the City of New York, 1820–1885*, ed. Cephus Brainerd and Eveline Warner Brainerd, 2 vols. (New York: Century, 1901), 1:231, 243, and Charles Brickett Hadduck, "The Elements of National Greatness," ibid., 272–73.

37. Quotations in order: Emma Willard, *Abridged History of the United States*, improved ed. (New York: A. S. Barnes, 1846), 42; Samuel G. Goodrich, *A Pictorial History of the United States: with Notices of Other Portions of America; for the Use of Schools* (New York: Huntington and Savage, 1843), 374; Willard, *Abridged History of the United States*, 114, 23, 42; S. Goodrich, *Pictorial History*, 374, 362.

38. Quotations in order: Selma Hale, *History of the United States: From Their First Settlement as Colonies, to the Close of the War with Great Britain in 1815, to Which Are Added Questions, Adapted to the Use of Schools* (Philadelphia: Uriah Hunt, 1835), 17–19; Lossing, *Pictorial History of the United States*, 50; Noah Webster, *Elements of Useful Knowledge: Containing Historical and Geographical Accounts of the United States, for the Use of Schools*, 3rd ed., vol. 1 (New London: Printed for O. D. Cooke by Ebenezer P. Cady, 1807), 89.

39. Strictly speaking, Massachusetts Bay Colony included the present state of Maine and the eastern shore of Rhode Island and excluded present-day Plymouth County. The nonstandardized approach that many of the authors take to the historical boundaries of both Virginia and Massachusetts Bay Colonies makes exact comparisons difficult, but New England is clearly given the greater coverage in any configuration of the region, and Massachusetts receives the lion's share of the attention given to New England in any book.

40. Quotations in order: Webster, *Elements of Useful Knowledge*, 92; Charles Goodrich, *A History of the United States of America, on a Plan Adapted to the Capacity of Youth*, 2nd ed. (New York: Collins, 1825), 21; Goodrich, *Pictorial History of North and South America*, 405, 408, 401, 397; Emma Willard, *Abridged History of the United States, or Republic of America*, New and enlarged ed. (New York: A. S. Barnes, 1852), 114; Jedidiah Morse and Elijah Parish, *A Compendious History of New England*, 2nd ed. (Amherst, MA: Thomas and Whipple, 1809), 198. For similar descriptions, see also *Goodrich, History of the United States*, 21; Frederick Butler, *A Complete History of the United States of America* (Hartford: Frederick Butler, 1821), 107; and Jedidiah Morse, *The American Geography* (Elizabethtown, NJ: Shepard Kollock, 1789), xx. Ruth Elson also noted the regional biases in schoolbooks, particularly that the South as a region is "subject to sustained criticism." Elson, *Guardians of Tradition*, 173.

41. Joseph Emerson, *Questions and Supplement to Goodrich's "History of the United States"* (Boston: Jenks, Palmer, 1850), 8.

42. Emma Willard, "Introduction," in Willard, *History of the United States, or the Republic of America* (New York: White, Gallagher, and White, 1828). Goodrich, *History of the United States of America*, 35th ed. (1832), 2. The book had gone through thirty-five editions since 1823.

43. Butler, *Complete History of the United States of America*, 193. [Charles Prentiss] A Citizen of Massachusetts, *History of the United States of America* (Keene, NH: John Prentiss, 1822), 47.

44. Quotations in order: Rufus Adams, *The Young Gentleman and Lady's Explanatory Monitor* (1815), quoted in Elson, *Guardians of Tradition*, 214; Hale, *History of the United States*, 44; William Grimshaw, *History of the United States from Their First Settlement as a Colony to the Cession of Florida* (Philadelphia: Benjamin Warner, 1821), 58; Morse, *American Geography*, 191; and Samuel G. Goodrich, *Peter Parley's Pictorial History of North and South America, by S. G. Goodrich: Illustrated with More Than Three Hundred Engravings* (Hartford, CT: Peter Parley, 1858), 492.

45. Quotations in order: Grimshaw, *History of the United States*, 57; Egbert Guernsey, *History of the United States, Designed for Schools* (New York: Cady and Burgess, 1851), 119; Goodrich, *Peter Parley's Pictorial History of North and South America* (1858), 469; Adams, *Abridgement of the History of New England*, 82; and Goodrich, Peter Parley's Pictorial History (1858), 464, 469. See also Abiel Holmes, *American Annals, or A Chronological History of America*, vol. 2 (Cam-

bridge, MA: W. Hilliard, 1805), 5; George Quackenbos, *Primary History of the United States, Made Easy and Interesting for Beginners* (New York: D. Appleton, 1868), 139-40; and Goodrich, *Peter Parley's Pictorial History of North and South America* (1858), 497 and 493.

46. Morse, *American Geography*, 192; Samuel G. Goodrich, *The First Book of History for Children and Youth* (Boston: Richardson, Lord and Holbrook, 1831), 37; J. L. Blake, The Historical Reader, Designed for the Use of Schools and Families (Rochester, NY: E. Peck, 1829), 263; Olney, *History of the United States*, 70; Goodrich, *Peter Parley's Pictorial History of the United States* (1858), 81; and John Howard Hinton, *The History and Topography of the United States of North America, Brought Down from the Earliest Period*, 2nd ed. (Boston: Samuel Walker, 1843), 71. For similar passages see, for example, Hale, *History of the United States*, 45; Samuel Goodrich, *Peter Parley's Book of the United States, Geographical, Political, and Historical* (Boston: C. J. Hendee, 1837), 139; Willard, *History of the United States* (1828), 127; and Webster, *Elements of Useful Knowledge*, 150.

47. Emerson, *Questions and Supplement to Goodrich's History* (1829), 89; Samuel G. Goodrich, *The First Book of History: For Children and Youth* (Cincinnati: C. D. Bradford, 1832), 37; Marcius Willson, *History of the United States, from the Earliest Discoveries to the Present Time* (New York: Newman and Ivison, 1853), 93; Webster, *Elements of Useful Knowledge*, 150; Grimshaw, *History of the United States*, 55; and Goodrich, *Peter Parley's Pictorial History of North and South America* (1858), 489.

48. Uncle Philip [Francis Lister Hawks], *History of the United States, or Uncle Philip's Conversations with the Children about Massachusetts* (New York: Harper, 1835), 210. Hinton, *History and Topography of the United States*, 71; Olney. *History of the United States*, 67; Goodrich, *First Book of History for Children and Youth*, 28; and *Olney, History of the United States*, 67.

49. Quotations in order: R. Thomas, *A Pictorial History of the United States, from the Earliest Discoveries* (Hartford: E. Strong, 1847), 200; Charles Goodrich, *History of the United States* (1825), 68; and Olney, *History of the United States*, 69–70.

50. Holmes, *American Annals*, 438. Holmes specifically refers to the Thomas Brattle letter from 1692 and to Hutchinson's history of the trials that was reprinted in the *Proceedings of the Massachusetts Historical Society* just before his own history was published. Holmes, *American Annals*, 6; Grimshaw, *History of the United States*, 57; Goodrich, *History of the United States*, 94–95; John *Frost, An Illuminated History of the United States, from the Earliest Period to the Present Time* (New York: Henry Bill, 1854), 255; and Adams, *Abridgement of the History of New England*, 82, 160.

51. Thomas Hutchinson, *The History of the Colony and Province of Massachusetts-Bay*, vol. 2, ed. Lawrence Shaw Mayo (Cambridge, MA: Harvard University Press, 1936), 25, 62, and passim. Hutchinson's entire original draft

was published privately in 1870. The editor of that version, William Poole, used it to promote the collections of the Massachusetts Historical Society. This version includes Hutchinson's notes on sources and his comments about other versions. Thomas Hutchinson, *The Witchcraft Delusion of 1692* [from an unpublished manuscript in the Massachusetts Archives] with notes by William Frederick Poole (Boston: Privately printed, 1870).

52. George Bancroft, *History of the United States, from the Discovery of the American Continent* (Boston: Charles C. Little and James Brown, 1844), 3:86, 87, 90, 95, 96, 98. For example, R. Thomas's *Pictorial History of the United States,* published in 1845, clearly shows that his compiling was done from the volumes of Bancroft already in print, such as this one; see especially pages 200–208 in Thomas.

53. John Neal originally published *Rachel Dyer: A North American Story,* in 1828. It is available in a modern edition: John Neal, *Rachel Dyer* (New York: Prometheus Books, 1996). John William De Forest's 1856 *Witching Times* is currently out of print. John Greenleaf Whittier used Salem in a number of poems related to antislavery arguments, and he was also a descendant of Susanna Martin, hanged in 1692. His 1857 poem "The Witch's Daughter" is assumed to be about his ancestor. Nathaniel Hawthorne, a descendant of John Hathorne, a judge in the Salem court, produced a number of works based on Puritan themes; the most notable using Salem are the short stories "Alice Doane's Appeal" and "Young Goodman Brown." Both are available in modern anthologies: Nathaniel Hawthorne, *Tales and Sketches* (New York: Library of America, 1982). His novel of Salem's legacy in one family, *The House of the Seven Gables,* is included in Nathaniel Hawthorne, *Collected Novels* (New York: Library of America, 1983).

54. Buell, *New England Literary Culture,* 210–11.

55. Ibid.

56. Examples of these include the novel by Eliza Buckminster Lee, *Delusion, or The Witch of New England* (Boston: Hilliard, Gray, 1840); a novel published under two different titles by William L. Stone, *The Witches: A Tale of New England* (Bath, NY: R. L. Underhill, 1837) and *Mercy Disborough* [sic] (Bath, NY: R. L. Underhill, 1844); and the novel (credited to a likely pseudonym) Harry Halyard, *The Haunted Bride, or The Witch of Gallows Hill, a Romance of the Olden Time* (Boston: F. Gleason, 1848). Stage plays include Cornelius Mathews's *Witchcraft, or The Martyrs of Salem* produced in 1846–47, and, *Superstition* by James Nelson Barker, produced in 1824. Buell, *New England Literary Culture,* 213.

57. The studies of the development of Salem witchcraft as a subject for fiction and other literary genres are many. The best of these include Buell, *New England Literary Culture,* and Slotkin, *Regeneration through Violence.* Other useful studies that focus on either the general evolution of Salem witchcraft as a literary theme or examinations of specific repeating elements of the episode in American literature include David Levin, *In Defense of Historical Literature: Essays on American History, Autobiography, Drama, and Fiction* (New York: Hill and Wang, 1967),

and James D. Hartman, *Providence Tales and the Birth of American Literature* (Baltimore: Johns Hopkins University Press, 1999).

58. Nathaniel Hawthorne, "Main Street," in *Twice Told Tales* (Boston: Ticknor and Fields, 1854), 1.

59. Hartman, *Providence Tales*, 102.

60. Buell, *New England Literary Culture*, 250. Buell also discusses at length the 1857 novel by Josiah Gilbert Holland, *The Bay Path*, which transplants the story of Salem witchcraft to western Massachusetts and is based closely on Holland's research for his nonfiction *History of Massachusetts*, published in 1855. For an analysis of Hawthorne's attitudes toward the Puritan past, see Michael Colacurcio, *The Province of Piety: Moral History in Hawthorne's Early Tales* (Cambridge, MA: Harvard University Press, 1984).

Chapter Three

1. "Comments on the Times," *New England Magazine* 7 (November 1834): 407–13, quotation on 408. The magazine misspelled his name, calling him Robert "Matthies." Paul E. Johnson and Sean Wilentz, *The Kingdom of Matthias: A Story of Sex and Salvation in 19th Century America* (New York: Oxford University Press, 1994), 145. See also Thomas M. McDade, "Matthias, Prophet Without Honor," *New-York Historical Society Quarterly* 62 (1977): 311–34. For coverage of the trial in the New York press from October 1834 through April 1835 in addition to the *Sun*, see *Evening Post; Commercial Advertiser; and New-York Observer*. For periodical coverage of the trials, see "Matthias and His Impostures," *North American Review* 89 (1835): 307–27. Several pamphlets and books quickly appeared detailing the most scandalous aspects of belief and conduct, which include *Memoirs of Matthias the Prophet, with a Full Exposure of His Atrocious Impositions, and of the Degrading Delusions of His Followers* (New York: New York Sun Press, 1835); [Margaret Matthews], *Matthias: By His Wife* (New York, 1835); G[ilbert] Vale, *Fanaticism: Its Source and Influence, Illustrated by the Simple Narrative of Isabella, in the Case of Matthias, Mr. And Mrs. B. Folger, Mr. Pierson, Mr. Mills, Catherine, Isabella, &c., &c.*, 2 vols. (New York, 1835); W. E. Drake, *The Prophet! A Full and Accurate Report of the Judicial Proceedings in the Extraordinary and Highly Interesting Case of Matthews, Alias Matthias* (New York, 1834); and William L. Stone, *Matthias and His Impostures, or The Progress of Fanaticism, Illustrated in the Extraordinary Case of Robert Matthews, and Some of His Forerunners and Disciples* (New York: *Sun* Press, 1835). See also *New York Daily Tribune*, December 5, 1849.

2. For a discussion of the role that print culture and particularly early daily newspapers (often called the "penny press") played in shaping public perceptions during the sensational trials of the nineteenth century, see Alexander Saxton, *The*

Rise and Fall of the White Republic: Class Politics and Mass Culture in Nine-teenth Century America (New York: Verso, 1988); Dan Schiller, *Objectivity and the News: The Public and the Rise of Commercial Journalism* (Philadelphia: University of Pennsylvania Press, 1988); and Patricia Cline Cohen, Timothy J. Gilfoyle, Helen Lefkowitz Horowitz, and the American Antiquarian Society, *The Flash Press: Sporting Male Weeklies in 1840s New York* (Chicago: University of Chicago Press, 2008). In regard to specific trials, one should start with the 1836 Helen Jewett murder, for which the Matthias scandal acted as a "dress rehearsal": Patricia Cline Cohen, *The Murder of Helen Jewett* (New York: Vintage, 1998); for a discussion of the moral dimension of the narratives of murder, see Karen Halttunen, "Early American Murder Narratives: The Birth of Horror," in *The Power of Culture: Critical Essays in American History,* ed. Richard Wightman Fox and T. J. Jackson Lears (Chicago: University of Chicago Press, 1993). Forty years after the Matthias trial brought sex, religion, and newspapers together, the Beecher-Tilton scandal showed the maturation of the form. See Richard Wightman Fox, *Trials of Intimacy: Love and Loss in the Beecher-Tilton Scandal* (Chicago: University of Chicago Press, 1999).

3. "Comments on the Times," 409; "Matthias and His Impostures," 324.

4. Salma Hale, *History of the United States: From Their First Settlement as Colonies, to the Close of the War with Great Britain in 1815; to Which Are Added Questions, Adapted to the Use of Schools* (Philadelphia: Uriah Hunt, 1835), 46–47.

5. "Infatuation and Imposture," *New-York Mirror,* October 11, 1834, 119. See also Karen Halttunen, *Confidence Men and Painted Women: A Study of Middle-Class Culture in America, 1830-1870* (New Haven, CT: Yale University Press, 1982).

6. Stone, *Matthias and His Impostures,* 321 and 16. On his friendship with and sympathy for the Folgers, see Johnson and Wilentz, *Kingdom of Matthias,* 165-67. Although Johnson and Wilentz do not mention this link (or Stone's novel), they mention Ann Folger's maiden name in their discussion of her background (29). There was in fact a historical basis for naming an accused "witch" Mercy Disborough, as Stone himself notes in the introduction to the novel.

7. Alon Confino, "Collective Memory and Cultural History: Problems of Method," *American Historical Review* 102 (December 1997): 1388.

8. Jon Butler, *Awash in a Sea of Faith: Christianizing the American People* (Cambridge, MA: Harvard University Press, 1990), 247, 236–37. On various antebellum religious movements discussed in this chapter, see especially Nathan O. Hatch, *The Democratization of American Christianity* (New Haven, CT: Yale University Press, 1989); Paul E. Johnson, *A Shopkeepers' Millennium: Society and Revivals in Rochester, New York, 1815–37* (New York: Hill and Wang, 2004); Richard L. Bushman, *Joseph Smith and the Beginnings of Mormonism* (Urbana: University of Illinois Press, 1985); Kenneth H. Winn, *Exiles in a Land of Liberty: Mormons in America* (Chapel Hill: University of North Carolina Press, 1989); Jan Shipps,

Mormonism: The Story of a New Religious Tradition (Urbana: University of Illinois Press, 1985); Terryl L. Givens, *The Viper on the Hearth: Mormons, Myths, and the Construction of Heresy* (New York: Oxford University Press, 1997); D. Michael Quinn, *Early Mormonism and the Magic World View* (Salt Lake City, UT: Signature Books, 1987); R. Laurence Moore, *Religious Outsiders and the Making of Americans* (New York: Oxford University Press, 1986); Bret E. Carroll, *Spiritualism in Antebellum America* (Bloomington: Indiana University Press, 1997); and David Chapin, *Exploring Other Worlds: Margaret Fox, Elisha Kane, and the Antebellum Culture of Curiosity* (Amherst: University of Massachusetts Press, 2003).

9. Quotations in order, all from the *Evangelical Magazine and Gospel Advocate*: "*History* vs. Millerism," 14 (March 17, 1843): 85; "The End of the World," 13 (September 16, 1842): 293; "Millerism Coming at Last," 13 (August 12, 1842): 234. See also "Comments on the Times," 409. In addition, the words "infatuation," "delusion," and "imposture" were used repeatedly in the review of Stone's book on the scandal by the *North American Review*. See Stone, "Matthias and His Impostures," 307-27 passim. The uproar over the Matthias case in the New York press was about his ability to "dupe" the Piersons and the Folgers and the sexual innuendo involved in the case. The possible murder of Pierson was spoken of more as a consequence of the crime than as the primary crime itself. See "Matthias the Prophet," *Christian Secretary* 13 (October 4, 1834): 151; "Infatuation and Imposture," 119; "Memoirs of Matthias the Prophet, with a Full Exposure of His Atrocious Imposture," *Workingman's Advocate* 6 (May 16, 1835).

10. "The Rebuke of the Spiritualists," *New York Times*, September 29, 1854, 6; Charles G. Leland, "The Ash Tree," *Continental Monthly* 2 (December 1862): 684.

11. David Brion Davis, "Some Themes of Counter-subversion: An Analysis of Anti-Masonic, Anti-Catholic, and Anti-Mormon Literature," *Mississippi Valley Historical Review* 47 (September 1960): 204–24. For a discussion of this in relation to the Matthias case, see Johnson and Wilentz, *Kingdom of Matthias*, 152. In relation to the Latter-day Saints, see Winn, *Exiles in a Land of Liberty*, 73. Although many of the debates include the term republican as understood by the combatants and appeal to this vision of that philosophy, I argue that by the 1830s the invocation of "republicanism" itself was a metaphor of sorts. Evidence for this is in the competing visions found in the debates (although Winn makes no such claim for metaphor status in regard to republicanism, I am working from his original observations in his discussion of the role of "republicanism" as a concept in anti-Mormon rhetoric). See Winn, *Exiles in a Land of Liberty*, introduction.

12. Quoted in Elson, *Guardians of Tradition*, 340.

13. Butler, *Awash in a Sea of Faith*, 236–37.

14. William R. Hutchinson, *Religious Pluralism in America: The Contentious History of a Founding Ideal* (New Haven CT: Yale University Press, 2003), 32, 35.

15. Jenny Franchot, *Roads to Rome: The Antebellum Protestant Encounter with Catholicism* (Berkeley: University of California Press, 1994), xvii. Franchot argues that anti-Catholicism "operated as an imaginative category" that helped define a Protestant middle-class identity.

16. 6. Davis, "Some Themes of Counter-subversion," 224. Davis ascribes the use of these themes to anxiety over social and economic change in an era of national expansion as well as nativism. Kenneth Winn, however, sees the issue of "republicanism" coming into the "anti" literature only after the Latter-day Saints' arguments in defense of the church were made on those grounds. See Winn, *Exiles in a Land of Liberty*, 4–5. I argue that while these issues were certainly inherent in much of the usage, the fundamental issue was proscribing cultural boundaries. The idea of "outsider" religions, as defined both externally and internally by these groups, is of course from Moore's *Religious Outsiders and the Making of Americans*. See especially chapter 1 for a discussion of the use of oppositional self-definition by the Latter-day Saints. For a discussion of this approach in schoolbooks, see Elson, *Guardians of Tradition*, 62.

17. Elson, *Guardians of Tradition*, 47.

18. Judge Addison of Pennsylvania, quoted in Gordon Wood, *The Radicalism of the American Revolution* (New York: Vintage, 1991), 363.

19. Noah Webster, *A Grammatical Institute of the English Language* (Hartford, CT: Huntington and Hopkins, 1784), pt. 1, introduction, iii.

20. "Petition of John Procter from Prison," in Robert Calef, *More Wonders of the Invisible World* (Salem, MA: William Carlton, 1700), 105. The original document no longer exists except in the form printed in Calef's book.

21. Franchot, *Roads to Rome*, 18–20, population figures, 31n128. Many states did not keep the restriction on officeholding long, and Massachusetts dropped its own in 1833, shortly before the Charlestown riot. On Anti-Catholicism in colonial American, see also "The Image of the Beast: Anti-papal Rhetoric in Colonial America," in *Conspiracy: The Fear of Subversion in American History*, ed. Richard O. Curry and Thomas M. Brown (New York: Holt, Rinehart, and Winston, 1972), and Ray Allen Billington, The *Protestant Crusade, 1800–1860: A Study of the Origins of American Nativism* (Chicago: Quadrangle, 1964).

22. "The Roman Catholics," *Episcopal Watchman* 3 (July 25, 1829): 150. The article also says that the *Watchman* had no desire to use "abusive or opprobrious epithets" and instructs readers that Roman Catholics "exceedingly dislike the terms…papery, papist…Romanish" and "require that we call them by no other name than that of Roman Catholic." Roger Finke and Rodney Stark, *The Churching of America, 1776–1990* (New Brunswick, NJ: Rutgers University Press, 1992), 111. The 1830 Census provides a total United States population of 12,858,670. http://www2.census.gov/prod2/decennial/documents/1830a-01.pdf (accessed on August 28, 2005).

23. David Brion Davis, "Some Ideological Functions of Prejudice in Ante-Bellum America," *American Quarterly* 15 (Summer 1963): 115. The only literature

approaching it in intensity are the anti-Mormon publications, which use many of the same themes with appropriate alterations.

24. Billington, *Protestant Crusade*, 345.

25. "Popery and Paganism," *Religious Monitor and Evangelical Repository* 9 (December 1832): 429. This article was noted as reprinted from the *Christian Spectator; Dr. Scudder's Tales for Little Readers, about the Heathens* (New York: American Tract Society, 1849); Elson, *Guardians of Tradition of Tradition*, 62.

26. "The Question Stated: Political and Religious Romanism," *Baltimore Literary and Religious Magazine* 1 (August 1835): 234–36 passim.

27. Billington, *Protestant Crusade*, 67.

28. "Manuela, or The Victim of a Convent," *Boston Pearl and Literary Gazette* 4 (June 13, 1835): 321.

29. "Clerical Hostilities," *North American Magazine* 2 (July 1833): 193, 194.

30. Billington, *Protestant Crusade*, 361. "Narrative of Rebecca Theresa Reed," *Literary Gazette* 2 (April 17, 1835): 7.

31. Davis, "Some Ideological Functions of Prejudice," 119.

32. Daniel A. Cohen, "Passing the Torch: Boston Firemen, 'Tea Party' Patriots, and the Burning of the Charlestown Convent," *Journal of the Early Republic* 24 (Winter 2004): 538. See also Franchot, *Roads to Rome,* and Billington, *Protestant Crusade.*

33. Billington, *Protestant Crusade*, 73.

34. Cohen, "Passing the Torch," 580. Billington, *Protestant Crusade*, 101-6. Reed's story of her life in the Ursuline convent, however, was soon eclipsed by the publication of the more widely remembered and infamous Maria Monk's *Awful Disclosures of the Hôtel Dieu Nunnery of Montreal.* Monk was eventually discredited by her personal life and by journalist William Stone's expedition to the Hôtel Dieu to look for evidence of the "strangled infants" from "unholy unions," and she did not continue to enjoy her sympathetic notoriety. William L. Stone was the same New York editor who had made such a success of the Matthias story several years earlier.

35. Quoted in "Great Riot at Charlestown, Massachusetts: Burning of the Nunnery," *Workingman's Advocate* 6 (August 16, 1834): 3. The *Workingman's Advocate* and the *Man* were weekly newspapers associated with the first labor movement in the United States in the 1820s and 1830s.

36. Paul Gilje, *The Road to Mobocracy: Popular Disorder in New York City, 1763-1834* (Chapel Hill: University of North Carolina Press, 1987), vii. See also David Grimsted, "Rioting in Its Jacksonian Setting," *American Historical Review* 77 (April 1972): 361-97. Kimberly K. Smith, *Dominion of Voice: Riot, Reason, and Romance in Antebellum Politics* (Lawrence: University Press of Kansas, 1999), 76-82. Smith rejects Paul Gilje's conclusion that hegemonic forces in the shape of middle-class values eventually quelled mob action in favor of institutional force in the form of police. While debates continue about whether social pressure from emerging middle-class notions of order, propriety, and property quelled the riots

of the 1830s and 1840s or whether it was the establishment of police forces, what we can see is a recurrent pattern of post-Revolutionary concern for order and control as virtues reflecting a rational society.

37. Paul O. Weinbaum, *Mobs and Demagogues: The New York Response to Collective Violence in the Early Nineteenth Century* (Minneapolis: UMI Research Press, 1979), 1; "Important Events and Occurrences, during the Year A.D. 1834," *American Magazine of Useful and Entertaining Knowledge* 1 (January 1, 1835): 216. Accounts of the riots were spread from local newspapers to other regions. See, for example, "Riots in Philadelphia," *Maine Farmer and Journal of the Useful Arts* 2 (August 22, 1834): 254. The latter article was noted as originally appearing in the *Philadelphia Pennsylvanian*.

38. "The Late Outrage at Charlestown," *Christian Examiner and General Review* 17 (September 1834): 134.

39. "The Charlestown Riots," *Workingman's Advocate* 6 (August 1834): 2. This was reprinted from the Charlestown local newspaper the *Bunker Hill Aurora* from October 25, 1835.

40. M. J. S., "Retrospect of the Past Year," *United States Catholic Magazine and Monthly Review* 4 (January 1845): 5.

41. Billington, *Protestant Crusade*, 85.

42. Rev. J. L. Blake, *A Geography for Children* (Boston: Richardson, Lord and Holbrook, 1831), 60. See also Caleb Alexander, *The Young Gentlemen and Ladies Instructor* (Boston: Larkin and Blake, 1797), 187; and By a Teacher, *The Village School Geography,* 3rd ed. (Hartford, CT: Reed and Barber, 1837), 43.

43. Samuel Goodrich, *A Pictorial History of America; Embracing Both Northern and Southern Portions of the New World* (Hartford, CT: House and Brown, 1847), 464.

44. M. J. S., "Retrospect of the Past Year," 5. This is one of the few times any "burning" claim arises in connection with Salem before the pro-slavery oratory of the late 1840s and into the 1850s, when it becomes an established part of the folklore about Salem in 1692. It is significant that it appears within a rebuttal to charges of European persecutions, since European witches were often executed by burning at the stake. But as in the use of "burning witches" by the pro-slavery forces in the 1850s, the assignment of this supposed fate for the convicted at Salem attempts to obscure the history of burning at the stake both in lynching and in the Inquisition by claiming that Salem's brutality matched that documented by their own historical episode under attack. It certainly is not part of the account of American colonial witchcraft cases by George Bancroft or either of the Goodriches, as the editorial asserts.

45. A Protestant, "Religious Liberty," *New York Times*, September 7, 1854, 2.

46. James D. Bratt, "Religious Anti-revivalism in Antebellum America," *Journal of the Early Republic* 24 (Spring 2004): 68-72. See also Jon Butler, "Enthusiasm Described and Decried: The Great Awakening as Interpretive Fiction," *Journal of*

American History 69 (September 1982): 305–25; Christine Leigh Heyrman, *Southern Cross: The Beginnings of the Bible Belt* (Chapel Hill: University of North Carolina Press, 1998); and Johnson, *Shopkeepers' Millennium.*

47. Joseph Emerson Worcester, "Religious Denominations," in *American Almanac and Repository of Useful Knowledge for the Year 1839* (Boston: Charles Bowen, 1838), 172. Worcester's numbers are hardly scientific, but what is critical is that the denominational reports and articles in the public press reflect what most people in the United States understood about the number of the churched from the individual sources they encountered. With publications such as Worcester's table, those assumptions (right or wrong) were reinforced.

48. Butler, *Awash in a Sea of Faith,* 247. For the "syncretism" of magic and other similar folk practices in many Christian denominations in this period, see ibid., 255.

49. Heyrman, *Southern Cross,* quotations from 64, 61, 73, 75. See also Butler, *Awash in a Sea of Faith,* 164–65.

50. Webster, *Elements of Useful Knowledge: Containing Historical and Geographical Accounts of the United States, for the Use of Schools,* 3rd ed., vol. 1 (New London: Printed for O. D. Cooke by Ebenezer P. Cady, 1807), 256. See also Hugh Murray, *The Encyclopaedia of Geography* (Philadelphia: Lea and Blanchard, 1839), 534, and Jedidiah Morse and Sidney Edwards Morse, *A New System of Geography, Ancient and Modern: For the Use of Schools* (Boston: Richardson and Lord, 1824), 262.

51. "West Indies Slavery," *Connecticut Courant,* January 6, 1824, and "Wyandott Indians," *Ithaca (New York) American Journal,* November 15, 1820, provide good examples of this common assumption.

52. "Eccentric Character," *Haverhill Gazette,* February 16, 1828.

53. Bratt, "Religious Anti-revivalism," 72, 94, 97.

54. "The Pioneer," *Correspondent* 4 (September 6, 1828): 111–12.

55. Carla Gardina Pestana, "The Quaker Executions as Myth and History," *Journal of American History* 80 (September 1993): 441–69. The most famous of the four executed Quakers (and undoubtedly the only one most of us could name if pressed) is Mary Dyer, who, since the tercentennial of her original conviction in 1959, is commemorated in bronze on the Massachusetts State House lawn as a "witness for Religious freedom."

56. S. Goodrich, *Pictorial History* (1850), 462.

57. Pestana, "Quaker Executions," 460.

58. "Address, Leonard Bacon, 1838," in The New England Society Orations: Addresses, Sermons, and Poems Delivered before the New England Society of New York, 1820-1885, vol. 1, collected and ed. Cephas Brainerd and Eveline Warner Brainerd (New York: Century, 1901), 196–97.

59. Benson J. Lossing, *A Pictorial History of the United States for Schools and Families* (New York: F. J. Huntington-Mason Brothers, 1854), 90–91.

60. Jedidiah Morse, *American Geography* (London: John Stockdale, 1792), 189.

61. Lossing, *Pictorial History,* 92 and 90. Many other histories referred to this example either explicitly or implicitly by speaking of some Quakers as violating "the decencies of social intercourse" in their actions. Charles Goodrich, *A History of the United States of America, on a Plan Adapted to the Capacity of Youths,* 35th ed. (Boston: Richardson, Lord, and Holbrook, 1832), 56. See also Pestana, "Quaker Executions," 445. George Bancroft, whose account of Puritan Massachusetts Bay Colony would become a significant part of the historical community's long-running "indictment of the Puritans," claimed that the "common mind disenthralled itself" from religious "superstition" to end the witch hunt. Emma Willard similarly finds the Puritans becoming "convinced of their error" and ending the arrests and executions of Quakers. George Bancroft, *History of the United States, from the Discovery of the American Continent* (Boston: Charles C. Little and James Brown, 1844), 3:93–98; Emma Willard, *History of the United States, or the Republic of America* (New York: White, Gallagher, and White, 1828), 183, 115.

62. J[ohn] G[reenleaf] W[hittier], "Evangeline—the Puritans," *National Era,* January 27, 1848, 13. Schoolbook authors also viewed with distaste the appearance of courting martyrdom. See Charles Goodrich, *History of the United States,* 56; Hale, *History of the United States,* 37; and Lossing, *Pictorial History of the United States,* 91.

63. E. B. H., "Fanaticism," *Monthly Miscellany of Religion and Letters* 9 (October 1843): 193–95. As mentioned earlier, for a good discussion of fearing the manner of action more than doctrinal heresies, see Hutchinson, *Religious Pluralism,* esp. 32–35.

64. Ann Braude, *Radical Spirits: Spirtualism and Women's Rights in Nineteenth-Century America,* 2nd ed. (Bloomington: Indiana University Press, 2001), 10.

65. Ibid., chap. 1; Butler, *Awash in a Sea of Faith,* 25.

66. "Modern Necromancy," *North American Review* 80 (April 1855): 513. John W. Hurn, letter to the editor, *New York Tribune,* February 25, 1850.

67. Butler, *Awash in a Sea of Faith,* 252–54.

68. Ibid., 253.

69. Braude, *Radical Spirits,* 7; Butler, *Awash in a Sea of Faith,* 253. For this reason it is unknown exactly how many Americans ever regularly or occasionally dabbled in Spiritualist practices. Historians have, however, disagreed about the source of Spiritualism's appeal to mid-nineteenth-century Americans. Ann Braude finds diverse reasons that range from grief reactions to entertainment to rebellion against both authority and mortality. Braude, *Radical Spirits,* 2. Jon Butler emphasizes that Spiritualism served to "satisfy" the search for "supernatural medical regimens" and the interest in millennialism. Butler, *Awash in a Sea of Faith,* 253.

70. Jon Butler stresses that Spiritualism was considered part of a Protestant-based faith system before 1870, in part because ministers regularly inveighed against it, demonstrating that it was seen as drawing followers from their congregations. Butler, *Awash in a Sea of Faith*, 253.

71. "Mesmer and Swendenborg," *United States and Democratic Review* 20 (February 1847): 107.

72. "Forthcoming Dramatic Novelty," *United States and Democratic Review* 32 (June 1853): 551.

73. "A Convention of Spiritualists," *Philadelphia Public Ledger,* August 11, 1852, 2; "To Diamonion, or the Spiritual Medium," *National Era* 6 (December 9, 1852): 200. In this article the author draws no fewer than five analogies between Salem and Spiritualism.

74. "Salem Witchcraft," *Littell's Living Age* 145 (August 15, 1868): 408.

75. "The Wakeman Tragedies—Popular Delusions and Superstitions," *Brooklyn Daily Eagle*, January 5, 1856, 2.

76. The spirits contacted came under criticism as well for "behaving no better than loafers and rowdies up town on New Year's Eve." "The Disembodied Spirits at Rochester," *New York Herald,* January 23, 1850.

77. "Modern Spiritualism," *Putnam's Monthly Magazine* 1 (January 1853): 1, 62.

78. "Are the Phenomena of Spiritualism Supernatural?" *New Englander and Yale Review* 18 (May 1860): 405.

79. *New York Herald*, January 23, 1850. This is a common theme that appears repeatedly in the 1850s and 1860s in various forms. See also "Column for the Curious," *Brooklyn Daily Eagle*, March 26, 1855, 2.

80. Joseph Smith's family had lived in Topsfield, Essex County, Massachusetts, near Salem for at least four generations by the early nineteenth century. See Shipps, *Mormonism*, 4-5, for genealogical information.

81. Jeffrey A., "European Emigration and New England Puritanism," *Southern Literary Messenger* 37 (August 1863): 467.

82. "Convention of Spiritualists."

83. Benjamin Park, "Letter from New York," *Southern Literary Messenger* 16 (July 1850): 450. Some critics, like W in a letter to the editor of the *New York Tribune* on February 4, 1850, before the Fox sisters arrived in New York City, were more direct in their condemnation and charges of fraud: "These girls would rather tell a lie than the truth." In 1885, in her memoir of the heady days when her sisters were the talk of New York, A. Leah (Fox) Underhill directly compared what she called "the mob" that criticized them to those who hanged witches in Salem almost two hundred years before. See A. Leah Underhill, *The Missing Link in Modern Spiritualism (*New York, 1885), 178.

84. "Curiosities of Puritan History: Witchcraft," *Putnam's Monthly Magazine* 9 (April 1857): 251.

85. "Are the Phenomena of Spiritualism Supernatural?" 405.

86. Hannah Adams, *An Abridgement of the History of New England* (Boston: Gray, 1806), 160. Similar sentiments are found in Charles Goodrich, *History of the United States*, 68, and Uncle Philip [Francis Lister Hawks], *History of the United States, or Uncle Philip's Conversations with the Children about Massachusetts* (New York: Harper, 1835), 150.

87. "Modern Necromancy," 523.

88. Ibid., 524. Clairvoyance was also occasionally mentioned along with Spiritualism as "repeating the history of witchcraft." Such things "Cotton Mather loved." See George M. Beard, "The Delusions of Clairvoyance," *Scribner's Monthly* 18 (July 1879): 433.

89. "On Somnambulism," *Living Age* 61 (October 1, 1859): 3.

90. Stone, *Matthias and His Impostures*, 325; "Matthias and His Impostures," *North American Review* 41 (October 1835): 326.

91. For a general overview of the history and practices of Joseph Smith and the Church of Jesus Christ of Latter-day Saints, and the opposition to them, see Bushman, *Joseph Smith*; Winn, *Exiles in a Land of Liberty;* Shipps, *Mormonism*; Givens, *Viper on the Hearth*; Quinn, *Early Mormonism*; and Moore, *Religious Outsiders*. The specific threats to social, political, and economic order believed to be posed by Mormons are also addressed in Sarah Berringer Gordon, *The Mormon Question: Polygamy and Constitutional Conflict in Nineteenth-Century America* (Chapel Hill: University of North Carolina Press, 2002), esp. chap. 3, and Gregory Pingree, "The Biggest Whorehouse in the World": Repression of Plural Marriage in Nineteenth-Century America," *Western Humanities Review* 50 (Fall 1996): 213–32.

92. Allen G. Campbell, "Utah: Has It a Republican Form of Government?" *Century* 23 (March 1882): 712. The political dimensions of the anti-Mormon activities are well documented in all the general histories of the Latter-day Saints mentioned in this chapter, but two particularly good discussions are found in Gordon, *The Mormon Question,* and Klaus J. Hansen, *Quest for Empire: The Political Kingdom of God and the Council of Fifty in Mormon History* (Lincoln: University of Nebraska Press, 1974).

93. "Mormon" or "Mormonite" was meant to be distinctly pejorative in the nineteenth century. Members of the Latter-day Saints more commonly referred to themselves as "Saints" (as did the Plymouth colonists in the seventeenth century) to mark their determination to follow Christ like the early church. The Utah-based church has reclaimed the term in the twentieth century, attesting to the power of language in shaping experience and effectively removing it from the arsenal of critics. Although commonly written as "Latter Day Saints," the church officially adopted the lowercase *d* in its name in the 1850s, and that form is used here except where specifically quoted from other print sources.

94. "The Mormonites," *Evangelical Magazine and Gospel Advocate* 2 (October 19, 1833): 335. The article is attributed to an unspecified edition of the *Sentinel*

and Star in the West. See Shipps, *Mormonism,* 158–59. Even twenty years later, when the anti-Mormon campaign was fully and nearly universally established in every print genre, there were still admissions within otherwise critical articles of the "outrages" suffered by Mormons. In Nauvoo, Illinois, for instance, one magazine claimed that problems there stemmed from local gentiles colluding in "a vast scheme of robbery in order to obtain the lands and improvements of the Mormons without paying for them." "Nauvoo and Deseret," *National Magazine* 4 (June 1854): 487.

95. Eber D. Howe, *Mormonism Unvailed [sic], or A Faithful Account of That Imposition and Delusion, from Its Rise to the Present Time, with Sketches of the Characters of Its Propagators* (Plainsville, OH, 1834), ix. Howe's book, according to Kenneth Winn, became the source for anti-Mormon writers well into the twentieth century. As Howe actively sought testimony in the form of affidavits from Smith's former neighbors, his projects, as he intended, took on the aura of careful and objective research.

96. *Philadelphia Christian Observer,* October 25, 1844, 170.

97. "The Many and the Few," *Ladies' Repository* 15 (September 1855): 526. It was also called "a sort of epidemic insanity," See "Mormon Theocracy," *Scribner's Monthly* 16 (July 1877): 393. 393, and "The Mormons," *Southern Literary Messenger* 17 (March 1851): 174. The usual epithets of "delusion" and "fanaticism" are also prominent in the descriptions of Mormon converts. See, for example, "The West," *Emerson's Magazine and Putnam's Monthly* 7 (September 1858): 319; "Brigham Young," *Brooklyn Daily Eagle,* August 30, 1877, 2; and "The Mormon Exodus, Emigration and Religious Fanaticism," *Brooklyn Daily Eagle,* June 17, 1858, 2.

98. Jeffrey A., "European Emigration," 467. For similar references, see "The Two Prophets of Mormonism," *Catholic World* 26 (November 1877): 315, and "History of the United States," *United States Democratic Review* 26 (January 1850): 44–49.

99. "Brigham Young," 2, and "The Mormon Exodus," 2.

100. George Rutledge Gibson, "The Origin of a Great Delusion," *New Princeton Review* 1 (September 1886): 203.

101. S. Goodrich, "*Pictorial History of the United States,* 314.

102. Quoted in Elson, *Guardians of Tradition,* 59.

103. Ibid., 288.

104. "Mormonism," *Vermont Gazette,* June 5, 1832.

105. C. C. Goodwin, "The Mormon Situation," *Harper's New Monthly Magazine* 62 (October 1881): 759.

106. "Nauvoo and Deseret," 482. For charges of everything from poor character to chicken stealing, see also Frederic G. Mather, "The Early Days of Mormonism," *Lippincott's Magazine* 26 (August 1880): 198. W. J. A. Bradford, "The Origin and Fate of Mormonism," *Christian Examiner and Religious Miscellany* 53

(September 1852): 202; "Historical Sketches: History of Mormonism," *Cincinnati Mirror*, September 10, 1836, 261, reprinted from the *New York Commercial Advertiser*. The attempt to denigrate Smith or Brigham Young (who was frequently referred to as simply "Brigham") was common, as were those who described them personally as mentally unstable or of violent temperament. This sort of description did not end with Smith or Brigham Young. In 1911 Joseph F. Smith, nephew of the founder, was described in a national magazine as "a man of violent passions; one could easily imagine him torturing heretics or burning witches to advance the kingdom of God." Burton J. Hendrick, "The Mormon Revival of Polygamy," *McClure's Magazine* 36 (January 1911): 259. On the use of "treasure digging" to discredit Smith and his family, see especially Quinn, *Early Mormonism,* and Alan Taylor, "The Early Republic's Supernatural Economy: Treasure Seeking in the American Northeast, 1780-1830," *American Quarterly* 38 (Spring 1986): 6–34.

107. Davis, "Some Themes of Counter-subversion," 221. Gary Alan Fine details this process from a sociological perspective. Gary Alan Fine, *Difficult Reputations: The Evil, the Inept, and the Controversial* (Chicago: University of Chicago Press, 2001), 6–9 and chap. 1.

108. Edward Ingebretsen, *At Stake: Monsters and the Rhetoric of Fear in Public Culture* (Chicago: University of Chicago Press, 2003), 4.

109. Quotations in order: Goodwin, "Mormon Situation," 759; Edwin De Leon, "The Rise and Progress of the Mormon Faith and People," *Southern Literary Messenger* 10 (September 1844): 526; and Howe, *History of Mormonism,* 399.

110. Leland, "Ash Tree," 684.

111. "A Nation's Right to Worship God," *Biblical Repertory and Princeton Review* 31 (October 1859): 672.

112. For a sampling of the schoolbooks that emphasize English control or influence over the courts at Salem, see Adams, *Abridgement of the History of New England,* 164; Jedidiah Morse, *American Geography* (Elizabethtown, NJ: Shepard Kollock, 1789), 192; and Jesse Olney, *A History of the United States: On a New Plan, Adapted to the Capacity of Youth* (New Haven, CT: Durrie and Peck, 1836), 70.

113. John Warner Barber and Henry Howe, *Our Whole Country, or The Past and Present of the United States. Historical and Descriptive,* 2 vols. (Cincinnati, OH: H. Howe, 1861), 1460.

114. Jeffrey A., "European Emigration," 467.

115. "The Origin and Fate of Mormonism," 202. "Brigham Young," 2.

116. "Disruption of the Federal Union," *DeBow's Review* 30 (April 1861): 432.

117. Joseph Richardson, *The American Reader* (Boston: Lincoln and Edmands, 1810), 100-101.

118. One newspaper article about grasshopper invasions in the West compared Mormons to "the Orientals" who eat "their insect enemies." *Brooklyn Daily Eagle,* August 23, 1855, 2.

119. "Nauvoo and Deseret," 484, 488. Untitled item in the *Brooklyn Daily Eagle*, August 23, 1855, 2. See also L. M. Lawson, "Popular Delusions," *Ladies' Repository* 4 (February 1844): 49.

120. Davis, "Some Themes of Counter-subversion," 224. For the use of Islam as a device to discredit the Latter-day Saints see also Givens, *Viper on the Hearth*, 130-33, and Timothy Marr, *The Cultural Roots of American Islamicism* (New York: Cambridge University Press, 2006), 186–89.

121. Goodwin, "Mormon Situation," 756.

122. Ibid. Undoubtedly the charges of "Eastern" practices that focused on the "Oriental" or the "Mohommadan" were meant to have racial implications as well.

123. J. D. Bell, "The Many and the Few," *Ladies' Repository* 79 (July 1859): 527.

124. Goodwin, "Mormon Situation," 760. Still, Territorial Representative W. H. Hooper found a use for Salem in his *defense* of polygamy. He appealed in this "age of great religious toleration" for allowing the religious practice of polygamy to remain legal. The antipolygamy bill then before Congress, Hooper said, recalled "the fearful days" in New England when witches were executed. Congress, House of Representatives, Territorial Representative W. H. Hooper of Utah speaking on Utah Statehood, *Congressional Globe*, 41st Cong., 2nd sess. (March 22 and 23, 1870).

125. "Comments on the Times," 409.

Chapter Four

1. *Congressional Globe*, 30th Cong., 2nd sess., February 23, 1849, 111–12. Horace Mann specifically complained of Bedinger's reference to Fisher's pamphlet, which "has been profusely scattered about this House." *Congressional Globe*, 30th Cong., 2nd sess., February 26, 1849. 318. The publication in question was the very popular pro-slavery polemic by Elwood Fisher, *Lecture on the North and the South Before the Young Men's Mercantile Library Association of Cincinnati* (Cincinnati, 1849). Fisher's lecture received wide distribution as a pamphlet, through lengthy reviews, and from excerpting in the *Southern Quarterly Review* 15 (July 1849): 273-11 and *DeBow's Review* 7 (August/October 1849): 134-45, 304-16. It appeared again in 1857 in *DeBow's Review* 23 (August 1857): 194-201. Elwood Fisher, raised an antislavery Virginia Quaker, had for a time practiced law in Cincinnati, where he appears to have had a change of heart. The creation of a pro-Southern daily newspaper, the *Southern Press,* in Washington, DC, gave Fisher a wider audience as one of the two founding editors in 1850. See Howard C. Perkins, "A Neglected Phase of the Movement for Southern Unity, 1847–1852," *Journal of Southern History* 12 (May 1946): 153–203. Perkins asserts that Fisher "popularized the selected-statistics method in the dialectics of the slavery controversy." Ibid., 165.

2. *Congressional Globe*, 30th Cong., 2nd sess., February 23, 1849, 112.

3. Ibid.

4. On the abolitionists' construction of the slaveholder figure, see Avery O. Craven, "The Coming of the War between the States, 1860–65: An Interpretation," *Journal of Southern History* 2 (August 1936): 313; *Revolution the Only Remedy for Slavery* (New York: American Anti-Slavery Society, 1855); and Ronald G. Walters, *The Anti-slavery Appeal: American Abolitionism after 1830* (Baltimore: Johns Hopkins University Press, 1976), 64–67.

5. Jan C. Dawson, "The Puritan and the Cavalier: The South's Perception of Contrasting Traditions," *Journal of Southern History* 44 (November 1978): 599. See also William R. Taylor, *Cavalier and Yankee: The Old South and American National Character* (Garden City, NY: George Braziller, 1963); Michael O'Brien, *Rethinking the South: Essays in Intellectual History* (Athens: University of Georgia Press, 1993); W. J. Cash, *The Mind of the South* (New York: Vintage, 1991); Frank Wesley Craven, *The Legend of the Founding Fathers* (New York: New York University Press, 1956); and Michael Kammen, *Mystic Chords of Memory: The Transformation of Tradition in American Culture* (New York: Vintage, 1993).

6. Craven, "Coming of the War between the States," 304–5. For an example of this cause-and-effect argument, see William Drayton, *The South Vindicated from the Treason and Fanaticism of the Northern Abolitionists* (Philadelphia: H. Manly, 1836), 180. Those fears were also subsumed within the Salem witchcraft metaphor. Craven wrote in opposition to the "avoidable" conflict model of historiography on the causes of the Civil War. See especially J. G. Randall, "The Blundering Generation," *Mississippi Valley Historical Review* 27 (June 1940): 4-16. On Sectional Crisis politics in general, see David M. Potter, *The Impending Crisis, 1848–1861*, completed and edited by Don E. Fehrenbacher (New York: Harper, 1976); William Freehling, *The Road to Disunion, 1776–1854* (New York: Oxford, 1990); and Alan Nevins, *Ordeal of the Union*, 2 vols. (New York: Charles Scribner's Sons, 1947).

7. For an example of the inclusion of the Inquisition with "burning witches," see "A Plea for the Fijians, or Can Nothing Be Said in Favor of Roasting One's Equals?" *Atlantic Monthly* 3, no. 17 (March 1859): 342–50, esp. 343.

8. Craven, "Coming of the War between the States," 313; Edward Ingebretsen, *At Stake: Monsters and the Rhetoric of Fear in Public Culture* (Chicago: University of Chicago Press, 2001), 1-10, quotations from 4 and 8.

9. On the persistence of witch-burning as a symbol of "ignorance and barbarity," see Bernard Rosenthal, *Salem Story: Reading the Witch Trials of 1692* (New York: Cambridge University Press, 1993), 209. I fully agree with his point about the motives for its use, but I argue that it enters the "story" of Salem witchcraft at this time and in this manner.

10. Quoted in James D. Hartman, *Providence Tales and the Birth of American Literature* (Baltimore: Johns Hopkins University Press, 1999), 44.

11. John McCardell, *The Idea of a Southern Nation: Southern Nationalism, 1830–1860* (New York: W. W. Norton, 1979), 179. Southern emphasis in the ante-

bellum period was on the development of tertiary institutions rather than on primary and secondary education.

12. For a quantitative analysis and discussion of Southern academies' use of schoolbooks written by Northerners, see Rolla M. Tryon, *The Social Sciences as School Subjects* (New York: Ginn, 1935). For a general overview of education in the nineteenth-century South, see Edgar W. Knight, *Public Education in the South* (Boston: Ginn, 1922), 271. Knight says that books by Northern authors were used "out of necessity." Both studies confirm the perception of antebellum editors who voiced concerns about the cultural effects of the schoolbooks in use and Tryon's conclusions about the national popularity of the authors listed in particular. For a study of Southern use of Northern publications, including schoolbooks, see also Jay Hubbell, *The South in American Literature, 1607–1900* (Durham, NC: Duke University Press, 1954), 354–66.

13. Drew Gilpin Faust, The Creation of Confederate Nationalism: Ideology and Identity in the Civil War South (Baton Rouge: Louisiana State University Press, 1988), 9–11.

14. Dawson, "Puritan and the Cavalier," 613. Dawson expanded on earlier studies of the various Yankee and Cavalier archetypes as sectional symbols found in the literary analyses of Rollin Osterweis and William R. Taylor by analyzing the Southern use of the Puritan and Cavalier as symbolic figures in nonfiction sources. Dawson delineated the use of the symbols in Southern periodical-based social commentary designed specifically to foster a historically legitimate basis for the Southern "sense of itself as a conscious minority and its hostility toward the North." She concluded that the archetypes of Puritan and Cavalier highlighted "the divided moral and religious heritage" of the two sections, which Southern social commentators asserted resulted in the evolution of two radically different cultures within the United States. Since Dawson's argument spans the general use from the early nineteenth century through the twentieth, her emphases and concerns diverge from my more specialized interest in a particular dimension of that use. For the mythology of the Virginia Cavalier and its adaptation as a Southern myth, see also Craven, *Legend,* and, Harlow W. Sheidley, *Sectional Nationalism: Massachusetts Conservative Leaders and the Transformation of America, 1815–1836* (Boston: Northeastern University Press, 1998).

15. Thomas Jefferson to John Taylor, June 4, 1798, in *The Papers of Thomas Jefferson* (Princeton, NJ: Princeton University Press, 2003), 30:287–90.

16. See Avery O. Craven, *The Coming of the Civil War* (Chicago: University of Chicago Press, 1957); Walters, *Anti-slavery Appeal;* and Steven Mintz, *Moralists and Modernizers: America's Pre–Civil War Reformers* (Baltimore: Johns Hopkins University Press, 1995).

17. Drayton, *South Vindicated;* quotations on 170, 161.

18. Ibid., 179.

19. Ibid.; italics mine. New Englanders were often described as speaking "nasally."

20. "The New England Character," *Southern Literary Messenger* 3 (July 1837): 412; "Misconceptions of the New England Character," *North American Review* 44 (January 1837): 237–60.

21. "New England Character," 416.

22. Ibid.

23. G., "Thoughts and Reflections," *Southern Literary Messenger* 5 (October 1839): 707.

24. Review, *Religion in America, Southern Quarterly Review* 7 (April 1845): 357.

25. Ibid., 358.

26. *Congressional Globe*, 30th Cong., 2nd sess., February 26, 1849, 161.

27. Ibid., 320.

28. Ibid., 316.

29. J[ohn] G[reenleaf] W[hittier], "The Reform School in Massachusetts," *National Era* 112 (February 22, 1849): 30.

30. Ibid. Giles Corey suffered such a fate at Salem.

31. "Slavery and Despotism," *National Era* 126 (May 31, 1849): 87.

32. Kinsley Scott Bingham, "Speech of Mr. Bingham of Michigan on the Admission of California, Delivered in the House of Representatives, June 4, 1850," *National Era* 6 (July 18, 1850): 116. For the full text of the speech see *Congressional Globe*, 31st Cong., 1 sess., June 10, 1850, 728-33.

33. Ibid.

34. The first of the articles to mention Salem in the *North Star*, "Salem Witchcraft and Slavery in the District, Etc.," was published on July 6, 1849, with the dateline "June 12, 1849, Washington." It appeared, of course, after the *National Era*'s spate of references, but it also began with a discussion of how, recently, "an editor of a Boston paper has favored his readers with long disquisitions on the subject."

35. "Biology—Moneyology—Etc.," *North Star*, October 29, 1849.

36. J[ohn] G[reenleaf] W[hittier], "Slavery in Massachusetts," *National Era* 204 (November 28, 1850): 190. Whittier also claims incorrectly in this article that slavery never had "the sanction and authority of law" in Massachusetts but "crept into the Commonwealth like other evils and vices."

37. "Calef in Boston, 1692," *National Era* 142 (September 20, 1849): 150.

38. "The Edinburgh Review and the Southern States," *DeBow's Review* 10 (May 1851): 512.

39. "The Conspiracy of Fanaticism," *United States Democratic Review* 26 (May 1850): 389–90.

40. The *Democratic Review* worried about the effect on the general population of a man who might "propound some stupendous dogma, to which he arrogates the sanction of Heaven, and they will batter down everything in its way." Ibid., 391.

41. Editorial, *United States Democratic Review* 35 (July 1855): 82.

42. Ibid., 8.

43. For a discussion of this in fiction and adult histories in the early republic, see Philip Gould, "New England Witch-Hunting and the Politics of Reason in the Early Republic," *New England Quarterly* 68 (1995): 58–82.

44. Dr. Van Evne, "Slavery Extension," *DeBow's Review* 15 (July 1853): 1.

45. E. Boyden, "The Epidemic of the Nineteenth Century," *Southern Literary Messenger* 31 (November 1860): 365; "Nella," Credulity of the Times," *Southern Literary Messenger* 20 (June 1854): 344.

46. Henry T. Tuckerman, "Nathaniel Hawthorne," *Southern Literary Messenger* 17 (June 1851): 348.

47. Review, "Bancroft's *History of the United States*," *DeBow's Review* 14 (August 1853): 178.

48. Ibid., 180.

49. Ibid., 181.

50. Robert Field Stockton, *Letter of Commodore Stockton on the Slavery Question* (New York: S. W. Benedict, 1850), 20. Stockton was the commander of the naval forces that captured the southern California coastal cities in the Mexican-American War and first U.S. governor of the territory, so many people assumed he had an informed opinion on the question.

51. Moses Stuart, *Conscience and the Constitution* (Boston: Crocker and Brewster, 1850), 61. Rufus W. Clark said that comparing the conscience of those resisting new fugitive slave laws with "that which the hangers of witches had" brings the whole concept on "conscience into contempt." See Rufus W. Clark, *A Review of the Revolution: Moses Stuart's Pamphlet on Slavery* (Boston: C. C. P. Moody, 1850), 78.

52. Samuel F. B. Morse to Sidney Morse, December 29, 1857, in *Samuel F. B. Morse: His Letters and Journals,* ed. Edward Lind Morse (Boston: Houghton Mifflin, 1914), 2:389–90.

53. *Congressional Globe*, 33rd Cong., 1st sess., March 14, 1854, 1517.

54. Charles Sumner, *Recent Speeches and Addresses, 1851–55* (Boston: Higgins and Bradley, 1856), 785. Sumner's own biographer notes Sumner's irritation with the earlier petition's going to Edward Everett for submission to the Senate. Sumner did not feel Everett was as strongly committed to the cause. His biographer, Edward Lillie Pierce, dates Sumner's public notice from this debate. His performance, Pierce says, let Southern senators know "they had a new kind of antagonist to deal with." See Edward Lillie Pierce, *Memoir and Letters of Charles Sumner* (Boston: Roberts Brothers, 1877–94), 3:379.

55. Sumner, *Recent Speeches,* 786.

56. Ibid.

57. *Congressional Globe*, 33rd Cong., 1st sess., June 28, 1854, 1555. I have yet to find a version that carries the text of this alleged "slur." This is an excellent example of the difficulty of recapturing oratorical references to Salem witchcraft even when the speech in question is purported to be published. Unless it was included

in a print version despite the editing allowed by congressmen before actual publication, we cannot know if Butler was lying or if Sumner was exaggerating.

58. Ibid.

59. The best study of the New England Societies remains Pershing Vartanian, "The Puritan as a Symbol in American Thought: A Study of the New England Societies, 1820–1920" (PhD diss., University of Michigan, 1971).

60. Cephas Brainerd and Eveline Warner Brainerd, eds., *The New England Society Orations: Addresses, Sermons, and Poems Delivered Before the New England Society in the City of New York, 1820–1885* 2 vols. (New York: Century, 1901), 1:193.

61. Charles B. Boynton, *Oration Delivered Before the New England Society of Cincinnati, on the Anniversary of the Landing of the Pilgrims, December 22d, 1847* (Cincinnati, OH: Collins and Van Wagner, 1848), 20.

62. Ibid., 8.

63. The 1820 meeting of the New England Society of the City of New York was marked by contention over the Congregational-Unitarian issue. Learning from this incident, the New York organization carefully avoided any topic that might split members' loyalties. As the Sectional Crisis intensified, this avoidance was increasingly impossible, as the 1855 orations show. Ironically, although the Civil War led to the dissolution of many local NESoc organizations, Charleston, South Carolina, navigated the political crisis to emerge as one of the strongest. See Vartanian, "Puritan as a Symbol," 73–76.

64. Brainerd and Brainerd, *New England Society Orations*, 2:74.

65. Oliver Wendell Holmes, *Semi-centennial Celebration of the New England Society in the City of New York, December 1855* (New York: Wm. C. Bryant, 1856), 35. Holmes called slavery "the detested social arrangement of our neighbors" and found "manly logic" in abolition. Ibid., 38.

66. Sumner, *Recent Speeches*, 390, 407. Sumner implied that the General Court also invalidated the laws against witchcraft in Massachusetts Bay Colony. It did not. Further, in another of Sumner's many errors in this address, the actions he approximately describes were taken not by the General Court but by the predecessor of the current Supreme Judicial Court, the Superior Court of Judicature, which was created specifically to oversee capital cases in the final days of the Salem investigations.

67. Ibid., 406.

68. Wendell Phillips, *Speeches, Lectures, and Letters* (Boston: James Redpath, 1863), 230.

69. Ibid., 236. Phillips made the very common error of conflating "Pilgrims" and "Puritans," which obviously continued in New England even among educated members of the "old families" at the annual dinner celebrating the Plymouth landing.

70. James Redpath, *Echoes of Harpers Ferry* (Boston: Thayer and Eldridge, 1860), 105, from an address originally delivered on December 19, 1859, at the Congregational Society, Boston, Massachusetts. Phillips also claimed that Brown acted out of the Puritan ethos of "action" both in Kansas and in Virginia.

71. "Duplicity Better Than Nationality," *Richmond Examiner*, April 24, 1855.

72. J. D. B. DeBow, "The War against the South: Opinions of Freesoilers and Abolitionists," *DeBow's Review* 21 (September 1856): 272.

73. Parker Pillsbury, "West Indian Emancipation," *Liberator*, August 12, 1859.

74. Phillips, *Speeches*, 231.

75. William Addison Phillips, *The Conquest of Kansas by Missouri and Her Allies* (Boston: Phillips, Sampson, 1856), 267–68.

76. "Editor's Table," *Southern Literary Messenger* 26 (January 1858): 77.

77. Ibid.

78. For historical accounts of the 1741 Negro Plot, See especially Jill Lepore, *New York Burning: Liberty, Slavery, and Conspiracy in Eighteenth-Century Manhattan* (New York: Alfred A. Knopf, 2005), xvi–xvii and 203–4; Peter Charles Hoffer, *The Great New York Conspiracy of 1741: Slavery, Crime, and Colonial Law* (Lawrence: University of Kansas Press, 2003); and Thomas J. Davis, *A Rumor of Revolt: The Great Negro Plot in Colonial New York* (Boston: University of Massachusetts Press, 1985). The chief judge in the trials also wrote a history of the episode, See Daniel Horsmanden, *The New York Conspiracy, or The History of the Negro Plot, 1741–42* (New York: Southwick and Pelsue, 1810).

79. Davis, *Rumor of Revolt*, fig. ix; appearance in histories, 251–53, "astonishment," 253. For New England and slavery, see especially Joanne Pope Melish, *Disowning Slavery:Gradual Emancipation and "Race" in New England, 1780–1860 (Ithaca, NY: Cornell University Press, 1998).*

80. William Smith Jr., *The History of the Province of New York*, ed. Michael Kammen (Cambridge, MA: Harvard University Press, 1972). It also was featured in another schoolroom history of New York State, William Dunlap, *A History of New York for Schools,* 2 vols. (New York: Collins, Keese, 1837), 2:54–65. See also Benson J. Lossing, *A Pictorial History of the United States for Schools and Families* (New York: F. J. Huntington, 1854), 111. It was also included in the few texts produced for black schools and homes; one notable volume in the early twentieth century was Leila Amos Pendleton, *A Narrative of the Negro* (Washington, DC: R. L. Pendleton, 1912). According to the preface, the author was a schoolteacher in Washington. She also says of the New York cases, "This period has been likened to the time when so many innocent persons were burnt as witches, at Salem, Massachusetts" (83).

81. The best study of New England's conscious and unconscious erasure of its regional slaveowning and slave-trading past is Melish, *Disowning Slavery.*A current history of slavery in New York City also offers a useful fully contextualized account. See Leslie Harris, *In the Shadow of Slavery: African Americans in New York City, 1626-1863* (Chicago: University of Chicago Press, 2003). For some examples of the refutation of the "burning" charge every time it appeared in print, see letters from readers in *Chicago Tribune*, February 18, 1895, 9 and February 18, 1895, 9; *New York Times*, May 26, 1874, 4 and October 20, 1895, 9; and *New York Times*, January 19, 1915, 10. Although Horsmanden's book was a poor seller, there is a rare notice about the reissued edition's being available at the Boston Athenaeum in *the Monthly Anthology and Boston Review* in May 1810.

82. Howell Cobb, *A Scriptural Examination of the Institution of Slavery in the United States, with Its Objects and Purposes* ([Perry?]: GA: Howell Cobb, 1856), 114.

83. Redpath, *Echoes of Harpers Ferry*, 112. From an address originally delivered on December 19, 1859, at the Congregational Society, Boston, Massachusetts. Phillips also claimed that Brown acted out of the Puritan "ethos of action" both in Kansas and in Virginia.

84. Ibid., passim. For an example of this sentiment from a nonprofessional abolitionist, see also Charles Henry Van Wyck, *True Democracy—History Vindicated* (Washington, DC: Republican Executive Committee, 1860), 11. For an evaluation of both Northern and Southern responses to the raid, see Paul Finkleman, ed., *His Soul Goes Marching On: Responses to John Brown and the Harpers Ferry Raid* (Charlottesville: University of Virginia Press, 1995).

85. *Raleigh (North Carolina) Register*, December 3, 1859.

86. Ibid.

87. Daniel Robinson Hundley, *Social Relations in Our Southern States* (New York: H. B. Price, 1860), 16.

88. Ibid. In various parts of this book Hundley also linked Salem witchcraft to "blue laws" and the "rejection of institutions."

89. J. T. Wiswall, "Delusions of Fanaticism," *DeBow's Review* 29 (July 1860): 46, 47. The root of such problems, according to the author, were the long New England winters, which preyed on the mind and produced "hypochondria and querulousness." It was also troubling that "in their colonies we find a large number of ministers." Ibid., 47.

90. *Congressional Globe*, 30th Cong., 2nd sess., February 26, 1849, 161.

91. *Congressional Globe*, 36th Cong., 1st sess., February 19, 1860, 158.

92. Van Wyck, *True Democracy*, 1.

93. Ibid., 11.

94. Ibid., 12.

95. Ibid.

96. *The Despotism of Slavery*, delivered June 16, 1860, by Congressman Charles Henry Van Wyck of New York in the House of Representatives (Washington, DC: Republican Executive Committee, 1860); quotations from version in *Congressional Globe*, 36th Cong., 1st sess., April 25, 1860, 434.

97. Ibid., 435. Van Wyck was also angry that Davis had challenged him to a duel over the comments in March. That Davis did so over "a mere utterance in a free country" was evidence, Van Wyck claimed, of the state of society in Mississippi owing to the violent influence of slavery. Ibid., 435–37.

98. Ibid., 435, 436. Van Wyck advanced the Republican platform of 1860 position here in that he acknowledged that he "disclaim[ed] any right to interfere with slavery where it exists," but he did reserve the right to comment on what "deadens your own sensibilities and brutalizes your own people," referring both to the

challenge to a duel and to the several Southern newspaper excerpts relating to mob violence against blacks that he read into the record to support his argument in the earlier session.

99. A. Clarkson, "The Basis of Northern Hostility to the South," *DeBow's Review* 28 (July 1860): 9. This was shown by "the fierce fanatic intolerance of his opinions" on slavery.

100. Ibid., 7. Clarkson went so far as to advocate restoring the Mason-Dixon line—to separate the two fundamentally different white races.

101. Ibid., 8.

102. Ibid.

103. "The Difference of Race between the Northern and Southern People," *Southern Literary Messenger* 30 (June 1860): 404.

104. Ibid., 407.

105. Ibid., 405.

106. "The Election in November," *Atlantic Monthly* 6 (October 1860): 501.

107. The editor of the *Richmond (Virginia) Examiner* certainly harbored no illusions: "The idle canvass prattle about Northern conservation may now be dismissed. A party founded on the single sentiment, the exclusive feeling of hatred to African slavery, is now the controlling power." November 9, 1860.

108. "Editorial Miscellany," *DeBow's Review* 28 (December 1860): 797. The "bloody shirts" of Harpers Ferry and Kansas were waved and the hated trio of Seward, Garrison, and Sumner was mentioned within this passage, but there was no elaboration of the reference to witch-burning.

109. Ibid.

110. Craven, "Coming of the War between the States," 304.

Chapter Five

1. Pennsylvania New England Society, Fifth Annual Festival, December 22, 1885 (Philadelphia: Times Printing House, 1885), 54.

2. Blight, *Race and Reunion: The Civil War in American Memory* (Cambridge, MA: Belknap Press, 2001), 2, 221, 390.

3. Drew Gilpin Faust, The Creation of Confederate Nationalism: Ideology and Identity in the Civil War South (Baton Rouge: Louisiana University Press, 1988), 7.

4. Ibid., 14.

5. J. Quitman Moore, "The Attitude of the South," *DeBow's Review* 29 (July 1860): 27. See also "The Non-slaveholders of the South," *DeBow's Review* 30 (January 1861): 73.

6. B. M. Palmer, "Why We Resist, and What We Resist," *DeBow's Review* 30 (February 1861): 232. See also "The Southern Confederacy, *DeBow's Review* 30

(April 1861): 475. The claim for continuation and fulfillment of the American Revolution was apparent in both words and deeds. Jefferson Davis's inauguration as president of the Confederate States of America was scheduled for George Washington's birthday, and Washington appeared both on the design for the CSA's Great Seal and on the postage stamp. In his inaugural address Davis appealed specifically to the Declaration of Independence by claiming that the move to secede was in accordance with the "inalienable" rights claimed in the original document. Calling on "the God of our fathers to guide and protect" the nation, Davis appealed for this new generation to assume the burdens of "the principles which by his blessing they were able to vindicate, establish, and transmit." See James D. Richardson, *A Compilation of the Messages and Papers of the Confederacy, Including the Diplomatic Correspondence, 1861–65* (Nashville, TN: United States Publishing, 1905), 33.

7. Senator [Andrew Pickens] Butler, "The South's Sacrifices in the Revolution," *DeBow's Review* 21 (August 1856): 198. See also Mr. Garnett, "The South and the Union," *DeBow's Review* 18 (August 1855): 440.

8. D. J. McLord, "How the South Is Affected by Her Slave Institutions," *DeBow's Review* 11 (October 1851): 351–52.

9. George Fitzhugh, "The Times and the War," *DeBow's Review* 31 (July 1861): 4.

10. J. Quitman Moore, "Southern Civilization, or The Norman in America," *DeBow's Review* 32 (January–February 1862): 5.

11. George Fitzhugh, "The Huguenots of the South," *DeBow's Review* 30 (May–June 1861): 517.

12. Frank B. Alfriend, "A Southern Republic and a Northern Democracy," *Southern Literary Messenger* 37 (May 1863): 285. See also "The Conflict of the Northern and Southern Races," *DeBow's Review* 31 (October–November 1861): 391–95.

13. "Southern Authors—School Books and Presses," *American Publishers' Circular and Literary Gazette*, November 22, 1856, 713.

14. Ibid.

15. Editorial, *Southern Literary Messenger* 33 (October 1861): 353. See also Editorial, *Southern Cultivator* 19 (November 1861): 291.

16. J. W. Morgan, "Our School Books," *DeBow's Review* 8 (September 1850): 436, 438, 440.

17. Ibid., 438.

18. Dr. [Samuel] Cartwright, "The Existing Crisis," *DeBow's Review* 32 (January--February 1862): 109. And the census records reflect this deficiency, showing a 10:1 ratio in favor of the North for mechanical infrastructure for the manufacture of books in 1860. Alice Fahs, *The Imagined Civil War: Popular Literature of the North and South, 1861–65* (Chapel Hill: University of North Carolina Press), 21.

19. For a general discussion of the effort to produce schoolbooks by Confederate authors and an annotated bibliography, see Stephen B. Weeks, *Confederate*

Text Books, 1861–65 (Washington, DC: U.S. Government Printing Office, 1900). For a contemporary acknowledgment of the problems of disseminating information among a population that is primarily "a talking people," see "Editor's Table," *Southern Literary Messenger* 38 (May 1864): 315.

20. A South Carolinian, *The Confederate* (Mobile, AL: S. H. Goetzel, 1863), 10.

21. Ibid., 15, 3.

22. Ibid., 33, 102, 10.

23. Ibid., 10.

24. Jeffrey A., "European Emigration and New England Puritanism," *Southern Literary Messenger* 37 (August 1863): 100.

25. "The Catholic Church," *Richmond (Virginia) Enquirer*, May 29, 1863. See also "The True Question: A contest for the Supremacy of Race, as between the Saxon Puritan of the North, and the Norman of the South," *Southern Literary Messenger* 33 (July 1861): 19.

26. "Editor's Easy Chair," *Harper's New Monthly Magazine* 22 (March 1861): 556.

27. Ibid.

28. James L. Crouthamel, *James L. Bennett's "New York Herald" and the Rise of the Popular Press* (Syracuse, NY: Syracuse University Press, 1989), 114.

29. "The Reign of Economy and Temperance Inaugurated at Washington," *New York Herald*, March 14, 1861.

30. "The Story of Puritanism—Real Origin of Southern Secession," *New York Herald,* January 26, 1861.

31. Ibid.; italics mine. See also Crouthamel, *Bennett's "New York Herald,"* 113-15.

32. "Story of Puritanism."

33. Ibid.

34. "Activity and Cause of Puritan Antislavery Propagandism," *New York Herald*, January 20, 1861.

35. Ibid.

36. Ibid.

37. "The Reaction against the Abolitionists—American Civilization versus Puritan Fanaticism," *New York Herald*, February 3, 1861.

38. Crouthamel, Bennett's "New York Herald," 116.

39. Ibid., 118.

40. "Recruiting in Danger in the North from Secession Sympathizers and Abolition Fanatics," *New York Herald,* September 28, 1861.

41. "Invasion of the South—the Inauguration of Civil War," *New York Herald*, April 8, 1861. See also "The Fate of the Negro Decided," *New York Herald*, December 29, 1863.

42. William Howard Russell, "What South Carolina Wants," *Philadelphia Christian Recorder*, June 15, 1861.

43. C. Chauncey Burr, "The Puritan War," *Old Guard* 1 (March 1863): 61, 62. For information on Burr's newspaper, see F. L. Mott, *A History of American Magazines, 1850–1865* (Cambridge, MA: Harvard University Press, 1938), 544–46. "Copperhead," of course, was a term created by Republican editors and politicians to cast doubt on the loyalty and aims of opponents (most notably Democrats); it still tends to generically label any Union opposition. Burr is on the extreme end of the spectrum, advocating for slavery, and as such personifies the slur aimed at more temperate and specific critics.

44. C. Chauncey Burr, Editorial, *Old Guard* 1 (January 1863): 23. Burr regularly printed an engraving of New York's Democratic governor Horatio Seymour, who was very critical of the war during his brief time in office. By 1864, however, Burr appears to have judged Seymour as too moderate, and he had fallen out of favor. Burr may have picked up his terminology anywhere in the print world of 1861, but since he regularly appears to "compile" from the New York dailies, including the *Herald,* their January articles might well have inspired him.

45. C. Chauncey Burr, "Civilization of the Tropics," *Old Guard* 3 (January 1865): 44.

46. Middletown (New York) Banner of Liberty, 1864.

47. Ibid.

48. Among others, see *Puritania: A Satire* (New York, 1865); and *Quevedo Redivicus: The South Church Council* (New Haven, CT, 1863). Both use prominent abolitionists and politicians as well as passages to illustrate the Puritan "lack of tolerance to all who differed."

49. James McPherson, *Battle Cry of Freedom: The Civil War Era* (New York: Oxford University Press, 1988), 592–93.

50. Samuel Sullivan Cox, *Puritanism in Politics: Speech of Hon. S. S. Cox, of Ohio, Before the Democratic Union Association, January 13, 1863* (New York: Van Evrie, Horton, 1863), 4, 29.

51. Ibid., 569.

52. At least two other articles that quoted "planters" in the two years after the war ended use Salem in the same way. See John C. Delavique, "Cotton Supply, Demand, Etc.," *DeBow's Review,* rev. ser., 4 (December 1867): 569, and J. W. DeForest, "Chivalrous and Semi-chivalrous Southrons," *Harper's New Monthly Magazine* 38 (January 1869): 199.

53. Scholars have emphasized the "ideologically expedient salvaging of a nationally appealing 'Pilgrim' split from the more oppressive legacy of 'Puritan' history," and particularly the role of these celebrations and men "in the construction of a New England–centered national identity," but they have differed on when and how that occurs. Although Udo Hebel states this most explicitly in his work on the New England Societies, he does not systematically pursue the full context for this "salvage" work by the men he studies or by others like them. Udo J. Hebel, "New England Forefathers' Day Celebrations between the American

Revolution and the Civil War," in *Ceremonies and Spectacles*, ed. Teresa Alves, Teresa Cid, and Heinz Ickstad (Amsterdam: VU University Press, 2000), 128. For a general acknowledgment of the contextual issues surrounding the new primacy of the "Pilgrim" in literature and other historical sources, and what Michael Kammen has called the "disarray" in the status of the symbols of Puritan and Pilgrim after the war, see Michael Kammen, *Mystic Chords of Memory: The Transformation of Tradition in American Culture* (New York: Vintage, 1993), 63–64, 208–11, and Lawrence Buell, *New England Literary Culture: From Revolution through Renaissance* (New York: Cambridge University Press, 1986), 450–51. For a complete evaluation of the place of the Puritan image in American intellectual history, see especially Jan Dawson, *The Unusable Past: America's Puritan Tradition, 1830-1930* (Chico, CA: Scholars Press, 1984).

54. Benjamin Scott, *The Pilgrim Fathers neither Puritans nor Persecutors* (London: Elliot Stock, 1891), 36, 18, 21. Scott's argument was not entirely new even to audiences in the United States. Another English minister, John Waddington, made a similar case for differentiating between Puritan and Pilgrim during the height of the Sectional Crisis in 1859, while Southerners routinely invoked Salem as the prime example of what they saw as the extremism of the Puritan expressed within his contemporary descendants. During his extensive tour of the United States, Waddington told his audiences at each stop: "The Puritans had half learned their lesson. The Pilgrims learned it all. They were not persecutors when in England or New England." Yet even in 1859 this seemed a minority position despite the barrage of anti-Puritan, Salem-laden rhetoric. John Waddington, *Track of the Hidden Church, or The Springs of Pilgrim Movement* (Boston: Congregational Board of Publications, 1863), xxiii–xxiv. For an evaluation of the same issues that Waddington mentions in relation to the Pilgrim as a desirable national icon, see Frank Wesley Craven, *The Legend of the Founding Fathers* (New York: New York University Press, 1956), 86–101. Peter Gomes attributes this shift to "liberal historians" who were "forced to resort to a useful distinction which would provide them a set of respectable ancestors to whom they could attribute their own values." I argue that this is a broader cultural phenomenon arising out of particular historical circumstances. See Peter Gomes, "Pilgrims and Puritans: 'Heroes' and 'Villains' in the Creation of the American Past," *Proceedings of the Massachusetts Historical Society* 95 (1983): 12.

55. Quoted in Mark Walgren Summers, "'With a Sublime Faith in God, and in Republican Liberty,'" in *Vale of Tears: New Essays on Religion and Reconstruction*, ed. Edward J. Blum and W. Scott Poole (Macon, GA: Mercer University Press, 2005), 128.

56. For a comprehensive examination of the Pilgrim in American culture, see John Seelye, *Memory's Nation: The Place of Plymouth Rock* (Chapel Hill: University of North Carolina Press, 1998). Seelye argues that the Pilgrim was much more of a presence in American culture before 1880 than I think is true. I reached my

conclusions based on the visibility of a distinct use in print or oratory of the Plymouth Pilgrim. Before 1865, the "Pilgrim," as I argue in the text, was more likely to be either a conflated Massachusetts colonial settler figure or a label applied to a colonist in histories and fiction whose location and history were clearly those of the Massachusetts Bay Colony Puritan. In regard to the role of Thanksgiving in the iconography of the Pilgrim settler since the establishment of the holiday in 1863, see Matthew Dennis, *Red, White, and Blue Letter Days: An American Calendar* (Ithaca, NY: Cornell University Press, 2002). For a consideration of the various debates about the primacy of Jamestown and Plymouth as founding colonies and icons, see also Ann Uhry Abrams, *The Pilgrims and Pocahontas: Rival Myths of American Origin* (Boulder, CO: Westview Press, 1999). For a contemporary presentation along these lines, see Tryon Edwards, "Pilgrims and Puritans," *Scribner's' Monthly Magazine* 12 (July 1876): 212–19.

57. Craven, Legend of the Founding Fathers, 101.

58. Kammen, *Mystic Chords of Memory*, 211–15; on the problem of the Puritan "paper trail," see 64. Kammen also mentions the postwar desire to valorize the male veteran; see 299–341. Earlier writers had also assigned these characteristics to the Plymouth settlers, but in that context of enthusiasm for market revolution, it was seldom an unqualified endorsement. Francis Baylies in 1840 described the Pilgrims as having "placed little value on rank or wealth." "An Historical Memoir of the Colony of New Plymouth," *North American Review* 50 (April 1840): 356. George Bancroft praised the Plymouth colonists highly as well; the Pilgrims he said, were important to the nation, since they "formed the mould for the civil and religious character of its institutions." George Bancroft, *History of the United States of America, from the Discovery of the American Continent* (Boston: Charles C. Little and James Brown, 1839),1:323.

59. For full newspaper coverage of the New York NESoc observance and the festivities in Massachusetts, see I. N. Tarbox, "Winthrop and Emerson on Forefathers' Day," *New Englander* 230 (1870): 175–203; "The Pilgrims' Jubilee Year," *New York Times,* January 18, 1870, 2; "The Pilgrim Fathers," *New York Times,* December 19, 1870, 2; and "Sons of the Pilgrims," *New York Times,* December 23, 1870, 1.

60. Robert C. Winthrop, "Address," in *New England Society Orations: Orations, Sermons, and Poems Delivered Before the New England Society in the City of New York, 1820–1885,* ed. Cephus Brainerd and Eveline Warner Brainerd, 2 vols. (New York: Century, 1901), 2:239, 231, 243. In his 1841 speech before the same organization, Charles Brickett Hadduck, a professor of literature and political economy at Dartmouth, had made the same claims for the national character's foundation in the "Yankee traits" rather than the "Old World" traits of the Virginian. He too had "no patience" with those who think only of "the witches and the Quakers." Charles Brickett Hadduck, "The Elements of National Greatness," in *New England Society Orations: Orations, Sermons, and Poems Delivered Before*

the New England Society in the City of New York, 1820–1885, ed. Cephus Brainerd and Eveline Warner Brainerd, 2 vols. (New York: Century, 1901), 2:272–73, 281.

61. *The Proceedings at the Celebration by the Pilgrim Society at Plymouth, December 21, 1870, of the Two Hundred Fiftieth Anniversary of the Landing of the Pilgrims* (Cambridge, MA: J. Wilson, 1871), 83, 86–87. It is helpful to recall here that Plymouth and Massachusetts Bay were once separate colonies, which most of his audience would have been well aware of, hence the "other Colonies" remark. Ironically, it was in the midst of the 1692 witchcraft episode in Salem that the new royal charter arrived, permanently joining the two into what would later become the state of Massachusetts.

62. Ibid., 129.

63. Abrams, *Pilgrims,* 252. Abrams claims that at this moment Plymouth attains emblematic status as a national rather than a regional icon of patriotism. I disagree not so much with her general chronology as with her reading of the meaning and context of Everett's poem. This was clearly not a lighthearted change from the old "hair-splitting" arguments. Reading all the orations at Plymouth demonstrates that the Puritan was surrendered reluctantly, even if by 1870 the "Puritan" was so damaged that there might have been an element of relief in the gesture.

64. This was Cephas Brainerd's statement about the reason for suspending the orations at the New York dinners in 1859. Given Brainerd's "Introduction," (which is philiopietism at its most devoted), there is no reason to doubt his evaluation. Further, coverage in the *New York Times* in the late 1850s shows that the members of the New York chapter clearly were split on the question of abolition and that the meetings were becoming uncomfortably rancorous.

65. Moncure Daniel Conway, *Emerson at Home and Abroad* (London: Trubner, 1883), 251. There is some dispute about Emerson's exact wording, but Conway reports that he asked Emerson himself, and Emerson replied: "That's about what I said."

66. *New England Society of New York, 1870 Annual Festival* (New York: New England Society, 1870), 32.

67. See Ralph Waldo Emerson's address in Brainerd and Brainerd, *New England Society Orations,* 2:375.

68. The New York New England Society probably best shows the transformation of the organization's membership from a merchant elite to an industrial elite. It also showed the most generalized persistence of the Puritan as a well-regarded symbol. As the members attempted to mold him into a man of business "associated with industrial growth," they did acknowledge his "limitations" but stood more firmly behind the symbol than most other chapters as in 1885 they enthusiastically financed a memorial statue by John Quincy Adams Ward in Central Park and (to a man) reviled Henry Adams's *Emancipation of Massachusetts* in 1887. See Pershing Vartanian, "The Puritan as a Symbol in American Thought: A Study of

the New England Societies, 1820–1920" (PhD diss., University of Michigan, 1971), 132–33, and chap. 5 passim.

69. Blight, *Race and Reunion*, 200. The *Columbus (Georgia) Enquirer's* announcement that Grady's upcoming calendar for his Northern trip was "crowded with club invitations" was reprinted approvingly in the *New York Times*. "Mr. Henry Grady," *New York Times*, December 26, 1886.

70. "A Message from the South," *New York Times*, December 23, 1886.

71. "Boasting of Puritan Sires; The Proudest Festival of New England's Sons," *New York Times*, December 23, 1886.

72. "A Message from the South." When Henry Grady died in 1889, the same paper would eulogize him as "an eloquent interpreter of the new spirit which had awakened and possessed the South." "Henry W. Grady," *New York Times*, December 24, 1889.

73. Blight, *Race and Reunion*, 90.

74. New York NESoc speakers and programs also prominently mentioned any Southern guest or speaker within their programs, and the *New York Times* dutifully listed them in its coverage of the annual Forefathers' Day dinners, along with a description of the enthusiastic reception they received from the members. See, for example, "Praising Yankee Stock," *New York Times*, December 23, 1887, and "Plymouth's Greatest Day," *New York Times*, August 2, 1889.

75. Sven Beckert, *The Monied Metropolis: New York City and the Consolidation of the American Bourgeoisie, 1850–1896* (New York: Cambridge University Press, 2001), 300; see also Blight, *Race and Reunion*, esp. 200. For a good discussion and contextualization of Henry Grady's speech, see Edward L. Ayers, *The Promise of the New South: Life after Reconstruction* (New York: Oxford University Press, 1992), 81-103; Gaines M. Foster, *Ghosts of the Confederacy: Defeat, the Lost Cause, and the Emergence of the New South* (New York: Oxford University Press, 1987); and Paul M. Gaston, *The New South Creed: A Study in Southern Mythmaking* (New York: Alfred A. Knopf, 1970). Oliver Wendell Holmes, *Semi-centennial Celebration of the New England Society in the City of New York, December 1855* (New York: Wm. C. Bryant, 1856), 35, 43.

76. *Annual Reunion, New England Society of St. Louis* (St. Louis: New England Society, 1886), 10, 18.

77. *Thirteenth Annual Festival of the New England Society of Pennsylvania at the Continental Hotel, Philadelphia, December 22, 1893* (Philadelphia: New England Society, 1893), 27.

78. An 1879 *New York Times* review of a new biography of Puritan Robert Pike by James S. Pike began with a complaint about the current reputation of the historical Puritans: "Until a comparatively recent period it was the general habit of American people to speak of the Puritans in terms of unmeasured eulogy. They were venerated as the champions of civil and religious liberty, and as illustrious examples of heroic virtue and daring enterprise ... it is now becoming as much the fashion to disparage and despise the Puritan as it was formerly to praise and honor

him." "New Publications: *The New Puritan: New England Two Hundred Years Ago*," *New York Times*, March 31, 1879. Also in 1879, Plymouth resident John Goodwin published an extended defense of Pilgrims over Puritans, highlighting the Pilgrims' separatist nature and their failure to use the witchcraft statutes that he admitted existed. John A. Goodwin, *The Pilgrim Republic: An Historical Review of the Colony of New Plymouth* (1879; Boston: Ticknor, 1888), 3, 393.

79. James McPherson, "Long-Legged Yankee Lies: The Southern Textbook Crusade," in *The Memory of the Civil War in American Culture*, ed. Alice Fahs and Joan Waugh (Chapel Hill: University of North Carolina Press, 2004), 67. See also Blight, *Race and Reunion*, 277–82.

80. John Bach McMaster, *A School History of the United States* (New York: American Book Company, 1897); John Fiske, *A History of the United States for Schools* (Boston: Houghton, Mifflin, 1899); Edward Eggleston, *The Beginners of a Nation* (New York: Appleton, 1899); and Edward Eggleston, *A History of the United States and Its People: for the Use of Schools* (New York: American Book Company, 1899).

81. Joel Dorman Steele, *A Brief History of the United States* (New York: A. S. Barnes, 1871), 316. John Fiske asked a similar question that divided the Massachusetts settler groups into two semidistinct bodies: "What was the difference between the Pilgrims and the other Puritans?" Fiske, *History of the United States for Schools,* 120. William Swinton, *First Lessons in Our Country's History: Bringing Out Its Salient Points and Aiming to Combine Simplicity with Sense* (New York: Ivison, Blakeman, Taylor, 1872), 52.

82. Steele, *Brief History of the United States*, 53. See also Edward Eggleston, *The Household History of the United States and Its People, for Young Americans* (New York: D. Appleton, 1889), 37. This idea of wishing only for a home and to be left undisturbed by others with different views also appears in postbellum literature in and about the South. See especially Nina Silber, *The Romance of Reunion: Northerners and the South, 1865–1900* (Chapel Hill: University of North Carolina Press, 1993); Blight, *Race and Reunion*; and Fahs, *Imagined Civil War.*

83. Quotations in order: Fiske, History of the United States for Schools, 94. Eggleston, Household History of the United States and Its People, 44.

84. McMaster, *School History of the United States*, 41. Joel Dorman Steele is less enamored with Mrs. Hutchinson and has a decidedly gendered view of her public notoriety, including describing her preaching as a "scandal" and, particularly, asking in his chapter questions, "Why did Mrs. Hutchinson become obnoxious?" Steele, *Brief History of the United States*, 57, 316. Many of the lower-level schoolbooks praise both individuals as challenging Puritan orthodoxy, but most concentrate on Williams's redemption with the founding of Rhode Island, leaving Anne Hutchinson to take refuge in Williams's new colony when she is banished.

85. Fiske, History of the United States for Schools, 97.

86. Quotations in order: Steele, *Brief History of the United States*, 60; Swinton, *First Lessons in Our Country's History*, 52. John Bach McMaster's very popular

school history instead discussed the political issues facing the colony in 1692, but others, including Joel Dorman Steele, covered the episode in a paragraph or less.

87. Swinton, *Brief History of the United States*, 52. A particularly interesting narrative development is the way the reconciliationist viewpoint (and perhaps, the wider geographical origins of postbellum authors) permeates the story of colonial Virginia. No longer was Virginia settled primarily by men who were "licentious"; rather, they were men who were "not used to work." They did not refuse to work as they had in the antebellum narratives, but instead struggled to learn to "'rough it' in the woods." See, for example, Swinton, *First lessons in Our Country's History*, 37, 51, and Frederick Butler, *A Complete History of the United States of America*, 3 vols. (Hartford, CT: Butler, 1821), 8.

88. William Frederick Poole, "The Mather Papers," *North American Review* 109 (April 1869): 337.

89. Ibid. Among the books he reviewed in this essay were Longfellow's *New England Tragedies*, Charles Upham's *Salem Witchcraft*, and *The Mather Papers*, vol. 8.

90. Much of the mapping that Upham did was based on local tradition and also has errors from confusing common names. Benjamin Ray has recently done a more modern study using GPS technology and more accurate records. This work promises to significantly alter some assumptions about the spatial relations of the accusers and the accused. For some initial findings about church membership and residence, see Benjamin C. Ray, "Satan's War against the Covenant in Salem Village, 1692," *New England Quarterly* 80 (March 2007): 69–95.

91. Poole, "Cotton Mather and Salem Witchcraft." Upham responded to Poole in "Salem Witchcraft and Cotton Mather," *Historical Magazine,* 2nd ser. 6 (September 1869): 129–220. For a complete evaluation of Mather's cultural reputation, see William Van Arragon, "Cotton Mather in American Cultural Memory, 1728–1892" (PhD diss., Indiana University, 2005).

92. Upham, *Salem Witchcraft;* quotations on 2:564 and 2:565n. In the original there is an apparent typographical error, with "ambitions" in place of "ambitious." Upham is nearly universally considered by historians to have originated the idea that Parris's slave Tituba was practicing "fortune-telling" or "magic" with the young girls of Salem, but this was a standard feature of many antebellum schoolbook versions long before Upham came to the topic. Likely he himself used one in school. See, for example. Hannah Adams, *An Abridgement of the History of New England* (Boston: Etheridge and Bliss, 1807), 82, and William Grimshaw, *History of the United States from Their First Settlement as a Colony to the Cession of Florida* (Philadelphia: Benjamin Warner, 1821), 58.

93. Poole, "Cotton Mather and Salem Witchcraft," 395. Poole much preferred the picture of Mather offered by Longfellow, which was as anachronistic and inaccurate as anything Upham offered but more flattering. William Poole also published the draft version of Thomas Hutchinson's chapter on Salem in 1870 to promote the collections of the Massachusetts Historical Society. He noted the

damage to the original manuscript pages that occurred when Hutchinson's house was ransacked during the "Stamp Act" riot of August 1765. "Portions of it were much defaced, and bore the marks of being trampled in the mud." William Frederick Poole, "The Witchcraft Delusion of 1692, by Gov. Thomas Hutchinson, from an Unpublished Manuscript (an Early Draft of His History of Massachusetts) in the Massachusetts Archives," *New England Historical and Genealogical Register and Antiquarian Journal* 24 (October 1870): 381.

94. Brooks Adams, *The Emancipation of Massachusetts* (Boston: Houghton, Mifflin, 1886), 222.

95. Ibid., 224.

96. Ibid., 236.

97. Ibid., 228.

98. The Puritan, however, would be the preferred colonist of many intellectuals precisely because of his ideology. See especially Richard Hofstadter, *Anti-intellectualism in American Thought* (New York: Alfred A. Knopf, 1963); Alan Simpson, *Puritanism in Old and New England* (Chicago: University of Chicago Press, 1955); and Perry Miller, *The New England Mind: From Colony to Province* (Cambridge, MA: Harvard University Press, 1953). For a full discussion of the Puritan tradition in American thought, see Dawson, *Unusable Past,* and Sacvan Bercovitch, *The Puritan Origins of the American Self* (New Haven, CT: Yale University Press, 1977).

99. Miller, *New England Mind,* 192.

Epilogue

1. For the history and the conflicts over morality involved with both Prohibition and legislation directed toward other moral issues, see Norman H. Clark, *Deliver Us from Evil: An Interpretation of American Prohibition* (New York: W. W. Norton, 1976); James A. Morone, *Hellfire Nation: The Politics of Sin in American History* (New Haven, CT: Yale University Press, 2003); and David E. Kyvig, *Repealing National Prohibition,* 2nd ed. (Kent, OH: Kent State University Press, 2000).

2. Eugene Brown, "Wet or Dry," *Los Angeles Times,* October 25, 1914; "Historical Ads about Liquors Found Illogical," *Christian Science Monitor,* August 20, 1915; "Fanaticism in Georgia," *Washington Post,* November 14, 1885.

3. Walt Mason, "Rippling Rhymes," *Los Angeles Times,* October 12, 1929.

4. "Punishment in the Good Old Days," *Chicago Daily Tribune,* April 27, 1928.

5. "June 30 to Be 'Daisy Day,'" *New York Times,* June 23, 1919. For similar statements, see Everett P. Wheeler, "Temperate Wine and Beer," *New York Times,* July 11, 1923.

6. Henry Morton Robinson, "Is the Lid Off?" *North American Review* 238 (August 1934): 110, 112.

7. H. L. Mencken, "The Yearning to Save," *Chicago Daily Tribune,* January 9, 1927; "The Day of the Mocker," *Los Angeles Times,* June 26, 1927. See also S. T. Joshi, ed., *Mencken's America* (Athens: Ohio University Press, 2004).

8. For a general history of the trial, its context, and its cultural legacy, see Paul Keith Conkin, *When All the Gods Trembled: Darwinism, Scopes, and American Intellectuals* (New York: Rowan and Littlefield, 2001); Edward J. Larson, *Summer for the Gods: The Scopes Trial and America's Continuing Debate over Science and Religion* (Cambridge, MA: Harvard University Press, 1998); and Constance Areson Clark, "Evolution for John Doe: Pictures, the Public, and the Scopes Trial Debate," *Journal of American History* 87 (March 2001): 1275–1303.

9. "Monkey Business," *Los Angeles Times,* May 19, 1925. The claim that "witch trials" were the obvious parallel with the Scopes trial appeared in all regions of the country; for instance, see Arthur Brisbane, "Today," *Wisconsin Rapids Daily Tribune,* July 14, 1925. The arguments about evolution, along with the warning of ignorance leading to a Salem-like end, continued sporadically for several years after the trial. See "Adds Billion Years to Life of World," *New York Times,* November 18, 1928.

10. "Text of Darrow's Speech," *Washington Post,* July 14, 1925. Also reported/reprinted in "Argument by Clarence Darrow at Dayton Assailing Foes of Evolution," *New York Times,* July 14, 1925, and Philip Kinsley, "Darrow Rips into Bigotry," *Chicago Daily Tribune,* July 14, 1925.

11. Joseph McCarthy's reputation goes through cycles of vilification and rehabilitation, which supports my argument that his reputation is still too much a matter of contemporary political controversy for any real adoption of "McCarthyism" as a cultural metaphor. A (qualified) scholarly defense of McCarthy can be found in Arthur Herman, *Joseph McCarthy: Reexamining the Life and Legacy of America's Most Hated Senator* (New York: Free Press, 1999). Other discussions of McCarthy's reputation include Ellen W. Schrecker, *Many Are the Crimes: McCarthyism in America* (Princeton, NJ: Princeton University Press, 1998); "Revisionist McCarthyism," *New York Times,* 23 October 1998; "Spy Stories: The Times vs. History," *New Republic,* November 16, 1998, 15–16; and John Earl Haynes and Harvey Klehr, *Venona: Decoding Soviet Espionage in America* (New Haven, CT: Yale University Press. 1999).

12. Some even invoked Salem in McCarthy's defense, citing the "the hysteria of witch-hunting" as driving his critics. See "Attacks on McCarthyism," *New York Times,* June 1, 1953; "Academic Freedom Discussed," *New York Times,* May 17, 1951.

13. Jill Lepore, "The Red Scare," *New York Times,* November 3, 2002.

14. Brooks Atkinson, "*The Crucible,*" January 23, 1953.

15. "Fraternities Take Subversion Stand," *New York Times,* November 26, 1950; "Red Probe Backed by Optometrists," *Los Angeles Times,* January 27, 1952.

16. Edmund S. Morgan, "*The Devil in Massachusetts*: A Modern Inquiry into the Salem Witch Trials," *American Historical Review* 88 (April 1950): 617.

17. John Proctor, who was about sixty years old, and Abigail Williams, who was eleven in 1692, were (with age adjustments) made into characters with a history of adultery. In the drama, Proctor confesses to indulging in adultery but refuses to sin by lying to the court or to name "other" witches.

18. Frank Rich, "Capital Shrink Rap," *New York Times*, October 7, 1998.

19. Bruce Handy, "As Seen on TV: Starr Shows Us His Fuzzy-Wuzzy Side, *Time*, December 7, 1998.

20. "A Falling Starr," *Newsweek*, October 5, 1998.

21. Frank Rich, "The Joy of Sex," *New York Times,* February 4, 1998. See also Joe Sharkey, "Witch Hunters' Manual," *New York Times*, January 24, 1999. While Starr played Cotton Mather in the public imagination and Linda Tripp was the nosy Puritan neighbor, a group of high school students preparing a stage production of *The Crucible* offered their own evaluations of the comparison between the witch hunts of the 1690s, the 1950s, and the 1990s. One student provided an obvious choice for casting the role of Abigail Williams, in Miller's version of Salem the young partner in adultery and accuser of witches: "She reminds me of Monica Lewinsky." Lynne Ames, "Students Find Parallels to Life in 'The Crucible,'" *New York Times*, November 1, 1998.

22. Brian Creech, "The Starr Report," *Time*, October 12, 1998.

23. Frank Rich, "Hardest Sell on Earth," *New York Times*, April 25, 1998.

24. Arthur Miller, "Salem Revisited," *New York Times*, October 15, 1998.

25. Michael J. Gerson and Karen Roebuck, "America's 'Puritan' Press: Journalists Wonder Why the Public Isn't Outraged, Too," *U.S. News and World Report*, October 5, 1998.

26. John M. Broder, "Donors Offer Cash and Compassion to Clinton," *New York Times,* September 28, 1998. Reporters appeared to scour the streets of Arkansas, New Haven, and other locations associated with Clinton for the "hometown" view, and they reported with various degrees of confusion or horror that most Americans did not share their "outrage." See, for example, Alison Mitchell, "With Echoes of Watergate in the Air, House Members Take a Historic Vote," *New York Times*, September 12, 1998; Rick Bragg, "In the President's Home State, a Sense of Sorrow and Satisfaction," *New York Times*, December 20, 1998; and R. W. Apple Jr., "Yale, Clinton's Alma Mater, Is Little Moved by Drama," *New York Times,* October 18, 1998. For the Democratic Party view of the trial and the charges, see, for example, Alison Mitchell, "Frustrated with the President, but a First Line of Defense," *New York Times*, October 4, 1998.

27. "Clinton's Enemies Use Frightening and Unfair Tactics," *St Petersburg (Florida) Times*, January 14, 1999.

28. Quoted in Edward Ingebretsen, *At Stake: Monsters and the Rhetoric of Fear in Public Culture* (Chicago: University of Chicago Press, 2001), 25.

Index

abolition: clergy and petitions, 107; as irrational, 106; public opinion and, 107; abolitionists as fanatics, 95

Adams, Brooks, 147

Adams, Hannah, 85

Adams, John, 35–36, 84

affirmative symbols, 39, 55

Alden, John, 14, 18, 19

Alfriend, Frank A., 122–23

American colonial past. *See* British: colonial past

American nationalism: schoolbooks and, 4, 142; creation of "American type," 51, 61; use of British colonial past in, 42; moral progress and, 47, 55; role of print in, 6; terms, 160n4, 173n6; virtue as central value, 41

American Revolution: in Confederate nationalism, 121–22, 204n6; in definition of national virtue, 43; as keystone memory in American nationalism, 40–41, 172n3; use in Charlestown riot editorials, 73

anti-Catholicism, 71–74, 76; defense against attacks, 74–75; newspaper attacks against, 71, 75–76; pope and tyranny, 47, 56; threat to republic, 69, 72; as false religion, 70; as foreign influence, 70–71, 72, 74. *See also* Roman Catholics; Inquisition

anti-Communism, 151–53

Arnold, Benedict: treason of, 41–42; use as negative symbol, 41–42, 54; use in

Confederate nationalism, 122; use in Roman Catholic press, 74

Atkinson, Brooks, 153

Backus, Isaac, 31

Bacon, Leonard, 80, 109

Bancroft, George, 60–61, 107

Baptists, 31–32

Barber, John Warner, 91

Bedinger, Henry, 94, 95, 101

Beecher, Henry Ward, 130

Beecher, Lyman, 71, 73

Belknap, Jeremy, 39

Bennett, James, 129

Bingham, Kinsley Scott, 102

Bishop, Bridget, 17, 27

Blight, David, 119

Boggs, Lilburn W., 87

Boone, Daniel, 5

Boyden, E., 106

Boynton, Charles, 109

Brattle, Thomas, 28–29, 30–31, 168n47

British colonial past: as frame of moral reference, 48; as measure of nation's moral progress, 55; as national cautionary tale, 147; as prologue, 147; repudiation of, 80, 147; selective use of, 147; settlers valorized, 147; symbolic role in American nationalism, 40, 43, 147. *See also* American nationalism; Cavalier; Puritan; Pilgrim

Brown, John: Harper's Ferry raid, 114–15; as Puritan, 115

Buell, Lawrence, 62, 175n21

Burr, C. Chauncey, 131

Burroughs, George, 19, 22
Butler, Andrew Pickens, 109, 121
Butler, Frederick, 55

Calef, Robert, as challenger to official
    narrative, 30–31; as historical source,
    146–47
Carrier, Martha, 27
Cavalier symbol: as alternative colonial set-
    tler symbol, 97–99, 122; Americanization
    of, 98–99; Confederate nationalism and,
    98; gentility and, 98; in opposition to
    Puritan symbol, 122–23; racial character-
    istics of, 122; as republican model, 122;
    in Southern rhetoric, 97, 99–100, 117.
    See also American nationalism; Puritan
    symbol; Pilgrim symbol
Cavalier-Puritan model: 95–100, 115–17. See
    also Puritan symbol; Cavalier symbol
Chalmers, George, 31
Choate, Rufus, 62
Civil War: English, 99–100
Clinton, William Jefferson, 154–57
Cobb, Howell, 113
Cohen, Daniel, 73
collective memory: as common point of
    reference, 134–35; and contemporary
    narratives of trials, 20–31; in creation of
    cultural symbols, 4; learned, 47; limits
    of, 81; living memory and, 20; narra-
    tive and, 26–29; petition language as
    source of, 20–26; as reinforcement of
    social norms, 31; selectivity of, 31, 78–
    81; social context for, 4; sociologists
    and, 161n10; and trauma, 19, 20, 30–31,
    160n7
Confederate States of America: and Cava-
    lier symbol, 122; print and the creation
    of nationalism, 123, 125; as republi-
    can restoration, 121; schoolbooks and,
    123–26; witchcraft trials in nationalist
    rhetoric, 121, 125–26
Confino, Alon, 4
Copperheads, 131–32
Corwin, Jonathan, 12, 21
Cox, Samuel Sullivan, 133
Craven, Avery O., 95, 118
Craven, Wesley Frank, 137
Cromwell, Oliver, 99–100
Crucible, the: anti-Communism and,
    151–54; impeachment crisis and,

155, 215n21; narrative distortions of,
    154; plot, 154; introduction of sexual
    themes by, 155, 156. See also Miller,
    Arthur

Darrow, Clarence, 151
Daughters of the Confederacy, 142
Davis, David Brion, 68
Davis, Reuben, 115–16
DeBow, James, 105–7
DeForest, John William, 61
Democratic party: in sectional debates,
    105
devil. See Satan
Douglas, Stephen A., 108
Douglass, Frederick, 102–3
Douglass, William, 32–33
Drayton, William, 99–100
Dyer, Mary, 80

education: public schools, 49; memorization
    and pedagogy, 68; in southern states,
    97; teacher preparation and, 49. See also
    schoolbooks
Eggleston, Edward, 143
Emerson, Joseph, 54
Emerson, Ralph Waldo, 140
English, Mary, 14, 18
English, Phillip, 14, 18
Enlightenment, 5
Europe, 48, 70
Everett, William, 138–39

Faulkner, Abigail, 23
Faust, Drew Gilpin, 97
Federalists, 44
Fenning, Daniel, 49
Finney, Charles Grandison, 78
First Great Awakening, 33
Fisher, Elwood, 94
Fiske, John, 143
Fitzhugh, George, 122, 134
Folger, Benjamin, 65, 67
folk magic, 13, 164n9
Forefather's Day, 139
Foster, Abraham, 23
Fox, Kate, 82, 84
Fox, Margaret, 82, 84
Franklin, Benjamin, 33
Franklin, James, 32–33
fraternities, college, 153

Frost, John, 97
Fugitive Slave Act, 104, 110

Gardner, Nathaniel, 32
geographies: as nationalizing influence, 48; defining national characteristics, 68. *See also* schoolbooks
Godbeer, Richard, 20
Good, Sarah, 12, 13, 14, 19
Goodrich, Charles A., 50, 54, 59, 97
Goodrich, Samuel G., 39, 89, 97, 153
Gould, Philip, 159n2
Grady, Henry W., 140–41. *See also* New South; racialized reconciliation
Greene, Nathanael, 42
Grimshaw, William, 58, 59
Guy Fawkes Day, 71

Hale, John: 10, 15, 19, 167n47
Hale, Salma, 50, 56, 97
Halyard, Harry, 38
Hathorne, John, 12, 21
Hawks, Francis Lister (Uncle Philip), 58
Hawthorne, Elizabeth, 38
Hawthorne, Nathaniel, 37–39, 62–63, 153
Hebel, Udo, 206n53
higher law, 107, 110–11
Hinton, John Howard, 58
history: popularity of in early republic, 40; as authority for memory, 31. *See also* schoolbooks
Holmes, Abiel, 60
Holmes, Oliver Wendell, Sr., 110, 141
Hoover, J. Edgar, 3
Horsmanden, Daniel, 112
Howe, E. D., 88
Hubbard, Elizabeth, 13
Hundley, Daniel, 115
Hutchinson, Anne: 144, 211n84
Hutchinson, Thomas, 34, 55, 146, 212n93
Hutchinson, William, 69

impeachment: media and, 155–56; as moral drama, 155; persecution as theme, 156; and public opinion, 156
Ingebretsen, Edward, 42, 96
Inquisition (Spanish), 151; in response to use of Salem, 56; in anti-Catholic literature, 74–75; compared to Lincoln administration, 131–32. *See also* anti-Catholicism
interest: as vice, 56

Jamestown Colony. *See* Virginia.
Jefferson, Thomas, 99
Jim Crow (laws), 141

Kammen, Michael, 137, 176n21
Kansas statehood, 111
King, Alexander, 170n59

Latter-day Saints, Church of Jesus Christ of: and American identity, 86–89; and anti-Catholicism, 86, 92; central authority and, 86, 88, 90–91; critics of, 7, 68, 86, 88, 92; converts as irrational, 88, 89; as fanatics, 88; as foreign, 90–92; founding of church, 87; geographic origins, 84; Mormon as pejorative term, 89, 192n93; polygamy and, 72, 92; public sympathy for, 87–88; as superstitious, 90. *See also* Smith, Joseph.
Lawson, Deodat, 166n37
Leacock, John, 35
LeCompte, Samuel D., 111
Leighton, George, 142
Leonard, Daniel, 35
Lewinsky, Monica, 155
liberty, 158
Lincoln, Abraham, 118
Locke, John, 49
Long, John D., 119
Lossing, Benson J., 50, 112
Lutherans, 76

Mann, Horace, 49, 94, 101, 115
Marshall, George, 153
Mason, James M., 108
Massachusetts: in school histories, 51, 53–56; in sectional rhetoric, 121; settler colonies in national mythology, 51, 44–46. *See also* Puritan; Pilgrim; New England; schoolbooks.
Mather, Cotton: defense of trials, 10–11, 26–28, 167n38; in memory of trials, 7; and method of escaping execution, 16–17; as personification of witch-hunter, 145, 147; and petitions for redress, 7, 25; and public trauma, 27–28; opinion of Robert Calef, 29–30; reaction to contemporary opinion about trials, 169n54; in sectional rhetoric, 107; as villain, 56, 145–47. *See also* Puritan.
Mather, Increase, 26, 30

Mathews, Cornelius, 38
Matthews, Robert. *See* Matthias, the
    Prophet.
Matthias, the Prophet, 64–68, 93
McCarthy, Joseph, 151–53
McCarthyism, 152, 214n11
McMaster, John Bach, 143
McPherson, James, 133
memory. *See* collective memory.
Mencken, H.L. 150
metaphor: function of, 161–62n12. *See also*
    witchcraft metaphor, Salem.
Methodists, 77
Milbourne, William, 25
Miller, Arthur, 151–53
Miller, Perry, 148
Miller, William, 67, 83
Millerism, 67, 83, 84
Moore, J. Quitman, 122–23
Morgan, Edmund S., 153
Morison, Samuel Eliot, 29–30
Mormons. *See* Latter-day Saints, Church of
    Jesus Christ of.
Morse, Jedidiah, 57
Morse, Samuel F.B., 108

nationalism. *See* American nationalism.
Neal, Daniel, 31
Neal, John, 61
negative symbols: function of, 39, 55; as
    mythical devils, 99; social boundaries
    and, 42, 55; Salem witchcraft as, 39,
    55, 67, *See also* affirmative symbols;
    witchcraft metaphor, Salem.
New England Society (NESoc): of Cincin-
    nati, 109; on distinctions between found-
    ing Massachusetts colonies, 138–42; of
    Philadelphia, 142; postbellum defense
    of Puritan symbol, 210n78; purpose,
    109–10; of New York City, 109–10,
    111, 137–38, 140–41; of St. Louis, 141–
    42, and Salem witchcraft, 109, 138–39,
    142
New England: influence of authors on na-
    tional histories, 7; political and cultural
    ambitions of, 43–44; regionalism as
    American nationalism, 43, 176n16; in
    schoolbooks, 53
New Jersey Teachers and Friends of Educa-
    tion, 47

New South, 140–41. *See under* New England
    Society: of New York City; Grady,
    Henry W.
New York Negro Plot of 1741, the: and
    cultural forgetting, 113, 116; historical
    accounts, 112–13; New England slavery
    and, 116; racialized memory of, 113
Norton, Mary Beth, 18, 164n9
Nurse, Rebecca, 14, 17, 19, 27

Olney, Jesse, 50, 58, 59
optometrists, 153
Osburn, Sarah, 12, 14, 19

Palfrey, John, 94, 101, 102
Parris, Betty, 10, 12
Parris, Samuel: involvement in trials, 10, 21;
    as villain, 56, 61, 107, 145–47. *See also*
    witchcraft trials, Salem.
Pestana, Carla, 79
Phillips, Wendell, 110–11, 114, 130
Phips, William, 15, 17–18, 21
Pierpont, John, 110
Pierson, Elijah, 65, 67
Pilgrim symbol: ascendancy in postbel-
    lum histories, 135–36, 142–44, 206n53;
    commemoration of, 45; conflation with
    Puritan settler, 45–46, 53, 136, 208n56;
    as founder of democracy, 54, 137, 147; as
    individualist, 137; Pilgrim Society, 110;
    religious tolerance and, 136; separation
    of settler symbols, 138; as settler symbol,
    8, 45, 176n21
Pillsbury, Parker, 111
Plymouth Colony: 250th Anniversary, 137–
    39
political socialization, 40
Poole, William Frederick, 145–47
Prentiss, Charles, 55
press: abolitionists and, 127, 129–30; censure
    of radicals, 127; compiling and, 65;
    northern press and Puritan symbol,
    129–30; penny press, 64–65; opposition
    to Lincoln administration, 127; and
    southern secession, 129
Proctor, John, 14, 71
Proctor, William, 71
Prohibition, 9, 149–51
Protestant: United States as, 70; danger of
    religious extremists, 75–6

public opinion: reconstructing, 20; understanding of guilt in witchcraft cases, 27–28

publications: ban during trials, 25–26; official narratives after trials, 26–29

Puritan, symbol: as abolitionist, 95–100; and anti-modernism, 150; as bigot, 138; compared to Pilgrim, 138–39; conflation with Pilgrim, 45–46; consequences of use in slavery debates, 120; in creation of national identity, 8, 39, 44; decline as dominant settler symbol, 120, 135, 144–45; as dominant settler symbol, 45–46; as fanatic, 99–100, 138–47; in First Great Awakening, 33; and governmental power, 120, 147; as intolerant, 120, 126–27, 145, 147; northern wartime press and, 132–34; as northerner, 97–100; as persecutor, 138, 145; in postbellum schoolbooks, 143; as racial threat, 113–17, 125; religious delusions and, 145, 147; in sectional rhetoric, 95–100; as un-American, 122; 117, 122–23; as witch hunter, 144–45; as witch burner, 138–39; Yankee as, 126–27. See also witchcraft metaphor, Salem; witch hunt.

Quakers: anti-slavery activity of, 81; civil disorder, 79; denominational memory of executed Quakers, 79; gender and memory, 80–81, 211n84; as intensifier of Puritan negative symbol, 79, 81; as Puritan victims, 75, 78–81, 114, 138–39, 144

racialized reconciliation: New England Societies and, 140–41; New South, 140–41; Pilgrim symbol in, 136, 142; sentimentalism and, 119; tolerance as rhetoric within, 137; white nostalgia and, 120, 136

Ray, Benjamin, 212n90

red scare: See anti-Communism; McCarthyism

Reed, Rebecca, 73

Reis, Elizabeth, 169n50

religion: antebellum innovations, 68–69; charges of fanaticism, 65, 68, 80; fear of Protestant extremism, 76, 80; heathens, 69, 70, 72; "Hindoos," 69, 70, 72; as

measure of civilization, 70; pagans, 77; "religious delusions," 65, 68; religious outsiders, 186n16; revivals, 65, 68, 77–78

republicanism, 56, 185n11

Rhode Island, 53, 144

Rich, Frank, 155

Richardson, James, 141

Robinson, Henry Morton, 151

Rockwell, Julius, 108

Roman Catholics: physical violence against, 71–74; population, 71; Catholic colonies and religious freedom, 75; and national identity, 69. See also anti-Catholicism.

Rosenthal, Bernard, 159n2

Rush, Benjamin, 47

Russell, William Howard, 131

Salem metaphor. See witchcraft metaphor: Salem.

Salmon, Thomas, 31

Satan: as tormentor of accused, 13; plot against colonists, 27; nature of threat, 28; in antebellum evangelical preaching, 76; as physical presence, 169n50

schoolbooks: authorship, 49–51; British colonial history as a subject of, 143; civics, 143; compiling and, 50; as conduit of memory, 4; cultural weight of, 7, 46, 48, 50–51; defining national virtues, 68; influence on memory, 49–50; influence of New England-based authors, 50; Massachusetts settlers in, 53–56, 180n39; national identity and, 46–50; morality and, 7, 47, 143; moral progress as subject, 55; pedagogical approach and, 49–50; Plymouth Colony in, 143; postbellum changes in, 51, 143; Salem witchcraft in, 49–50, 55, 143–45; sales, 177n22; stability of narrative in, 51; Virginia settlers in, 51–54

schools. See education; schoolbooks.

Scopes, John, 151

Scott, Benjamin, 136

Scott, Jonathan, 62

Scott, Walter, 97

Second Great Awakening, 33, 76–78

Sewall, Samuel, 24, 26–27

Seward, Charles, 118

Shakers, 76

Slotkin, Richard, 5

Smith, John, 52. *See also* Virginia.
Smith, Joseph: assassination of, 87; as
    founder, 67, demonization of, 90, 92;
    ridicule of, 89, 90. *See also* Latter-day
    Saints, Church of Jesus Christ of.
Smith, William, Jr., 112
spectral evidence: misuse in trials, 16,
    166n37; definition of, 16; challenges
    to in petitions, 20–27; ministers criti-
    cal of, 24; Brattle and, 28–30; Calef on,
    29–30. *See also* witchcraft trials: Salem.
Spiritualism: as religious innovation, 82–
    84; religious anxieties of critics, 68,
    83; geographic origins of, 84–85; as
    progressive idea, 85; as delusion, 84
St. Bartholomew's Day Massacre, 74
Starkey, Marion L., 153
Starr, Kenneth, 155
Stockton, Robert Field, 107
Stone, William L., 65
Story, Joseph, 42
Stoughton, William, 15, 26–27
Stowe, Harriet Beecher, 97
Strong, George Templeton, 130
Stuart, Moses, 108
Sumner, Charles, 108–9, 110, 118
superstition: and race, 77–78; and class,
    77–78; and mental illness, 78

Taylor, John, 99
Tituba: accused of witchcraft, 12; back-
    ground of, 12, 14, 163n5; confession of,
    12–13; imprisonment of, 17; as likely
    suspect, 12, 14, 19; in sectional rhetoric,
    104; value as witness, 13
tolerance: American religious practices,
    67–69, 70, 87–89
Torquemada, 131. *See also* Inquisition;
    anti-Catholicism.

United Confederate Veterans, 142
Upham, Charles Wentworth, 31, 36, 84,
    212n90

Vallandigham, Clement L., 133
Van Wyck, Charles Henry, 115–16
Venable, Abraham W., 115
Virginia: acceptance of tyranny, 51; colonial
    witchcraft laws in, 100; portrayal of set-
    tlers in schoolbooks, 51–54; rejection of

settlers as symbols of virtue, 51; settlers
    as "self-interested," 51
virtue. *See* American nationalism.

Waddington, John, 207n54
Washington, George, 84, 111
Webster, Daniel, 107
Webster, Noah, 47, 52
Whittier, John Greenleaf, 61, 81, 102, 104
Willard, Emma, 50, 54, 89, 97
Williams, Abigail, 10, 12
Williams, Roger, 144–45
Willson, Marcius, 50, 58, 177n22
Wilson, Deborah, 81
Winthrop, John, 158
Winthrop, Robert C., 137–38
Wise, Henry, 111, 114
Wiswall, J.T., 115
witch burning: adoption by northern press,
    132; in Catholic press, 96, 188n44; use
    by Democratic newspaper, 105; as for-
    eign practice, 96; invention of, 8; and
    lynching association, 97, 115; as part of
    Salem metaphor, 94–96; persistence of
    in popular imagination, 96; as symbol of
    barbarism, 96
witchcraft: antebellum religious ideas about,
    76; colonial cases, 11–12; danger of not
    prosecuting, 19, 26–27; *maleficium* and,
    12; as practice, 83; non-Salem uses of,
    83
witchcraft metaphor, Salem: abolitionist
    intolerance and, 125–26; addition of idea
    of witch burning in Salem, 94–96; use in
    anti-Communism campaign, 3, 151; as
    articulation of social and political anxi-
    eties, 3, 55; associated with persecution,
    3, 9; charge of bigotry, 3, 80, 125–26;
    claim of delusions within public contro-
    versies, 7, 59, 76, 83; claim opponents
    are irrational, 3, 63, 88; emergence in
    antebellum public controversies, 66;
    fanaticism within social and religious
    movements and, 7, 76, 80, 82, 88; to
    mark subject as foreign, 50–51, 57, 58,
    76; marking cultural boundaries, 157;
    narratives and the creation of, 153; in
    oratory, 199n57; in pro-slavery rhetoric,
    8, 101; in Prophet Matthias scandal, 64–
    68; in Prohibition controversy, 149–51;

postbellum decline of metaphor, 148; in rhetoric during American Revolution, 35–6; re-emergence in twentieth century, 149; in religious controversies, 56, 76; in coverage of Scopes trial, 151; shift in meaning during Civil War, 101, 125–26; use in smallpox epidemic, 32–33. *See also* individual controversies; schoolbooks.

witchcraft trials, Salem: accusation patterns and, 14; as capital crime, 11; courts and, 15, 18, 21; empirical evidence, 16, 17; executions, 17; historians' interpretations of, 2, 10; legal procedures, 15; local memory, 171n61; local tensions as catalyst for, 11; repentance, 24; spectral evidence, 16, 26–30; petitions for redress, 20–26, 157, 165n23; political and social consequences of, 18; charges of witness fraud, 60. *See also* spectral evidence; Parris, Samuel; Mather, Cotton.

witch hunt: anti-Communism as, 153; impeachment as, 155; postbellum use of term, 9, 120; Prohibition, 149–51; and witch-hunter, 9, 120, 147

Worcester, Joseph Emerson, 76

wrestlers, professional, 153

Yankee. *See* Puritan.

Young, Brigham, 91